DEDICATION

This book is dedicated to my parents, Eduardo and Helena, who gave me life; and to my husband, Mike Flaxman, who has been my greatest supporter and friend during the writing of this text and throughout my career.

ACKNOWLEDGMENTS

I would like to thank all my students for inspiring and helping me to write this book. In particular I am very grateful to Michael Melo for donating his Henry character to the book, modeling the targets for the facial expressions, and checking the accuracy of many of the tutorials. Aharon Charnov wrote the Simple Guy tutorial. Meng-Yang Lu rigged Henry and created the Happy and Sad animations. Jason Friedman, Steve Gagne, and Ezra Schwepker reviewed portions of the manuscript for clarity and technical accuracy.

Several students allowed me to use their class assignments as examples: Aaron Walsman donated his Jump animation; David Suroviec his Weight animation, and Marcos Romero his Push animation. William Robinson provided a sample of his *Astrobucks* animation storyboard. Brittany Lee created the storyboard for the sack jump scene. Jiunnfu Su provided his graceful Koi animation.

Thank you all for your contributions to this book.

ABOUT THE AUTHOR

Tereza Flaxman teaches 3D modeling and animation at the Harvard Extension School and Northeastern University. She has been teaching animation for the past seven years at both undergraduate and graduate levels and is a Certified Alias Maya Instructor. Additionally, she has taught at the School of Film and Animation at the Rochester Institute of Technology (RIT) and at the State University of New York (SUNY). She also works as a freelance animator. She has more than 15 years of experience with high-end 3D animation software, and has used Maya since version 1.0. Her work has been published in several books and magazines and exhibited in shows throughout the U.S. She has an MFA in Computer Animation from the School of Visual Arts in New York City and a BFA from the University of Oregon.

CONTENTS

CHAPTER 4   RIGGING AND ANIMATING A SIMPLE CHARACTER   **129**

INTRODUCTION

Maya 2008 Character Modeling and Animation: Principles and Practices is an introductory-to-intermediate–level text designed for anyone who wants to learn 3D character modeling, rigging, and animation using Autodesk Maya software. The book is intended to support both classroom use and the independent learner.

The organizational approach is based on my classroom teaching experience over the past seven years. It was motivated by a lack of texts that effectively integrate the principles of animation with their technical implementation in Maya. Each chapter starts with a section (or sections) that describes the relevant principles. These are largely software independent, although sometimes include illustrations or mini-tutorials demonstrating the concepts using Maya. The second part of each chapter is composed of one or more detailed tutorials. These tutorials lead you step by step through an example, and are supported by additional materials on the CD-ROM.

This book does not attempt to replace or duplicate the Maya manuals or to run through every feature available in the program. It is expected that you are somewhat familiar with the Maya interface. If you are not, or if you need a brief refresher, please see Appendix A, "Maya Boot Camp: Creating Your First Maya Scene," which provides a basic introduction.

This book is organized as a series of projects in which you learn how to model, rig, and animate your characters. The chapters are designed to be read sequentially, because each project is of progressive difficulty and relies on techniques taught earlier.

I believe that character modeling, rigging, and animation are so tightly integrated that they should be approached together. This way, you learn to build characters that animate well. Some institutions, however, teach separate courses on modeling and animation. It is possible to use this text in such courses by skipping over chapters. For example, a modeling course would skip the animation chapters. An animation course would just use the sample rigged characters provided and skip the chapters describing their modeling and rigging. Examples of curricula that illustrate how this might work for various quarter- or semester-long courses are provided as Appendix B, "Sample Syllabi."

THE ANIMATION PRODUCTION PROCESS

In This Chapter

- Overview of Production
- Preproduction Process

In this chapter, you will be introduced to the character animation production process. The first part of the chapter gives you an overview of the process from beginning to end and introduces basic terminology. Next, basic concepts of cinematography and lighting are introduced. This is followed by two tutorials in which these concepts are applied within the Maya interface.

OVERVIEW OF PRODUCTION

The overall production process is divided into three major phases: preproduction, production, and postproduction.

Preproduction

Preproduction is the process of planning, organizing, researching, and working out the details of the animation. As tempting as it may be to jump straight into production, experienced animators realize that good preproduction not only improves overall quality, but it also actually speeds up the production process. The time spent modeling something unseen or an object seen only in the distance is time better spent on important details. The time spent animating an unneeded shot is not only time wasted, but also it can get in the way of a clear-headed editing decision.

An animation starts with an idea that develops into a story. Often the idea is clear enough in the animator's head. However, the story needs to be well planned to communicate with an audience. If more than one person is involved with the production, the preproduction process is also critical in developing a shared vision of the desired end product. This process is so important that major studios often spend at least a third of their overall project time on preproduction. Fortunately for the independent animator, the main things required in this phase are the power of observation and a simple sketchpad.

The basic process is to start with creative brainstorming, followed by careful and selective research and observation. Collected ideas and observations are then gradually structured into forms useful for animation production. For example, the concept for a character may grow from the need for a particular role within a story but eventually needs to be honed into a tangible physical form that the audience will relate to. Similarly, general ideas about pacing and mood will end up in cinematographic form as lighting and camera decisions. When the various elements are prepared, they are brought together in sequence using a technique known as *storyboarding*. Based on the storyboard, an *animatic* is produced, which is a crude form of movie in which elements such as dialogue and music can be added. When the animatic is tested and refined, the animator can have strong confidence that a piece will convey the desired message to its audience.

Production

The simplest way of thinking about the animation production process is as a sequence of steps; each step must logically be completed before subsequent steps. The first production steps are the modeling of digital sets and props and the creation of digital characters. These start as surface models, but in the case of digital characters, they must be *rigged*. Rigging is the process of creating a skeleton used to animate the character. The skeleton must then be attached to the surface model (a process known as *skinning* or *binding*). After the digital characters are rigged, the next steps are *blocking*, which is the placement of the characters on set at key points in time, and *layout*, which is the positioning of characters, sets, and props relative to the camera. At this point, the entire movie sequence can be viewed digitally in crude format, a process akin to a digital animatic and usually referred to as a *previs*. After the previs is done, the process of character animation can start. In practice, this is often conducted in numbered passes such as first pass, second pass, and so on. After animation is complete, timings are final, and sound work can begin. Also at that point, final texture and lighting can be implemented. Finally, with all the previous elements in place, rendering can take place.

Postproduction

Although most of the necessary work in animation is usually completed during the production phase, there is often a follow-up phase known as *postproduction* or *post*. If production is done well, post is a much briefer process in animation than in other types of filmmaking. For example, there should be no major editing component because most edit decisions should long since have been worked out. However, little fixes are almost always needed, so it is wise to schedule time for them.

The largest task in animation post is usually *compositing*—bringing together all of the production elements. In particular, animations are often rendered as a series of passes (note that this is a second meaning of this term in animation). The *beauty pass* contains basic color information only, and separate layers are used for shadows, particles, dirt and grime, and even sweat. The reason for rendering things in this way is that it allows much more flexibility in the final compositing process. For example, lighting can be adjusted to improve continuity between scenes. After all of the various render layers have been composited, and the final sound mix is added, the animation is technically complete.

The balance of this chapter will discuss key ideas in preproduction, whereas the rest of the book will talk mostly about production issues. Postproduction is typically done using editing, compositing, and sound-production software not addressed in this book.

PREPRODUCTION PROCESS

Now that you've gotten an overview of the full process, let's consider some of the more detailed steps that go into preproduction.

Story Concept and Development

A good animation story starts with a strong idea. You should explore many ideas or variations before deciding on a single story line. Your first idea may not be the best one, or it might require production elements outside of your time frame or budget. Start by brainstorming 10 story ideas. From those ideas, choose five, and from those, pick one. It is often helpful to get the opinions of others about your story idea.

When brainstorming, remember that a good story involves theatrical reality. The audience will react to your story depending on how emotionally moved they are. If your character is strongly likeable and has an obstacle to achieving his goals, the audience most likely will sympathize with him. Theatrical reality has a stronger structure than real life. One way of thinking about this is that in drama, a character starts with an objective that leads the character to action. However, for the story to be interesting, there are usually one or more obstacles that impede the realization of the objective. Finally, in classic story structure, there is a single climactic moment that is followed by a resolution.

Write a few brief sentences summarizing your story idea as you might explain it to a friend. In the movie business, this is known as an "elevator pitch." You don't need to give away the ending. Actually, you want to leave things a bit ambiguous to spark curiosity. For example:

> The story is about a swallow that falls in love with a mean cat. The swallow dreams of marrying the cat, but the cat has other ideas.

> Clarence is an almost unbearably shy guy. But when a new kid shows up at school, Clarence helps him out. Soon he finds that by helping his new friend, he has helped himself.

Now you need to think a bit more about the story details. For each idea, identify where the story takes place, the character's motivation, the obstacles your character will have in achieving his goals, and the final resolution (see Table 1.1).

Table 1.1

IDEA #	LOCATION	MOTIVATION	OBSTACLE	RESOLUTION
1	A lush pine forest	The bird loves the cat	The cat wants to eat the bird	After several close calls, love triumphs
2	School playground	Clarence desires companionship	Painful shyness	New best friend

At this point, you also need to start thinking about some important practical concerns of animation. How many characters are required? How long would the piece have to be to tell this story? Do aspects of the plot require technically challenging special effects? For example, the bird would require feathers and the cat would need fur, both of which could increase render times.

When you have decided which story you want to animate, write two to three pages describing the plot. At this point, you should be thinking dramatically. Pay special attention to the escalation of obstacles and to the climactic moment of the story. Do you want the audience be tense? Surprised? Laughing?

CHARACTER DESIGN AND CHARACTER SKETCHES

Visually and conceptually interesting characters such as those in Figure 1.1 are a hallmark of animation.

FIGURE 1.1   An old man and a boy. (Courtesy of Michael Melo.)

Part of the fun of working within this medium is that you can use your imagination to design wild caricatures and fantastic creatures. However, building a lively and interesting character requires more than physical design. Some people find it easier to start by brainstorming and refining character concepts and then drawing things out; others prefer to grab a pencil and think things through visually while sketching. In either case, developing a *backstory* is often a useful way to generate ideas, some of which will have physical attributes and others of which will be apparent in animation or story development.

To start developing a character history, try coming up with creative answers to the following questions. These questions may not apply to all characters. (Perhaps your character is a clonal android with no parents, in which case that is relevant background as well.)

- Is your character male or female?
- What is his age and state of health?
- What is his name? The name is an important part of the character because it gives the audience its first idea of what the character is about.
- Where did he grow up? The kind of place and its influence on the character is more important than a specific location.
- What education and work history does he have? Has he been a slave since childhood, working in the mines?
- What kind of relationship does he have with his parents? Is he a rebel? Is he a momma's boy?
- What does he like to eat?
- How far out of his way will he go to obtain his favorite item?
- What does he like to do in his spare time? Consider sports, games, reading, travel, and so on.
- Is he shy, outgoing, or in between?
- What situations would cause the character to feel intimidated or especially confident?
- What makes him happy? Is he looking for friends? Anxious to make money? Looking for adventure?
- What is the character's greatest fear or weakness? Is he afraid of losing his teeth? Is he afraid of heights?
- What is his greatest strength? Does he realize it, or might it be only discovered under a particular circumstance?
- Is he kind or aggressive?
- Is he a goody two shoes or the black sheep of the family?

There are no right or wrong answers to these questions. Just avoid creating a boring character.

Start a project notebook or sketchbook. This can be any format that is convenient but should be legible enough to show a friend, colleague, or classmate to ask advice. Sketch and collect and annotate clippings for the physical design of your character. For example, you might find another character with design elements you want to borrow. Take a clipping, circle or blow up a detail of the important portions, and paste it into your notebook. Make sure the physical characteristics of your character match with its environment. For example, a cave woman would probably have long, uncombed hair and long nails. She most likely would wear clothes made with animal skins and accessories made of plants or seeds.

Rough out some preliminary ideas of how your character might look and act. One common and useful technique is to imagine what poses might be most characteristic. A pose is simply a character frozen in time at a key moment. For example, if your character has been a bookkeeper for 25 years, you might picture him working in the office, walking his dog, getting a haircut, or at home watching television. By visualizing the character in several situations you can begin to see the character's personality emerge (see Figures 1.2 and 1.3).

FIGURE 1.2   The character in the office and watching television.
(Courtesy of Michael Melo.)

FIGURE 1.3   The character walking the dog and getting a haircut.
(Courtesy of Michael Melo.)

Is the character frenzied or relaxed? Confident or nervous? What body posture might best show these characteristics? Which camera viewpoint might accentuate them?

The physical appearance of your character should vary according to the story. Make sure the gender and approximate age of your character are clear. Females not only look different than males, but they also behave differently. This is true of "realistic" characters but also of an animated sack. To start with, never be afraid of exaggerating these characteristics. It is easier to pull back a bit later than to start out overly subtle.

One way of thinking about this is that a character should never be boring to look at or watch. If you need inspiration in this area, look carefully at the performance of a great actor when the actor is *not* speaking. You will find that even if the actor is doing nothing more than listening or waiting around, he is likely to still be active and engaged. How he acts at a particular moment is a function of his motivation. This is partly what he is actually doing and partly what he is thinking about or has concluded.

Your job as an animator is to make your audience react to your characters. Usually, you will want them to empathize and will want to make your character likeable. On other occasions, you will want them to hate or fear a character. You will almost always be better off making a character with strong feelings (wearing his heart on his sleeve). Rarely would you want them to be neutral or disengaged.

Create a character with imperfections. The imperfections can be either physical or psychological. Physically, your character may be missing a tooth, an arm, or an eye, and so on. Psychologically, he may be hyperactive, shy, aggressive, or lazy. Interesting characters have several imperfections, some of which they are aware of and others not. A good example of this is how Indiana Jones is afraid of snakes.

Environments and Sets

Unlike live action production, animation takes place within an environment entirely created by the filmmaker. While sets can range from simple to elaborate, they provide essential visual support for the story. Sets combine with lighting and prop design to put characters in appropriate historical and emotional perspective. For example, a piece taking place in a shabby, dark room would convey a very different feeling from one set outdoors in bright sun with beautiful mountain views. Sets also establish where characters live geographically, and even the personality of a character. For example, setting a scene in a character's home allows background details to convey a character's preferences. A little boy's room might have baseball posters indicating a love of sports. If useful to the story, the period of the décor could make clear the historical time when the action takes place.

Cinematography

Cinematography is the art of telling a story through the camera lens. Telling a story using the camera is in some ways similar to telling a story with text. When you read a book, the words have an impact on you depending on the writing style and structure. When you watch a movie, the camera shots have a similar impact.

In a movie, the director uses camera movements to signal to the audience. The audience decodes these meanings and reacts to them emotionally, sometimes without even being aware of the direction. For example, if two characters are arguing in a scene, and the camera shows a close-up of a knife, the audience anticipates that the knife may be used.

Directors and cinematographers use a series of camera shots to establish when and where the action is taking place and characters' reactions and feelings. In animation, the viewer tends to identify with the camera—a phenomenon known as *transference*. Basically, when the camera moves, the audience feels that it is moving too.

In live-action film, a director works in the physical world, often together with a large crew. The production team must find appropriate locations, build sets, pick exactly the right time to shoot to get the desired light, and so on. The default world in animation, however, is a boring featureless plane.

Basically, an animator has complete control of this world. This is both a great advantage and a difficult responsibility. Fortunately, many of the elements of cinematography are shared between live action and animation, and animators have much to observe and learn from film and television.

As with other aspects of animation, observation can be your best teacher. However, we are so used to watching television and film that distancing ourselves from the process enough to accurately observe it can be difficult. One very simple technique that often helps is simply to turn off the sound and watch a scene or segment repeatedly. After you do this, you may find it easier to observe camera motion, set design, or other elements of cinematography. If necessary, use a stopwatch and take notes. This kind of shot breakdown will start to give you a sense of how various directors treat material and how such treatments vary based on subject matter and media. Many DVDs have comment tracks that feature the director explaining the various shots. This can also be helpful.

Elements of Cinematography

The basic aspects of cinematography include point of view, camera distance and motion, color choice, transitions, shot pacing, and lighting.

The two basic positions, or points of view, that a director can choose are *in the action* and *out of the action*. If the camera is in the action, the viewer is placed directly in the scene. This makes it easier to see details, including facial expressions; however, it requires many shots or a lot of panning to keep up with the action. A director might also choose to pull the camera out of the action. This vantage point allows the viewer to understand the context of the scene and can provide some degree of emotional distance.

Framing refers to the position of a camera relative to objects in the scene. This aspect of cinematography terminology and principles is largely derived from the world of art. For example, objects in the scene are characterized as being in the foreground, middle ground, or background. Often shots are composed so that symmetry is avoided, and important elements are laid out dramatically relative to the frame. As in painting, the rule of thirds is often used in composition. The *rule of thirds* is when you draw imaginary lines dividing your scene in three equal parts horizontally and vertically. These lines create four intersections, and these can form anchor points for the placement of characters or other major scene elements (see Figure 1.4).

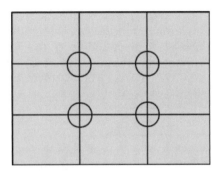

FIGURE 1.4   The rule of thirds graph.

Basic Camera Shots

There are many types of camera shots, but the most used ones are close-ups, over-the-shoulder shots, medium shots, long shots, and establishing shots (see Figure 1.5).

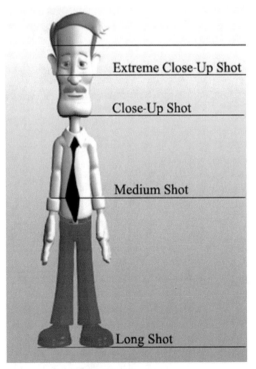

FIGURE 1.5   Shot types.

- A *close-up shot* is taken a short distance from the character's face or props. The close-up is intended to show the character's facial expressions, give importance to certain props, or direct the audience's attention to something important. Occasionally, an extreme close-up is used. For example, this might show only a character's eyes and brows (see Figure 1.6).

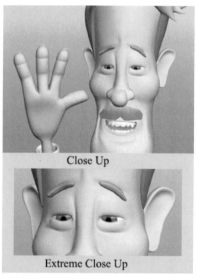

FIGURE 1.6 Close-up and extreme close-up shots.

- An *over-the-shoulder shot* is when the camera is over the shoulder of one character, showing the face of another. This shot is used to show two characters' conversation and focus the audience's attention on one character at a time instead of on both characters at once, as shown in Figure 1.7.

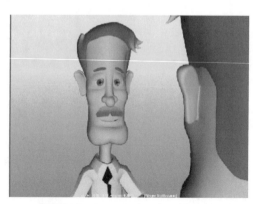

FIGURE 1.7 An over-the-shoulder shot.

- A *medium shot* shows the character from the waist up (see Figure 1.8). This shot is often used to show two characters interacting with each other such as talking, hugging, or arguing.

FIGURE 1.8   A medium shot.

- A *long shot* is shot from a distance but not from as far away as the establishing shot. In an interior scene, it typically shows the room and the character's full body (see Figure 1.9).

FIGURE 1.9   A long shot.

- An *establishing shot* is a view from a distance or a bird's-eye shot (see Figure 1.10). This shot is often used at the beginning of a film or location segment to show where the story takes place. An establishing shot can be followed by a long shot. For example, you can have a bird's-eye shot showing a house and its surroundings and then cut to a long shot inside the house, with the character standing in the living room .

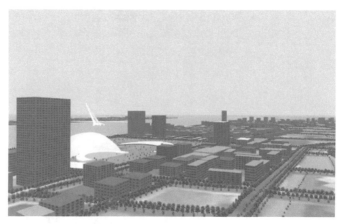

FIGURE 1.10   An establishing shot.

Camera Angles

The camera angle helps the director emphasize and deemphasize the importance of the subject. It sends a visual message to the audience about the subject's status of power and dominance.

The major camera angles are listed here.

- **Low angle.** In this shot, the camera is placed below eye level looking up to the subject. This camera angle makes the subject look bigger than it is to show the audience that the character is important, powerful, and imposing.
- **High angle.** In this shot, the camera is placed above eye level looking down to the subject. This camera angle makes the subject look smaller than it is and makes the character less dominant and more vulnerable and subordinate.
- **Eye-level angle.** In this shot, the camera is placed at the subject's eye level. It is a comfortable angle for the audience and is basically a neutral angle because we are used to seeing things at eye level (see Figure 1.11).

FIGURE 1.11   Low angle, high angle, and eye-level angle camera shots.

Camera Movements

The types of shots just described form the director's basic repertoire. However, the camera doesn't always need to stay still. The following terms and techniques are commonly used to describe camera motion.

- *Pan* refers to the camera rotating from side to side. The two types of pans are the *following pan* and the *surveying pan*. A following pan is when the camera follows the character; a surveying pan is when the camera looks for an existing subject in the scene. For example, the camera might pan across a table, stopping at a loaf of bread.
- A *tilt* is when the camera follows an action up or down. Although this is commonly done just to follow the action, tilting can also be used to emphasize height or depth. For example, you might start a shot at a character's feet and then tilt up gradually to show his face. This camera move is commonly used to indicate or emphasize a character's height.
- A *zoom* is when the camera stays in the same place, and the focal length of the lens is changed to bring the subject closer or farther. It is important to realize that changing the lens' focal length does not magnify elements uniformly—it changes their relative size in the frame based on their distance to the camera. When you zoom in, background elements in the scene appear larger relative to foreground elements.
- A *dolly* is when a camera moves toward or away from the subject. The term comes from the actual mechanism used to accomplish this with a physical camera, where the camera and cameraperson are slid back and forth. Superficially, a dolly might appear to be the same as zoom; however, these are two different movements. The relative sizes of objects change less using a dolly than when zooming (see Figure 1.12).

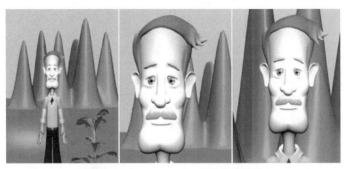

FIGURE 1.12   Comparison of zoom (middle) and dolly (right) shots.

- A *truck* is when the camera moves sideways and keeps the same depth of field. This camera movement is commonly used to follow a subject while maintaining a near constant perspective on the character.

Shot Sequences and Screen Orientation

With arbitrary camera angles, it is possible to confuse and disorient the audience. When you begin to plan the sequences of a shot, you usually want to keep your viewers oriented in space. (The exception is sequences intentionally designed to be scary or disorienting.) The *180-degree rule* helps keep your audience oriented. Think of your scene from top down, and draw an imaginary line through the center of the space occupied by your characters. If you keep the camera always on one side of this line, the characters and objects in the scene will always appear in a consistent spatial orientation within the camera frame. You can place this imaginary line anywhere in your scene that makes sense given the action, but if you want to maintain orientation, avoid alternating shots that are more than 180 degrees apart (see Figure 1.13).

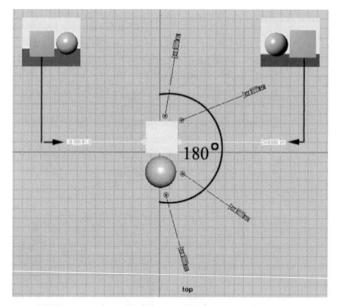

FIGURE 1.13   The 180-degree rule of camera placement.

Transitions

A film consists of a series of shots connected with transitions. The *transitions* are used to change from one camera shot to another. Most transitions are very short and are designed not to call attention to themselves. However, this is a matter of directorial style. Occasionally, transitions are made longer and visually obvious. Often this form of transition is used to indicate a change of time and place. The most common transitions are as follows:

- A *cut* is an abrupt change of camera shots. This is by far the most common transition. For example, cuts are commonly used in dialogue shots to show the speaker and then the person listening and reacting.
- A *dissolve* is when one shot fades out into another. This is used when a break in the visual continuity is desirable to indicate the passage of time. Dissolves typically vary from 15 to 120 frames.
- A *fade in/out* is when a shot is gradually changed to a static color, usually black or white. The purpose of a fade is fundamentally different from cuts and dissolves. Cuts and dissolves are used to connect shots; fades are used to separate them. Fades are commonly used to indicate the passage of time. Often cinematography is used to anticipate the fade, for example, when a shot ends with the character turning off the lights.

 Fades can be done from any color to any color, based on the intent of the effect. Fade out to white is often used to indicate bright blinding light such as the sun coming through a window. Fade in from white is intended to show bright light or an object fading into the shot.

- A *wipe* is when a new shot is gradually revealed while the previous shot is still on the screen. Wipes resemble the opening of a curtain. Wipes can move in any direction: horizontally, vertically, diagonally, across the frame, out of the center, and so on. The newly revealed shot can take many different shapes, including triangles, squares, circles, keyholes, and so on. Wipe effects were popular in the 1930s and 1940s Hollywood movies, but are rarely used today. This type of transition is very showy and can get tiresome, so it should be used with restraint.
- A *focus in/out* is when a shot ends with the images out of focus and dissolves into the next shot that dissolves in with the images blurred and coming into focus. When this effect is done properly, the dissolve is unnoticeable because the shots are connected while the images are unrecognizably blurred. This effect is often used to convey a sense of a character's loss of consciousness. For example, it might be used when a character is undergoing anesthesia for surgery.
- A *match shot* is a transition in which both shots share the same character but in a different location. The character passes from one shot to the other doing the same action identically. Sometimes the two shots are connected with a cut but often with a dissolve. A match shot is used to convey passage through space. For example, imagine a character walking in the desert day after day. A series of match shots

might be used in which the character is continuously walking, but the desert background changes between shots. The main focus of the match shot is the character's acting. The place is important only in relation to the character.

- A *jump cut* is similar to a match shot, except that what varies is time and not place. In a jump cut, two shots share the same character doing the same action at different times. For instance, the intention might be to show the character walking all day and into the evening. Both shots would have the character walking but with different lighting.
- A *freeze frame* is when the action is frozen momentarily to show the point of view of the character. This is commonly used to show a photographer's viewpoint when taking a picture.
- A *sound cue* is when visual and audio transitions are not in sync. In most common cases, the audio leads the visual transition—a form of anticipation in editing. Less commonly, the audio from one shot can bleed into a following shot. Sound cues can be used with any kind of visual transition. An example would be a color fade in which the sound (music, dialogue, laughing, etc.) is heard before the image appears.

Despite the wide range of transitions available, many of the best films ever made only used a couple of types of transitions, so don't feel compelled to use them all. Good direction, like good writing, should support the story and not call attention to itself. Think of transitions in terms of your control of continuity and the audience's sense of time and place.

Shot Pacing

Even a short animation is typically composed of many shots. The length of these shots, as well as the variation in their length, is frequently manipulated for effect. For example, a very slow pacing might be used to emphasize a feeling of laziness, whereas quick shots are used to add excitement.

Color Choice

In cinematography, color choices are often carefully considered. Usually, a consistent visual vocabulary is established for the film as a whole, and then various scenes or locales are given variations within the theme. These choices affect both the colors and textures given to objects and to the set lighting. In choosing colors, you should think first about the dominant colors as seen through the camera and not about every individual portion of each object.

One way of organizing this process systematically is first to identify the results that you want to achieve with color. The psychological effects of color vary a bit based on culture, but the following are some common generalizations.

- **Red.** Passion, excitement, aggressiveness
- **Green.** Nature, relaxation
- **Blue.** Stability, security (associated with ocean and sky)
- **Orange and yellow.** Joy, happiness
- **White.** Innocence, purity
- **Black.** Elegance, formality, death

After you have an idea of the overall mood you want to set, you can select either a main dominant color or a color scheme based around a central hue. For this purpose, you might consider one of several books on color harmony that include useful color schemes and variations. For example, the book *Color Harmony: A Guide to Creative Color Combinations* by Bride M. Whelan (Rockport Publishers, 1994) contains a useful set of images and color schemes.

Lighting

Lighting plays an important role in cinematography. The design, intensity, and color of lighting help to tell the story. Lighting can be used to establish mood, convey the time of the day and season, and emphasize or deemphasize elements within a shot.

In live-action film, lighting is an important element of the cinematography and must be designed and planned in preproduction. After filming starts, lighting decisions are completely committed. However, in 3D computer animation, lighting is a separate element, often considered in detail mostly during the later stages of production and into postproduction.

One of the most important overall aspects of lighting is the exposure ratio within a scene. Think of this as the difference between the brightest portion of the frame and the darkest. When a scene has little overall light and low contrast, it is referred to as *low key*. *High-key* scenes have the opposite characteristics—they are bright overall, with dark shadows and high contrast. Low-key scenes create a dark and somber mood. High-key scenes are associated with happy situations.

A lighting director can use several types of lights to adjust the mood of the scene. For the purpose of this book, the three most important types will be considered: key lights, fill lights, and back lights (see Figure 1.14).

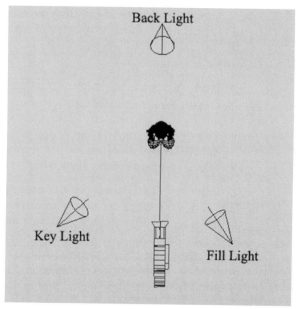

FIGURE 1.14   A figure with key, fill, and back light.

- The *key light* should be the strongest light in the scene. It should be immediately clear to the audience where the light comes from. Because its intensity is greater than any other light in the scene, it should cast shadows. The angle and density of the shadows serve as clues to the type of location and presumed source. In outdoor scenes, the key light often represents the sun. In lighting humanoid characters, the most flattering key light placement is from above and to one side. When the light strikes the face at an angle rather than straight on, it helps to bring out the depth and character of the face.

- A *fill light* is a light placed to soften the shadows created by the key light and illuminate objects not lit by the key light. The fill light is positioned on the opposite side of the key light. If the key light is on the left side of the character, the fill light should be on the right side of the character. It should be placed lower than the key light, up to the subject's height. The intensity of the fill light should be half of the key light. The fill light in computer graphics is used to simulate the light that in reality would be bounced from the ground and surrounding walls or objects back onto a character. Thus, its color is usually picked to reflect the environment.

- A *back light* is used to separate foreground objects from background. The back light is placed between the foreground object and the background object, facing toward the camera. Back lights are usually much weaker than fill lights, except where a distinct silhouette is desired. A common lighting technique is to use a single key, fill and back light—a strategy known as "three-point lighting."

Storyboarding

After you have developed a story and designed the characters, the next step is creating a storyboard. A *storyboard* contains one sample image for each shot in your movie. To the side or below the image should be a brief description of the setting, as well as notes on cinematography and sound—including dialogue, if present (see Figure 1.15).

FIGURE 1.15   *Astrobucks* animation storyboard. (Courtesy of William Robinson.)

A storyboard can be created with hand drawings, other computer software, or with Maya itself. Don't worry if you cannot draw well, however. The purpose of storyboarding is not artistic but organizational. The point is to have the film sequence worked out on paper. This is an important planning tool, even for an individual animator working alone. For a group project, the storyboard becomes a key working document referenced repeatedly by the full team.

The basic layout of a storyboard is chronological. If you are uncertain of the full sequence up front (which is common), consider using individual sheets of paper attached to an empty wall or even large index cards. After you are reasonably confident of the sequence, number your scenes and shots. Then review your storyboard and start to estimate shot and scene timings.

Finally, walk through your boards again from the perspective of each character; think about their emotional state(s) in each shot, and make sure the audience can see the character's anticipation, action, and reaction. A common problem is not leaving enough time for the audience to visually register a character's reaction to an event. Also, be sure to include enough close-ups so that these reactions are evident to the audience. There is no sense animating complex facial expressions in a long shot because the audience will miss them. Instead, use a long shot to establish context, and then cut briefly to a tight reaction shot.

The Animatic

The *animatic* is a 2D movie created with the storyboard images. A storyboard is a good organizing device, but until you are very experienced, it is hard to judge timing or continuity well in this format. Fortunately, these days it is relatively easy to create a short 2D movie from your storyboard images. Programs such as Adobe's AfterEffects and Premiere enable you to sequence a combination of scanned or digital images and then output them as a digital movie. You can also record a rough soundtrack, including dialogue, if present, and add it to the movie. Similar to the storyboard, the animatic should be treated as a working document. Don't waste time fussing with details; instead, concentrate on getting your overall scene timing correct and checking that your narrative makes sense in linear form. The animatic is also a good device to solicit feedback from friends and colleagues.

Sound Design

The animatic is the first time in the preproduction sequence when you will need to start thinking about sound. However, this topic is important enough to deserve special consideration. Sound is a key component in film, and beginning animators commonly underappreciate its importance. In medium to large productions, sound design is an independent specialty. In small productions, animators often recruit their friends to help with voices and sound effects. In all productions, animators should understand enough about sound to come up with at least preliminary sound ideas on their own. Typically, preproduction sound at the level of an animatic requires enough of a rough approximation to help guide the rest of the process forward. The three major components of sound that must be considered are dialogue, sound effects, and music.

Dialogue

Dialogue not only tells the story but also provides important clues to the audience about your characters' backgrounds, feelings, and emotions. It is not an accident that large animation productions feature Hollywood "A List" stars as their animated characters' voices. Even if your budget precludes hiring an Eddie Murphy for your production, thinking through who you would want to cast as one of your characters is useful. There is nothing to stop you from considering your character as a rabbit who acts and talks a bit like James Dean; this can help with your dialogue writing as well as preliminary reading and pacing.

If you cast friends or nonprofessional actors for your voice work, one additional suggestion is to cast with personality. In other words, don't ask an inexperienced person to play a character that is very different from the person. Professional actors can pull this off, but don't recruit your mild-mannered friend to play an aggressive loudmouth. You are probably asking for more than he can deliver, and the result will likely be unconvincing.

Another important consideration is the impact of dialogue on story timing and on character animation. Recording dialogue typically comes late in the preproduction sequence, after the storyboard and script are set. However, you should keep in mind that the recording sessions can provide valuable feedback. Obviously, you will be recording audio, but you should also consider videotaping these sessions. The expressions and body language of your actors can provide valuable reference for your animation. Observation of this reference footage will also be important in adjusting both timing and cinematography. This is a good opportunity, for example, to look for appropriate close-ups and cutaway shots.

Sound Effects

Sound effects can be categorized in two different ways, both of which highlight important aspects to consider in animation. The first is that sound effects can be either synchronous or asynchronous. The synchronicity here refers to actions visible onscreen. For example, if a character stumbles over a rock, you would typically want a synchronous sound effect timed to emphasize the hit. Asynchronous effects typically include environmental sound, such as the birds in a forest scene or traffic noise. However, asynchronous effects might also include important plot elements occurring offscreen.

The second main consideration is the location or prominence of sounds. A good strategy for composing effects tracks is to try layering sound similarly to the way you might layer graphics in an image composition. Try to think about sounds being not only in the background or foreground but also the midground. Also, consider when you want your audience to become aware of a sound. Often you will want to time this to just slightly lead what they are about to see. Classic horror films are full of good (but rather heavy-handed) examples of this technique.

There are two common techniques for generating sound effects. One is to purchase effects libraries, and the other is to create your own. Effects libraries have the advantage of providing numerous well-categorized effects with known distribution rights. The disadvantage is that these effects tend to be like clip art—a bit too generic and recognizable. For preproduction purposes, however, they are often a good start. In production or postproduction, you can often adjust these stock sounds using any of a number of relatively inexpensive sound programs.

Often you will want or need to create your own effects. When doing so, a lot of creativity and a little sound manipulator software become indispensable. The human voice is capable of amazing things, and you can get a lot of interesting effects just by banging on things. Often it is possible to create unique effects simply by speeding up, slowing down, and blending common sounds. For example, try crunching up paper and slowing down the sound loop significantly.

Music

Film music is itself the subject of many books. Here we will consider only a few specific issues that come up frequently with respect to animation production. The first is that most of the music familiar to you is likely to be copyrighted, and it can be difficult to obtain appropriate clearances, so for preproduction animatic purposes, go ahead and use a track from your favorite band—but don't assume that you will be able to use it for your final. Moreover, you should be aware that music rights include both a composition component and a performance component. Having your kid brother play the theme from the *Love Boat* for your sound track means that you don't need to worry about the performance rights, but you would still need to pay royalties on the composition. Similarly, you are not free to use a performance of a Mozart symphony from the London Philharmonic. In that case, the copyright on the composition has long since expired, but the performance rights still need to be negotiated. On the other hand, if you can coax your brother to play Mozart for you, you would likely be legally in the clear.

One important resource you might want to consult is the ASCAP (The American Society of Composers, Authors and Publishers) website at http://www.ascap.com. The site provides a searchable database that lets you enter the title or performer of a song or composition and find out who wrote it and who owns the rights. The site also provides contact information for the copyright holders.

Even if you can get appropriate permissions, a second common issue with the use of existing music for animation is that most music composed for other purposes is likely to be too long for use in short animations. This is not simply a matter of the full length of a piece. It has more to do with the length of phrasing and the build up of emotional expression within the music. One suggestion is to back your introductory credits and establishing shots with musical lead in. This gives your music a chance to establish a mood, sometimes before any visuals. Similarly, closing credits give you a chance to musically restate your themes.

However, repurposing existing music for animation can still be very difficult. As an alternative, you should give serious consideration to hiring a composer or musician with composing skills to create custom music for your piece. Given the brevity of most animations, this is not nearly as expensive as you might imagine, and it can greatly improve the work. If you don't personally know any suitable musicians, your local university music department can be an excellent source for both composers and musicians.

Motion Studies

Motion studies are to the animator what quick sketches are to an artist. They are quick experiments to capture the most important characteristics that distinguish one character from another. To create a motion study, you must be able to repeatedly observe the motion. Up until a few years ago, the equipment needed to do this was beyond the reach of any individual animator. Now any consumer camcorder or DVD player can provide you with the needed reference. There are two common sources of reference footage, and most productions use both.

The first is other films or videos, some of which you will already have identified in your character development work. If you haven't already done so, find a movie star persona appropriate to your character. Identify some reference clips from a movie or two that show the essence of your character. Pick scenes with emotional content that you want your character to express. Use your notebook to write a paragraph that describes the important mannerisms used by the actor in your reference footage. What are his facial expressions, body postures, hand gestures, vocal emphases? Also, how did the director and director of photography (DP) structure the shot? How was lighting used?

The second source of reference for motion studies is to create your own. This has the considerable advantage that you can record exactly the action you'll need. One difficulty is that you will need appropriate subjects to shoot. For small productions, the likely subjects include yourself and your friends, but even at major studios, animators must act out their characters. Don't worry if you are not a great actor. Acting things out yourself can be a big help in learning to feel your character's emotions and their physical manifestations. If your character is not human, ask how would the character behave if he were human? Give your character human emotional feelings. Act your character under different circumstances such as when he is hungry, afraid, happy, sad, or coerced.

TUTORIAL 1.1: CAMERAS AND CINEMATOGRAPHY

Because cinematography is so fundamental to animation, this first tutorial will start you off with a simple prepared scene and ask you to act as the DP. In the basic storyline, the character, Henry, comes home after a very hard day at the office. He opens the front door, enters his living room, and walks across to a bar counter. He shakes his head and pounds on the counter in frustration. You will create and position Maya cameras using basic cinematography to tell this small story visually.

Creating a Long Shot

You will start with a long shot. In this case, the long shot serves two purposes. First, it will introduce the character's environment—in this case, a room with a door and a counter. Second, it will show the full body of the character in motion, which will give the audience a chance to read the emotion of the character through his walking posture. To support this, we want the line of action to travel across the middle of the screen, with strong focal points in the upper-left and lower-right thirds of the screen. To show this action while also showing the room, the focal length of the camera was changed from the default (35) to 65. The action begins at approximately frame 70. From frame 70 to 250 (six seconds), we see the character opening the door and walking over to the counter.

ON THE CD

1. Open a file called camera_shots_tutorial.mb in the MayaWorking-
   Files subfolder from the chapter1 folder on the CD-ROM.
2. Select Create > Cameras > Camera and Aim (see Figure 1.16).

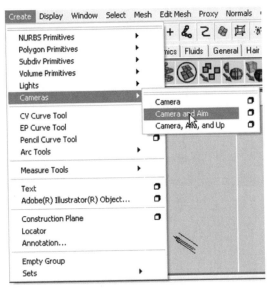

FIGURE 1.16   Create Cameras menu. By default, Maya creates the camera at the origin.

3. In the Top view menus, select Panels > Panel > Outliner.
4. Scroll down the Outliner window until you see camera1_group.
5. Click on the + sign of the camera1_group. You should see camera1
   and camera1_aim.
6. Double-click on camera1_group and change its name to longShotGroup.
7. Double-click camera1 and name it longShotCamera.
8. Double-click on camera1_aim and rename it longShotAim.
9. Select the longShotCamera and, in the Channel Box, type Translate
   X = 86.5, Translate Y = 35, and Translate Z = 150. The camera should
   move to the back of the room above the character's height.
10. In the Channel Box Shapes section, change the Focal Length value
    to 65.
11. Select the longShotAim and, in the Channel Box, type Translate X =
    21, Translate Y = 10, and Translate Z = 13.5. You should see the cam-
    era as shown in Figure 1.17.

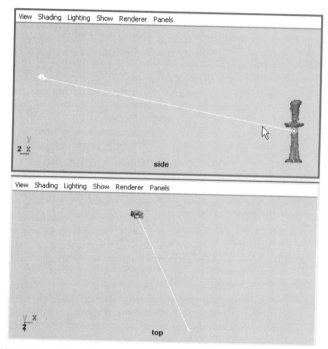

FIGURE 1.17   Side and Top views of camera and camera aim positions.

12. In the Perspective view, select Panels > Perspective > longShotCamera.
13. Play the animation to see the shot.

Creating a Medium Shot

The purpose of this medium shot is to show the upper body of the character as he is approaching the counter and to highlight the action when he pounds the counter in frustration. Because you started the action with the camera showing the character's right profile, continue on this side of the scene, following the rule of 180. Again, try to create a final composition where the line of action proceeds across the screen, ending about two-thirds of the way across the frame and avoiding symmetry. This shot goes from frames 250 to 400 (five seconds).

1. Select Create > Cameras > Camera and Aim.
2. Repeat steps 3 to 8 in the preceding section to rename the camera parts. Change camera1_group to mediumShotGroup, camera1 to mediumShotCamera, and camera1_aim to mediumShotAim.

3. Select the mediumShotCamera and, in the Channel Box, type Translate X = 64, Translate Y = 12, and Translate Z = 44.
4. Select the mediumShotAim and, in the Channel Box, type Translate X = 48, Translate Y = 14, and Translate Z = 28.5. You should see the camera and aim as in Figure 1.18.

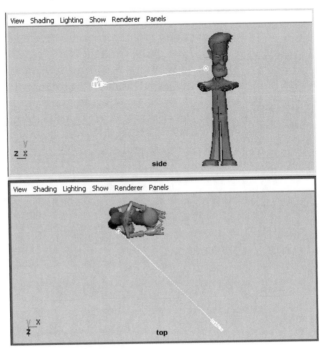

FIGURE 1.18   Side and Top views of camera and camera aim positions.

5. In the Perspective window, select Panels > Perspective > mediumShot-Camera.
6. Play the animation to see the shot.

Creating a Close-Up Shot

The purpose of this shot is to concentrate on the facial expression of the character (in this case, anguish). You already established where the character is and shown his frustration through the body language of his walk and by his action of pounding on the counter. You want to end the scene with as dramatic a shot as possible. You maintain the same overall position relative to the character (showing his right profile), and set up the composition so that the door frame is visible in the background. (In final rendering, this might be blurred using depth of field, and the facial expression might be highlighted using lighting.) This shot runs from frames 400 to 490 (three seconds). Reaction shots are generally much shorter than action shots, but this one ends the scene, so we need enough time for the audience to react before shifting to the next scene.

1. Select Create > Cameras > Camera and Aim.
2. Repeat steps 3 to 8 from the "Creating a Long Shot" section to rename the camera parts. Change camera1_group to closeUpGroup, camera1 to closeUpCamera, and camera1_aim to closeUpCameraAim.
3. Select the closeUpCamera and in the Channel Box, type Translate X = 61, Translate Y = 18, and Translate Z = 33.
4. Select the closeUpCameraAim and, in the Channel Box, type Translate X = 49.6, Translate Y = 16.53, and Translate Z = 27.6. You should see the camera and aim as in Figure 1.19.

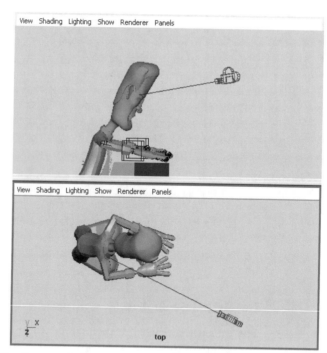

FIGURE 1.19   Close-up shot in the camera and aim position from Front and Top views.

5. In the Perspective view, select Panels > Perspective > closeUpCamera.
6. Play the animation to see the shot.

TUTORIAL 1.2: THREE-POINT LIGHTING

Let's apply a simple lighting design to a scene. As described earlier, the best starting lighting arrangement for simple scenes is three-point lighting because it uses three lights: a key, a fill, and a back light (see Figure 1.20). After getting basic lighting set up, you may want to create additional environment lights within the scene.

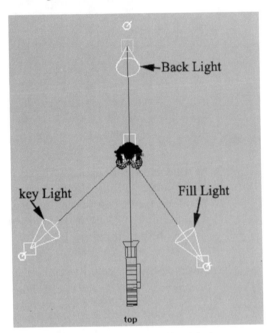

FIGURE 1.20   Key, fill, and back lights.

Creating the Key Light

To create the key light, follow these steps.

ON THE CD

1. Open a file called lighting_tutorial.mb in the MayaWorkingFiles subfolder from the chapter1 folder on the CD-ROM.
2. Select Create > Lights > Spot Light.
3. Name the light keyLight.
4. In Top view, move keyLight approximately 20 to 45 degrees to the left side of the camera.
5. Press T on the keyboard to activate the Show Manipulator tool. You should see the light manipulators and the point of interest of the light manipulators.
6. In the Side view, move the light above the character's height. Click on the point of interest of the light and move it on the character's nose (see Figure 1.21).

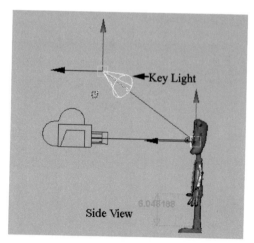

FIGURE 1.21   Key light position from Side view.

7. In the Channel Box, scroll down until you see the Intensity channel. Make sure the Intensity value is 1.
8. Render a frame test to see the results of keyLight. The character's face should be lit. The right side of his face should be lighter than the left side as shown in Figure 1.22.

 If you want to have the character cast a shadow, enable Use Depth Map Shadow in the Shadows section of the light's Attribute Editor.

FIGURE 1.22   The face lit with keyLight.

Creating the Fill Light

To create the fill light, follow these steps.

1. Select Create > Lights > Spot Light.
2. Name the light fillLight.
3. In the Top view, move the light 20 to 45 degrees to the right of the camera.
4. In the Side view, move the camera approximately to the character's height. fillLight should be lower than the keyLight
. 5. Move the light point of interest on the character's nose (see Figure 1.23).

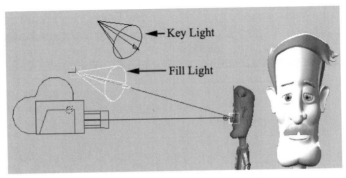

FIGURE 1.23   The fillLight position from the Side view.

6. In the Channel Box, scroll down until you see the Intensity channel.
7. Change the Intensity value to 0.5.
8. Click on the color field. You should see the Maya Color Chooser. Change the color to H = 219, S = 0.030, V = 1.0 (very light blue) and click Accept.
9. Render a frame test. The right side of the character's face should be lighter.

Creating the Back Light

To create the back light, follow these steps.

1. Select Create > Lights > Spot Light.
2. In the Top view, move the light to the back of the character.
3. In the Side view, move the light above the character's height.
4. Move the light point of interest to the bottom of his head (see Figure 1.24).

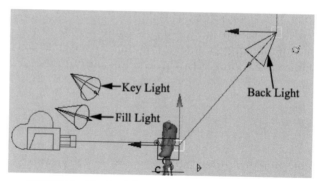

FIGURE 1.24   The back light position from the Side view.

5. In the Channel Box, change the intensity of the light to 5.
6. In the Side view, adjust the light until you see a rim of light highlighting the shoulders and hair.
7. Render a frame test.

You can use the three-point lighting method to light your characters and props.

ON THE CD
A scene with three-point lighting is included in the chapter1 MayaWorkingFiles folder on the CD-ROM.

SUMMARY

In this chapter, you were introduced to the character animation production process from beginning to end. Preproduction was discussed in detail, including cinematography and lighting. Two tutorials demonstrated the basic technical steps necessary to create a sequence of shots and three-point lighting.

In the next chapter, you will learn the art and science of animation.

CHALLENGE ASSIGNMENTS

1. Character and Story Development

Part A: Character Concept

Develop a new character using the backstory method described in the "Character Design and Character Sketches" section of this chapter. Try to answer the questions in that section in terms of your character. Pick a real-world actor who would be suitable to play the role of your character and explain why. Then summarize your character and his or her environment in a paragraph describing the "5Ws".

- **What.** What is it? (a bird, a fish, a horse, a woman, a man, a girl, a boy).
- **Where.** The environment where he or she lives.
- **When.** The time when he or she lives or lived.
- **Who.** The character's temperament and personality.
- **Why.** The whys of your decisions. Why does the character have a missing tooth? Why does the character have big ears?

Part B: Story Concept

Develop the story concept for a short animation with a single lead character. Try to summarize the concept in a sentence or two (you do not need to specify a full plot).

Examples:

This story is about a stylish pig that lives in a pig town and wants to be a famous skater.

The story is about an ugly piglet that is desperate to win the pig beauty contest at the county fair. With the help of several friends, she succeeds.

Part C: Physical Character Design

Given your conceptual character design from Part A and your general story from Part B, develop a series of preliminary physical character sketches and then narrow these down to a single proposed character design.

First, create a physical or digital character scrapbook. Collect reference materials from websites, magazines, snapshots, or video clips that illustrate design elements you find interesting and appropriate to your character.

Second, do a series of quick and rough character sketches that combine your design ideas in a variety of ways. For example, you might want to experiment with the proportions of your character's body or try several different designs for your character's clothes and accessories.

Third, pick your favorite among your rough sketches and develop a more carefully drawn or detailed character. Draw at least two full-body views: one from the front and another from the side.

Part D: Storyboarding

Create a storyboard for the story developed in Part B. Use index cards for each shot, laying them out on a table or wall. Develop a 15- to 30-second shot sequence. The story should show both weaknesses and strengths of your character.

Make sure your cinematography allows the viewer to see both character anticipation and character reactions by including tight shots where appropriate. Each shot/index card should have a phrase or sentence summarizing the action and a graphical or text notation about the camera work. For characters or objects in motion within a frame, you may want to draw beginning and ending positions with an arrow between them.

After your sequence is stable, number your shots and develop and note camera transitions between the shots.

Part E: Pitching Your Production

Develop and present the pitch for your proposed animation production. If you are working within the context of a class, be prepared to give this as a presentation to your classmates. If you are an independent learner, round up some friends and have them role-play studio executives (cigars optional).

Imagine that your audience has a very short attention span. Keep in mind the following points and be prepared to act out key portions such as your story's climax. Do not talk about why you chose to create the animation or about its techniques, camera shot decisions, or any other extraneous information during the initial story pitch. Encourage people to ask questions during the pitch.

Required Pitch Elements

- **Story concept.** Start with your story concept sentence to orient the audience to the basic idea first without giving away the climax or ending.
- **Character introduction.** Because storyboards do not easily convey the essence of characters, briefly introduce the main character before starting the story pitch to the audience. Tell the audience what actor you are using as a reference to give them an idea of the essence of the final character.
- **Storyboard walkthrough.** After the overall story concept and character information are established, take your audience through your storyboard panel by panel.

2. Cinematography and Lighting Design

Part A: Adding Drama

ON THE CD

Open the scene called shots_exercise.mb from the CD-ROM. This is the same scene used in Tutorial 1.1. Imagine that your director has reviewed your first pass of cinematography and wants "more drama." The simplest way to do this is to add more reaction shots and to bring the camera closer to the character. Using your tutorial scene, first create a medium shot of Henry just after he enters the door. This will give the audience an earlier chance to read Henry's facial expression. After a brief medium shot is inserted, you can go back to the existing long shot to show Henry walking across the room. Next, create an extreme close-up camera, and insert an extreme close-up before the final (normal close-up) shot.

Part B: Creating Spotlights

Using your cinematography scene, create three spot lights in the scene. Position and adjust the light parameters to be the key light, fill light, and back light. Your challenge as lighting designer is to reflect and highlight the frustrated and angry mood of the character. Pay particular attention to the ending shot with Henry at the bar.

FUNDAMENTALS OF COMPUTER ANIMATION

In This Chapter

- The Art and Science of Animation
- Basics of Keyframe Animation

The Art and Science of Animation

> I used to think that being an animator meant moving objects.
> Later, I learned that being an animator means moving the audience.
> —Anonymous

The word *animation* comes from the Latin word *animus*, which means the condition of being alive. To make a character alive, you need to consider the art and science of animation.

Science helps the animator understand how things work in the real world. Human beings have observed things in the real world for thousands of years and have expectations when seeing things in motion. Animators have to fulfill these expectations but not necessarily by imitating the real world exactly. Animators can suspend or distort reality for artistic purposes. For example, it is common to see a cartoon character run beyond the edge of a cliff, then look down and panic before gravity catches up with him. This is funny because it plays with our expectation of reality. However, if the character continued to float in thin air, the audience's illusion of reality would be shattered.

In this chapter, you will create a simple animation. You will start studying how things appear through observation and then make use of scientific principles that generalize observation. Finally, you will apply some artistic principles to give the animation additional impact.

Some Basic Principles of Animation

The principles of animation are technology-independent rules, or rules of thumb, which have proven useful for more than half a century of animation practice. These are different from scientific descriptions such as Newton's laws in that they are rooted in human perception. They also include issues that have proven important in the specific medium of film. When you create an animation, you are to some degree or another creating a film. Thus, you need to learn the conventions that have been found to work well in film. Two key concepts to consider are timing and weight.

Timing

When animators refer to *timing*, they are talking about both the general pacing of the animation and a specific character's action. Timing can be manipulated by the animator to show objects' weight and scale, and characters' emotions, personality, and moods. For example, to convey that a character is happy, you would time his actions faster than if he is sad. To convey that an object is heavy, you would time its motion slower than a light object.

Conveying a Sense of Object Weight in Animation

Weight can be conveyed with timing. Heavy objects have more momentum and usually move more slowly than light objects. The size and texture of an object can convey weight. For example, a large ball with a metal texture would look heavier than a small ball with a rubber texture.

Newton's Laws: The Physics of Bodies in Motion

The basic workings of gravity and mechanical behavior were first systematically studied by Isaac Newton many centuries ago. The resulting Newton's laws remain relevant to animation even today. Some animation systems, including Maya, provide dynamic functions that can simulate some of these kinds of behaviors for some objects. However, much of the time, an animator must manually simulate physical forces.

Newton's first law of motion is usually stated as follows:

> An object at rest tends to stay at rest, and an object in motion tends to stay in motion with the same speed and in the same direction unless acted upon by an opposing force.

This is basically a statement of the concept of *momentum*. Objects keep doing what they have been doing, unless something forces them to change. This is clear enough, but at first reading, it appears to ignore a very common observed characteristic of objects in motion: Most of the time in the real world, an object will not keep moving indefinitely. Without an energy source, objects tend to slow down gradually and then stop. Before Newton, most scientists thought objects had a natural resting state to which they always returned. So why do objects in the real world tend to slow down?

The answer according to Newton is in the "unbalanced forces," specifically, air resistance and friction. A book sliding along a table can slide a relatively short distance. The same book sliding on ice might travel much farther. Thus, the force stopping the book is not a characteristic of the book but rather of its environment.

Newton's second law describes in further detail what occurs when forces acting on an object are unbalanced. This law is most famously stated as follows:

> F = MA (where F is force, M is mass, and A is acceleration)

For animation purposes, this can also be expressed as

> A = F/M

In other words, the acceleration of an object depends on two things: the force being applied to it and the mass of the object. If all other things are equal, an object that is twice as massive should accelerate half as fast.

Also, to accelerate very quickly, you need to have a large force, a small mass, or both.

The most common real-world animation applications of this law are to convey relative differences in the weights of objects. For example, your audience won't believe a character is heavy unless they see that he starts and stops moving relatively slowly.

Finally, Newton's third law states that for each action, there is an equal and opposite reaction. These action-reaction pairs are common. For example, when you sit on a couch, you are putting a downward force on it proportional to your mass times your rate of acceleration. The couch also exerts a force back toward you (if it didn't, you'd fall through it). Birds can fly in part because when they press down on the air, the air pushes the bird back upward.

In practice, animators pay a great deal of attention to action and reaction. For example, if you were to animate a boat being rowed through water, you would have to balance the effort of the oarsman straining against the oars (action) with the forward progress of the boat (reaction).

BASICS OF KEYFRAME ANIMATION

In the old days, before computers, animations were created by a main animator and the tweeners. The main animator would draw the keys, or main poses, and the tweeners would draw the in-between drawings. With the advent of computer technology, the process of creating animations changed substantially. Now, the computer does the work of the tweeners, and animators act more like digital puppeteers. The animator composes the main poses or keys, and the computer generates all of the in between poses.

The basic process of animation in Maya includes two steps. First, the animator selects an object and sets one or more if its properties. Then the animator sets a *key* for those properties at a particular point in time. For example, the animator might position a character sitting down at time 1, then set a key, then move the character into a standing position and set another key at time 2. The computer calculates the intermediate positions and rotations using a process known as *interpolation*.

Most of the time, Maya interpolates things so well that an animator doesn't need to know the details of how the process is done. However, on occasion, you will get unexpected results, so you should understand what Maya is doing behind the scenes. The first thing to understand about interpolation is that it is clamped, by default, in Maya. This means that keyframes whose values vary by more than about five percent are connected using smooth curves. Keyframes whose values vary less than five percent are connected with linear curves. Let's set up a simple test animation to demonstrate the process.

1. Select File > New Scene.
2. Press F2 to go to the Animation mode.
3. Select Create > Polygon Primitives and uncheck Interactive Creation.
4. Select Create Polygon Primitives > Cube.
5. Set the end time of the playback range and the end time of the animation to 120.
6. Make sure the time indicator on the Time Slider is set to 1 (see Figure 2.1).

FIGURE 2.1   Time indicator.

7. Select the cube, and in the Channel Box, type Translate X = −7, Translate Y = 0.5, and Translate Z = 0 (see Figure 2.2).

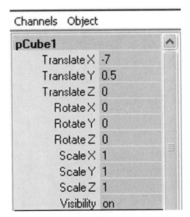

FIGURE 2.2   Channel Box.

8. Choose Animate > Set Key Option Box (see Figure 2.3).
9. In the options window Choose Edit > Reset Settings. This allows you to set keys for all manipulator handles and keyable attributes.
10. Press the Set Key button to set the first key.

FIGURE 2.3   Set Key menu.

11. Type 30 in the time indicator to indicate that you are on frame 30.
12. In the Channel Box, type Translate X = 0, Translate Y = 7, and Translate Z = 7.
13. Choose Animate > Set Key or press S on the keyboard to set a second key.
14. Move the time indicator to frame 60 and type Translate X = 7, Translate Y = 0.5, and Translate Z = 0.
15. Press S on the keyboard to set a third key.
16. Move the time indicator to frame 90 and type Translate X = 0, Translate Y = 7, and Translate Z = –7.
17. Set a fourth key.
18. Move the time indicator to frame 120 and type Translate X = –7, Translate Y = 0.5, and Translate Z = 0.
19. Set a fifth key.
20. Play back your animation. You should see the box moving at a constant velocity in between keyframes, but smooth motion as it eases in and out of the keys (see Figure 2.4).

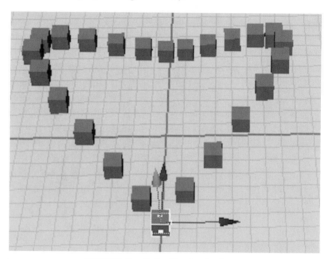

FIGURE 2.4   Cube linear motion.

The Graph Editor

The *Graph Editor* provides a different way of looking at animation. Instead of viewing object positions or attributes at a particular point in time, the Graph Editor lets you see the value of an attribute over time. For an example of this, try tweaking the simple animation in the previous section.

1. To launch the Graph Editor, first select your animated cube and then select Window > Animation Editors > Graph Editor. The editor has two panels. On the left, the *Outliner* has a hierarchical tree diagram (see Figure 2.5) representing the animated channels on the selected object.

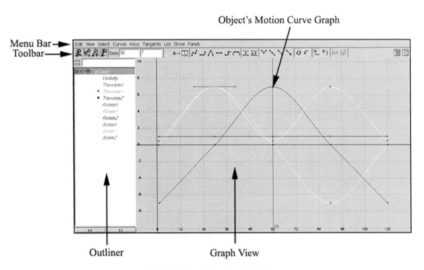

Object's Motion Curve Graph

Menu Bar →
Toolbar →

Outliner   Graph View

FIGURE 2.5   The Graph Editor.

 The Graph Editor can also be found under the Panels > Panel > Graph Editor on any of the four views windows.

2. From the Graph Editor's menus, select View > Autoframe (this will increase the visibility of your curves).
3. Select the Y translation channel of the box object by clicking on Translate Y in the Outliner. On the right, you should see a graph with an animation curve representing the position of the cube over time (see Figure 2.6). In the Graph Editor, time runs horizontally along the bottom axis. The vertical axis represents the values of the selected attribute. In this case, these should range from 0.5 (at frame 1) to 7 (at frames 30 and 90).

Note that as time increases (reading from left to right along the curve), the Y translation value increases as well. The curve continues moving upward until it reaches the horizontal location that represents frame 30 and then reverses direction and goes back down at frame 60. In this kind of graph, if an animation curve is horizontal, it means the value is not changing over time. Thus, unanimated channels (such as Rotate and Scale X, Y, Z) appear as horizontally flat lines. Conversely, curves that are very steep represent things that are changing very rapidly. A vertical line represents an instantaneous change. It may take a while to get used to, but the beauty of the Graph Editor view is that it gives you a visual indication of both speed and the rate of acceleration or deceleration. As it turns out, this information is very important for creating convincing animation and for correcting common errors made when animating in Perspective view.

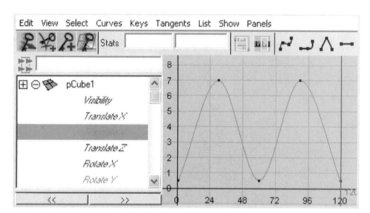

FIGURE 2.6   The animation curve represents the position of the curve over time.

Perhaps the most common use of the Graph Editor is to add *ease-in* and *ease-out* to motion. When an object starts to move, it usually does not get up to speed instantaneously. Depending on its weight and what is driving it, an object starting at a resting position takes a perceptible amount of time to start moving (ease-in). This effect can be exaggerated to convey the impression of heaviness. For intentional motion, the opposite effect occurs at the end of a range of motion. As you reach for a glass, you slow down as your hand approaches the glass (ease-out). Unintentional motion, by contrast, will keep going at the same pace until forced to stop or redirected. A ball hitting a wall does not slow down in anticipation—but a human would.

Let's apply these principles to our simple example. Imagine first that you want to create an impression of great weight. You want the motion to start out slowly and then gradually pick up steam. Conceptually, you want the Y translation curve to start out very flat and then curve upward gradually.

1. Make sure you have the Move tool selected. Select the first key on the Y translation curve by dragging a rectangle over it or by clicking on it (see Figure 2.7).

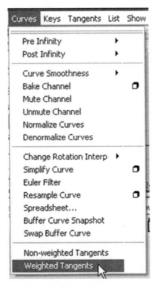

FIGURE 2.7   Selecting the first key.

2. In the Graph Editor, choose Curves > Weighted Tangents (see Figure 2.8). This changes the curve to allow you to have nonsymmetrical tangents.

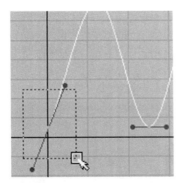

FIGURE 2.8   Weighted Tangents menu choice.

3. Click on the curve tangent's right grabber handle and then click on the Free Tangent Weight toolbar button (see Figure 2.9). This frees the specific handle for nonsymmetrical editing. The end point of the grabber handle should become an empty square.

FIGURE 2.9   Free Tangent Weight button.

4. Make sure you have the Move tool selected. Middle-click and then drag and pull the handle to the right and down until you flatten the beginning of your curve (see Figure 2.10).

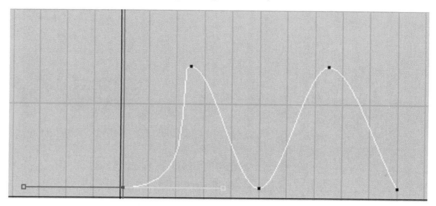

FIGURE 2.10   Flatten tangent to ease-out.

5. Now zoom in pretty close on your box at the origin and play back the animation. You should see a relatively slow start and then noticeable acceleration.

Arranged on the right of the Graph Editor's toolbar is a set of icons for various kinds of curve tangent modes (see Figure 2.11).

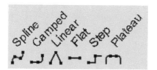

FIGURE 2.11   Different tangent type buttons.

Think of these as semiautomatic ways of adjusting how the curve approaches a key. The simplest form of tangent is *Linear* (third icon from the left). As noted earlier, this might make sense for unintentional motion such as one object hitting another. Another common mode is *Spline tangent*. This smoothes animation curves as they approach a keyframe but tends to cause problems where the curve overshoots the desired position. *Plateau tangent* mode is very good in a variety of situations, notably for footstep animations where you want feet to stick exactly on the ground. Change the tangent of the third key (frame 60) to Linear. Notice that the cube changes direction in a sharp curve (see Figures 2.12 and 2.13).

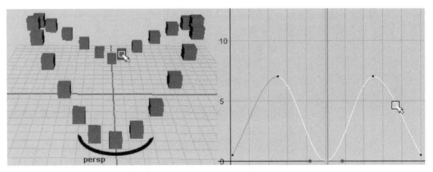

FIGURE 2.12   Frame 60 Spline tangent.

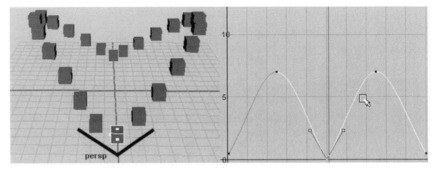

FIGURE 2.13   Frame 60 Linear tangent.

Breakdowns

Breakdowns are special keys you can set between keys. They have a nested relationship with the keys on either side of them, and they automatically shift when those keys are moved. You can think of a breakdown as a key where time is specified relative to surrounding keys. If you put a breakdown halfway between two normal keys, it will always stay halfway between those keys.

For example, in a biped character walk, when both feet are on the ground (contact position), a key is set for each foot. When the foot is passing, you set a breakdown key for the passing foot. You will learn how to set a breakdown later in this chapter.

TUTORIAL 2.1: LIGHT AND HEAVY BOUNCING BALL ANIMATION

Now that you have a set of physical principles and a set of animation techniques, you can combine the two to create a simple animation. Your animation will feature two balls, both starting out dropping from a similar position. One of the balls is large and heavy; the other smaller and lighter. You will want your animation to reflect the physical difference in the way those two objects might move.

To create the animation, you need to understand the Maya Time Slider. The *Time Slider* allows you to set the start and end times of the animation and playback. It also allows you to set a specific time for a key either by typing the key number in the Current Time field or by scrubbing (dragging the left mouse back and forth) on the Time Slider (see Figure 2.14).

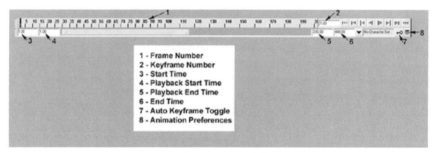

1 - Frame Number
2 - Keyframe Number
3 - Start Time
4 - Playback Start Time
5 - Playback End Time
6 - End Time
7 - Auto Keyframe Toggle
8 - Animation Preferences

FIGURE 2.14   Time Slider.

Animating the Translation of the Light Ball

To animate the translation of the light ball, follow these steps.

1. Select File > New Scene.
2. Press F2 to go to the Animation mode.
3. Create a NURBS (Non-Uniform Rational B Spline) sphere with the default setting options.
4. In the Channel Box, click on nurbsSphere1 and type lightBall.
5. Make sure the time indicator on the Time Slider is set to 1. In the Channel Box, type Translate X = –10 and Translate Y = 10.
6. With the sphere still selected, press W to get the Move tool.
7. Choose Animate > Set Key Options and click on All Manipulator Handles and Current Time. The All Manipulator Handles option allows you to set keys for all the handles of the selected manipulator. In this case, the Move tool is the selected manipulator (see Figure 2.15).
8. Click on Set Key.
9. Now you are going to translate the ball in X and Y and set keys and breakdowns as specified in Table 2.1. To set breakdowns, enter the keyframe number in the Current Time field on the Time Slider and select Animate > Set Breakdown.

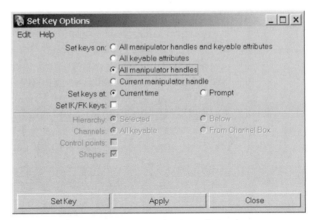

FIGURE 2.15   Set Key Options dialog box.

Table 2.1 Translating the Ball in X and Y and Setting Keyframes and Breakdowns

FRAME #	TRANSLATE X	TRANSLATE Y	KEYFRAME/BREAKDOWN
1	−10	10	Set key
34	−3.17	1	Set key
60	0	5.65	Set breakdown
82	1.68	1	Set key
102	4.25	3.21	Set breakdown
115	5.94	1	Set key
126	7.26	2.46	Set breakdown
141	9.08	1	Set key
155	10.48	2.08	Set breakdown
165	11.46	1	Set key
178	12.31	1.79	Set breakdown
185	12.77	1	Set key
194	13.246	1.55	Set breakdown
202	13.66	1	Set key
211	14	1.295	Set breakdown
217	14.14	1	Set key
223	14.28	1.23	Set breakdown
227	14.39	1	Set key
233	14.51	1.13	Set breakdown
235	14.55	1	Set key
241	14.7	1.035	Set key
245	14.79	1	Set key
247	14.83	1.015	Set key
249	14.87	1	Set key
251	14.91	1.003	Set key
253	14.93	1	Set key

10. When you finish setting all the keys and breakdowns for the ball translation, play the animation. The ball should move by bouncing from left to right and slowly decelerating. Notice that the ball is sliding when it hits the ground, and there is no ease-in and ease-out on acceleration and deceleration of the bouncing. To fix that, you will have to change the tangents of the keys.

11. Open the Graph Editor. Click on the Translate Y channel. Select all the keys of the Y channel with value 1, except the last two (253 and 251). Change their tangents to Linear (see Figures 2.16 and 2.17).

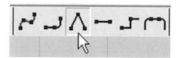

FIGURE 2.16   Linear tangent icon.

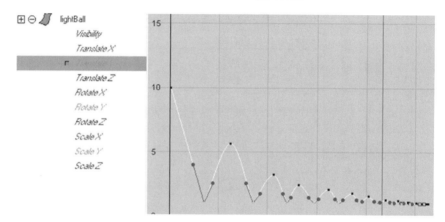

FIGURE 2.17   Key with Linear tangent.

12. Select all the breakdowns on the Translation Y channel. Change their tangents to Flat (see Figures 2.18 and 2.19).

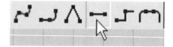

FIGURE 2.18   Flat tangent icon.

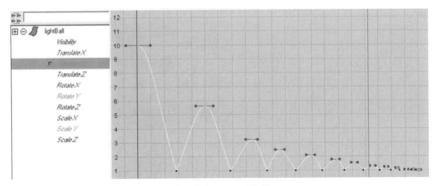

FIGURE 2.19   Breakdowns with Flat tangents.

13. Play the animation.
14. Save your work. Call the file light_ball.mb.

Animating the Rotation of the Light Ball

At this point, you have set all the translation keys for the ball. However, when the ball moves, it also rotates. In reality, a bouncing ball might rotate on X, Y, and Z. For the purpose of this exercise, however, you will animate the Z rotation only.

1. Go to frame 1 and make sure that Rotate X, Y, and Z are 0, 0, and 0.
2. Click on Rotate Z in the Channel Box to select it (see Figure 2.20).

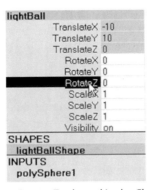

FIGURE 2.20   Rotate Z selected in the Channel Box.

3. Right-click on Rotate Z in the Channel Box. Choose Key Selected from the menu that appears to set a key for Rotate Z (see Figure 2.21). Notice that this is a different way to set a key. This method allows you set a key for a specific parameter only.

FIGURE 2.21   Key Selected in the Channel Box.

4. Go to frame 253.
5. Type Rotate Z = –1107. Set another key for Rotate Z.
6. In the Graph Editor, select key 1 and 253 of Rotate Z. Change their tangent to Flat to ease in and out the beginning and ending of the rotation (see Figure 2.22).

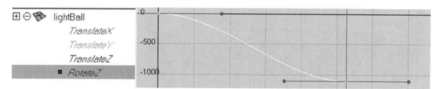

FIGURE 2.22   Rotate Z animation curve for the lightBall.

7. Play the animation.
8. Save your work.

Animating the Heavy Ball

As previously discussed, heavy objects often move more slowly than light objects, and they always accelerate and decelerate more slowly. In the real world, objects have mass and are affected by gravity. In key animation, you have to manipulate time to fake these attributes and create convincing motion.

To create the heavy ball animation, pretend that the heavy ball has approximately twice the mass of the light ball. Given Newton's law, F = MA, it follows that A = F/M. If the force is constant, this means that doubling the mass would halve the rate of acceleration. Keep in mind that this exercise represents an approximation of reality to convey the concept of weight.

Animating the Translation of the Heavy Ball

To animate the translation of the heavy ball, follow these steps.

1. Open the file in which you created the light ball animation and hide the light ball. Create a new layer. Click on the layer, and call it light-BallLayer. Right-click on the new layer and choose Add Selected Objects (see Figure 2.23). Press V to hide the layer.

FIGURE 2.23   Add selected object to a layer.

2. Create a NURBS sphere and call it heavyBall.
3. In the Channel Box, select makeNurbSphere under INPUTS. Change the radius to 2.
4. Translate the ball in X and Y and set keys as specified in Table 2.2.

Table 2.2 Translating the Ball in X and Y

FRAME #	TRANSLATE X	TRANSLATE Y
1	−10	10
32	−3.57	2
81	−0.26	4.73
104	0.8	2
132	1.81	3.1
156	1.97	2
179	3.92	2.7
202	4.86	2
389	11.61	2

5. When you finish setting all the keys, play the animation. Notice that the heavy ball moves more slowly than the light ball.

Animating the Rotation of the Heavy Ball

To animate the rotation of the heavy ball, follow these steps.

1. Go to frame 1 and make sure Rotate X, Y, Z are 0, 0, 0.
2. Set a key for Rotate Z in frame 1.
3. Go to the last key (389). Type Rotate Z = –448.
4. Play the animation. The ball rotation may look linear. Select keys 1 and 448 and change their tangents to Flat (see Figure 2.24).

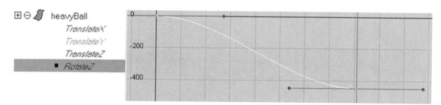

FIGURE 2.24   Rotation Z of the animation curve of the heavy ball.

5. Save your work. Call the file light_heavy_balls.mb.

ON THE CD   You can see an example of this exercise by accessing the file called light_heavy_balls.mb in the MayaWorkingFiles subfolder of the chapter2 folder on the CD-ROM.

OBJECT RELATIONSHIPS

Maya gives you two basic ways of organizing relationships between objects: parenting and grouping. These relationships can be established and visualized in a component of Maya known as the Hypergraph window. To open the Hypergraph, select Window > Hypergraph: Hierarchy.

All objects created in Maya have two separate representations. The first is the geometry, which has been the focus of our discussion so far. The second is a more abstract view, in which each object is represented by a node in a diagram, and relationships between objects are represented by lines between them. For example, create a new scene, and within it add a polygon cube. Within the Hypergraph:Hierarchy window, a single rectangular box appears, which is the node representing your polygon cube (see Figure 2.25).

FIGURE 2.25   A polygon cube node.

If you select a node in the Hypergraph, notice that the object geometry is also selected and vice versa. In complex scenes, the Hypergraph can provide a quick way to select things. Also, note that the normal Zoom and Pan command keys work within the Hypergraph window as they do in other views.

The node contains all the information about the object such as radius, height, width, sections, spans, shader, and so on. A group of connected nodes is called a *hierarchy*. Maya has two types of hierarchies. One is called the *dependency graph*, and the other is called the *scene hierarchy*. The dependency graph is an internal hierarchy that has the input and output connections. To see the dependency graph, select the node and click on the Input/Output Connections button in the Hypergraph window (see Figure 2.26). You should see something like Figure 2.27.

FIGURE 2.26   Input/Output Connections button.

FIGURE 2.27   The polygon cube dependency graph.

The dependency graph can also be viewed by selecting the object and selecting Window > Hypergraph: Connections. The scene hierarchy is a group of nodes parented to each other. The top nodes are the parents and grandparents of the nodes below. For example, when you create a human arm joint, you create the shoulder, elbow, and wrist joints. These joints are hierarchically connected as shown in Figure 2.28.

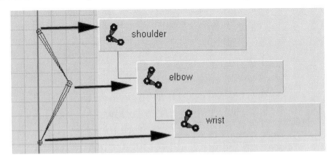

FIGURE 2.28   Arm joints hierarchy.

The shoulder joint is the parent of the elbow joint and grandparent of the wrist joint. If you move the shoulder joint, the elbow and wrist joints will move with it. However, when the wrist joint is moved, the nodes above it are not affected.

Understanding Parenting

In Maya, the term *parenting* has a special meaning. Maya allows you to create a relationship between two or more objects, in which the top-level object, called the parent, controls the transformation of lower-level objects, known as children. This relationship is not symmetrical. Moving the parent object causes the child object to move along with it. However, moving the child objects does not cause the parent to move. Transformations can include translation, rotation, and scaling. In the Hypergraph, a child object is represented as a node indented relative to its parent. To create a parenting relationship, you first select one or more desired child objects and then the parent. You can either use the Edit > Parent menu command or simply press the P key. Let's create a simple scene.

In a new scene, create a cube and a sphere primitive side by side. In our example, the cube is the parent object, and the sphere is the child.

1. Select the cube (child).
2. Hold down the Shift key and select the sphere (parent).
3. Press P on the keyboard. In the Hypergraph, nodes of the cube and sphere should be as shown in Figure 2.29

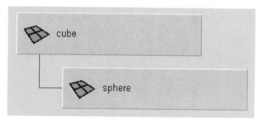

FIGURE 2.29   Parented object's nodes.

4. Now, switch to the Move tool (shortcut key W) and move the sphere. The cube should follow.
5. Switch to the Rotate tool (shortcut key E) and rotate the sphere. The cube should rotate about the sphere.
6. Switch to the Scale tool (shortcut key R) and scale the sphere. The cube should scale proportionally to the sphere.
7. By contrast, try any of these three operations on the cube. The cube itself will be transformed but not the sphere.

Parenting allows you to create logical groups of objects and transform them in a one step by manipulating the parent object.

Understanding Grouping

Grouping in Maya works a bit differently from parenting. When you group two or more objects, Maya creates a new node above the objects (see Figure 2.30).

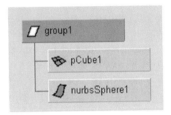

FIGURE 2.30   A group node.

This node has no geometry of its own, but it does have transformation information such as translation, rotation, and scaling. You can see this by creating a couple of objects, selecting them, and then grouping them (choose Edit > Group or press Ctrl+G). When you create a group, Maya keeps the position of the objects constant.

However, once grouped, you can move all the objects together as long as you select the group node and not the individual objects inside the group. The best way to do this is usually in the Hypergraph because, by default, Maya's screen picking always works on the individual objects, even when grouped.

In Maya, you can also group a single object. This creates a new transform node above the object but does not otherwise affect its location. Although not an obvious thing to do, you will see in a moment how this can be useful.

TUTORIAL 2.2: REFINING KEYFRAME ANIMATION

The output of Tutorial 2.1 is an animation in which basic physics is taken into account. Part of what makes animation fun, however, is your ability to artistically exaggerate for effect. In this tutorial, we will add some refinements to the initial animation, making use of a classic principle in animation known as *squash and stretch*. To accomplish this effect with rotating balls, you need to make some technical changes to your base animation. The changes require that you understand a couple of more technical topics in computer graphics, namely hierarchy and the order of animation evaluation. With this knowledge, you should be able to make a new version of the bouncing balls animation that is more interesting and more dramatic.

Squash and Stretch

Squash and stretch is one of the most important principles of animation. Most, if not all, living things squash and stretch when in motion. Only objects made of rigid materials such as metals or wood do not squash and stretch when moved. For instance, a rubber ball squashes and stretches when it hits the floor. The amount of squash and stretch depends on the material the object is made of and the object it hits. A rubber ball bouncing on a carpet squashes and stretches less than a rubber ball bouncing on a wood floor. Squash and stretch can be exaggerated for artistic purposes. This is one of the most common artistic mechanisms in classic 2D animation. It must be used with significantly more subtlety and care in 3D but is still very useful (see Figures 2.31 and 2.32).

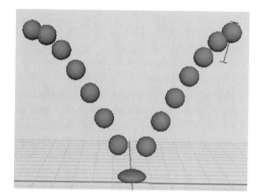

FIGURE 2.31   Ball with squash and stretch.

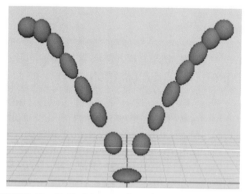

FIGURE 2.32   Ball with squash and stretch exaggerated.

Before you implement squash and stretch in Maya, you need to learn a bit more about a couple of technical topics.

Applying Squash and Stretch to the Existing Ball Scene

Now that you understand the concept of parenting, let's apply this technical concept and the animation notion of squash and stretch to your previous animation. The concept of parenting can be used not only between various geometric objects but also to make sure various transformations and controls move together. In this case, you will create a squash transformation on our ball, and you'll want the squash and its controllers to move along with the ball.

Squash and stretch is implemented in Maya as a tool. This tool not only scales an object along one axis, but it also maintains the illusion of object mass by expanding the object along the two other axes.

1. Open your light_heavy_balls.mb file from Tutorial 2.1.
2. Hide the heavy ball either by using a layer or by selecting the ball and selecting Display > Hide > Hide Selection. You also can use the shortcut Ctrl+H.
3. Go to frame 1.
4. Select the lightBall.
5. Choose Deform > Create Nonlinear > Squash. A squash handle should appear on the lightBall.
6. Move the squash handle down until the Move tool handles reach the bottom of the ball (see Figure 2.33).

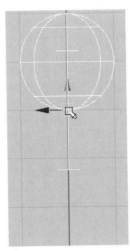

FIGURE 2.33   Squash handle moved down.

7. Scale the Y axis of the squash handle until it reaches the top of the sphere (see Figure 2.34).

FIGURE 2.34 Squash handle scaled on the Y axis.

8. Open the Hypergraph window by choosing Window > Hypergraph: Hierarchy.
9. Select squash1Handle as the child, select the lightBall as the parent, and press P on the keyboard. This parents the handle to the ball.
10. Move the sphere to the right. The squash handle should move with the lightBall.
11. Undo the action to make sure the ball is back to −10 on Translate X.
12. Go to frame 82. Click on the squash1 in the Channel Box.
13. Enter the Factor value of −0.5. The ball should squash.
14. Notice that the ball is not squashing the bottom, which is hitting the ground. The reason is that the ball is rotated −138.62 and so is the squash handle (see Figure 2.35).

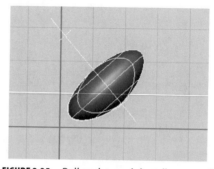

FIGURE 2.35 Ball and squash handle rotated.

The immediately apparent problem is that the squash transform is not being applied in the direction that you want. However, an even deeper and more general problem is lurking here. Let's take this opportunity to fix the immediate problem and also learn how to fix other similar ones that may come up later. The thornier issue here has to do with the order of evaluation of transforms. The current order of transformation is translate, rotate, and then squash. You want the order to be translate, squash, and then rotate. However, Maya does not provide a direct interface to change this order. Instead, you will need to understand the hierarchy that Maya uses to control the order of evaluation so that you can manipulate it.

Light Ball with Squash and Stretch

Now that you understand how hierarchy is organized inside Maya, let's return to the issue that prompted the discussion: How can you get your squash transformation to occur before the rotation? As it turns out, the answer has to do with the hierarchy. Maya evaluates transforms starting at the topmost level in the node hierarchy and working its way downward. In other words, the order always goes from parents to children and not vice versa.

To change the order of evaluation in Maya, you need to create a series of nodes ordered in the direction you want those transformations applied. You can use the group operation to create several group nodes above your geometry. Instead of doing translation and rotation directly on the geometry, you can instead do translation on a top-level node and rotation on a node below it. When you split up the transformations in this way, you are then finally able to control the order in which they are evaluated.

1. Make sure you are on frame 1 in the Time Slider.
2. Hide the heavy ball.
3. Select the lightBall and group it twice by choosing Edit > Group or pressing Ctrl+G (see Figure 2.36).

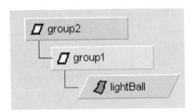

FIGURE 2.36   The lightBall grouped twice on itself.

4. Name group1 rotation and group2 translation (see Figure 2.37).

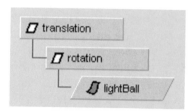

FIGURE 2.37   lightBall groups named translation and rotation.

5. Choose Window > Animation Editors > Graph Editor.
6. Make sure the lightBall is selected. In the Graph Editor, click on the Translate X channel. You should see the translation X animation curve only.
7. Select all the Translate X keys.
8. In the Graph Editor window, choose Edit > Cut. Make sure that the All is option selected (see Figure 2.38).

FIGURE 2.38   Cut Keys Options window.

9. Click on the Cut Keys button.
10. Select the translation node in the Hypergraph.
11. In the Graph Editor, choose Edit > Paste (see Figure 2.39).

FIGURE 2.39   Paste Keys Options window.

12. In the Paste Keys Options window choose Edit > Reset Setting to make sure you are using the default settings and click on the Paste Keys button. You should see all the keys pasted in the Graph Editor.
13. Select the lightBall Translate Y channel in the Graph Editor.
14. Repeat steps 7 through 11 to paste the Translate Y keys from the ball to the translation node.
15. You should see the Translate X and Y keys pasted on the translation node.
16. Select the lightBall.
17. In the Graph Editor, click on the Rotate Z channel. You should see the Rotation Z animation curve.
18. Select all the Rotate Z keys and choose Edit > Cut in the Graph Editor.
19. Select the rotation node in the Hypergraph.

20. In the Graph Editor, choose Paste.
21. At this point, the translation node should have the Translate X and Y keys, and the rotation node should have the Rotate Z keys.
22. Delete the flat channel keys left on the lightBall. The lightBall should have no keys.
23. Select the lightBall in the Channel Box and set the Translate and Rotate X, Y, and Z channels to 0, 0, 0. Make sure the lightBall node has no translation or rotation.
24. With the ball still selected, choose Deform > Create Nonlinear Squash.
25. Parent the squash handle to the translation node by clicking on the squash1Handle node first, then clicking on translation, and finally pressing P.
26. You should see the squash handle parented to the translation in the Hypergraph (see Figure 2.40).

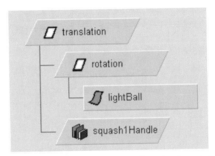

FIGURE 2.40   Squash handle parented to the translation node.

27. Go to frame 30.
28. Select the squash handle. Click on squash1 in the inputs of the Channel Box. You should see the squash1 channels (see Figure 2.41).

INPUTS	
squash1	
Envelope	1
Factor	0
Expand	1
Max Expand Pos	0.5
Start Smoothness	-0.08
End Smoothness	-0.08
Low Bound	-1
High Bound	1

FIGURE 2.41   Squash1 channels.

29. Click on Factor to select it. Right-click and choose Key Selected.
30. Go to frame 34. Change the Factor value to –0.3 and set a key by right-clicking.
31. Go to frame 38. Change the Factor value to 0 and set a key by right-clicking.

Notice that the ball hits the ground on frame 34, and you set a key for the Factor = 0 four frames before and four frames after the ball hits the ground. This is *not* physically realistic because the ball is starting to deform slightly before actually hitting the ground. However, this is classic artistic exaggeration. The extra frames of squash and stretch give the viewer's eyes time to notice something that in reality would occur more quickly.

Repeat the same procedure for the frames in Table 2.3.

Table 2.3 Changing the Order of Evaluation for Additional Frames

FRAME #	FACTOR VALUE
78	0
82	–0.25
86	0
111	0
115	–0.20
119	0
137	0
141	–0.15
145	0
161	0
165	–0.10
169	0

Now that you have a basic setup, try exaggerating the squash and stretch. Imagine that each ball, instead of being a mechanical object, is actually a character with an internal energy source and distinctive behavior.

Rendering the Animation

Rendering an animation is the process of producing an image for each frame. First you have to specify the rendering parameters in the Render Setting window. To open the Render Setting window, do the following. (First press F6 to go to the Rendering mode.)

1. Choose Window > Rendering Editors > Render Settings or click on the Render Settings button on the Status Line (see Figure 2.42).

FIGURE 2.42   Render Settings button.

2. The Render Settings window opens as shown in Figure 2.43.

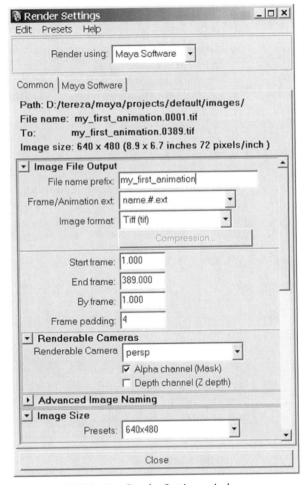

FIGURE 2.43   Render Settings window.

3. Make sure that the Render Using drop-down list is set to Maya Software. Then type my_first_animation in the File Name Prefix box. If you don't give it a name, Maya will give the working file name by default.
4. Change the Frame/Animation ext setting to name.#.ext.
5. In the Image Format list, choose either JPEG or TIFF. The default Maya file format is TIFF. However, other software packages do not understand this format. If you are going to use this frame on editing software such as AfterEffects, FinalCut Pro, or Premiere, make sure you render the frames using a format that the software understands.
6. In the Start Frame box, type 1; in the End Frame box, type 389 (the last key).
7. Make sure that By Frame is set to 1.
8. Change the Frame Padding value to 4. This will make Maya add zeros before the frame number. Click on the Close button.
9. Choose Render > Batch Render.
10. Look at the Command line to see the status of the rendering.

SUMMARY

This chapter gave you an understanding of the basic physical laws of mechanics applied to animation. You also learned about Maya hierarchy, parenting, and grouping, as well as how to use squash and stretch for artistic exaggeration. Finally, you learned how to render an animation.

CHALLENGE ASSIGNMENTS

1. Squash and Stretch

Create a 10-second animation demonstrating squash and stretch. Model a toy of your preference and animate it bouncing across an uneven surface. Texture the model and other objects in the scene. Light the scene with one or two spot lights. Render the animation.

2. Newton's Laws

Create two balls, one filled with air and the other with lead. Create an animation of 5 to 10 seconds that illustrates Newton's three laws. Show how each ball would move given an equal amount of initial force. Use timing and collisions to simulate the mass of objects. Be sure to use ease-in and ease-out on all objects. Texture the balls. Light the scene with two or three spot lights. Render the animation.

MODELING AND TEXTURING A SIMPLE CHARACTER

In This Chapter

- Modeling Using Polygons
- Modeling Strategies
- Advanced Modeling Techniques
- Polygon UV Coordinates and Texture Mapping

This chapter introduces you to polygon modeling in Maya. You will also learn how to create and work with texture maps. The final tutorial in this chapter will take you step-by-step through modeling and texturing a simple character.

MODELING USING POLYGONS

A polygon is a geometric figure with three or more sides. In Maya, different tools are available for manipulating the four geometric components of a polygon (see Figure 3.1).

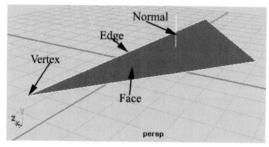

FIGURE 3.1   Polygon components.

- **Faces.** The interior surfaces of the polygons can be translated, rotated, scaled, and extruded. They are also used for putting textures on a model.
- **Edges.** The sides of the face are represented by a straight line and can be translated, rotated, scaled, and extruded.
- **Vertices.** Points connecting the edges of a face can be translated and extruded.
- **Normal.** A *surface normal*, or just *normal*, is a three-dimensional vector that is perpendicular to a surface. In Maya, the surface normal indicates which side of a surface is illuminated by default.

To speed lighting calculations, it is common to render carefully only the front side of all surfaces. This can lead to visual artifacts if you end up looking at the back side of a surface, however. Depending on the lighting model, such faces may be rendered with flat ambient lighting or even disappear entirely. Note that Maya's real-time rendering environment onscreen can give different results on back-facing surfaces than another renderer. When drawing polygons, Maya determines which side is the "front" based on the "right hand rule." If you look at your right hand and imagine drawing vertices in order from the base of your index finger toward its tip, the normal will point in the direction of your thumb. Another way to think of this is that if you draw a polygon with its vertices in counterclockwise sequence, Maya will put the surface normal facing you. Conversely, if you draw a polygon in clockwise order, its normal will point away from you. You can also "flip" polygon normals at any time or enable double-sided rendering.

Modeling with polygons is the process of creating, extruding, and attaching polygons to create an object. There are three fundamental polygon modeling methods. The first is to create flat polygons by using the Create Polygon tool, as shown in Figure 3.2.

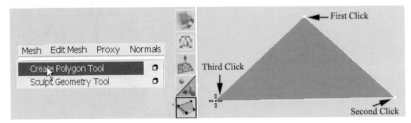

FIGURE 3.2   A flat polygon.

The second polygon modeling method is to start with a polygon primitive and progressively refine it (see Figure 3.3).

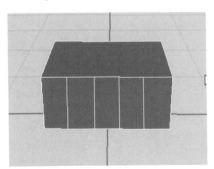

FIGURE 3.3   Polygon cube.

The third polygon modeling method is to use profile curves. You draw a series of profile curves and then use the Loft command to create a polygonal geometry between them, as shown in Figure 3.4.

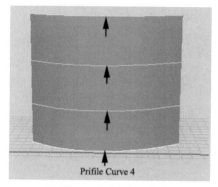

Prifile Curve 4

FIGURE 3.4 Lofted surface.

Exercise: Polygonal Modeling Starting from a Plane

One simple method of polygonal modeling is to begin with a plane:

1. Select File > New Scene.
2. Press F3 to go to the Polygons menu.
3. Select Mesh > Create Polygon Tool, as shown in Figure 3.5.

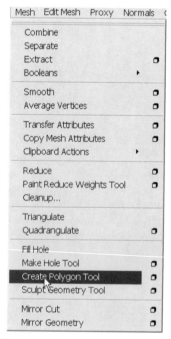

FIGURE 3.5 Create Polygon Tool selection.

4. In Front view, click in three places to create a triangle polygon, as shown in Figure 3.6.

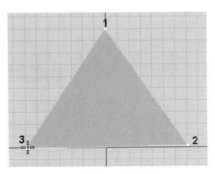

FIGURE 3.6   Triangular polygon.

5. Press Enter to exit the Create Polygon Tool.
6. Right-click the polygon and select Face, as shown in Figure 3.7.

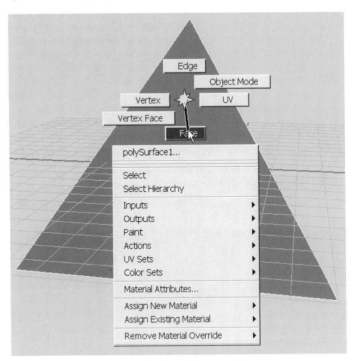

FIGURE 3.7   Polygon face-marking menu.

7. Click in the center of the polygon face to select it.
8. Select Edit Mesh > Extrude, as shown in Figure 3.8. Three extrude manipulators appear.

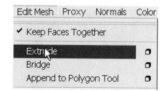

FIGURE 3.8   Extrude Face command selection.

9. Click the blue manipulator, as shown in Figure 3.9, and drag it out five units. This should develop a volume.

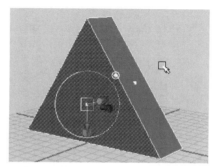

FIGURE 3.9   Extrude Face handles.

10. Right-click the polygon and select Edge (see Figure 3.10).
11. Click one of the edges of the polygon to select it.
12. Select Edit Mesh > Extrude.
13. Drag the blue manipulators to the right to create a new face (see Figure 3.11).
14. Save your work.

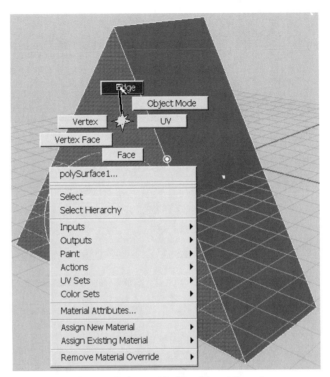

FIGURE 3.10   Polygon Marking Menus for edges.

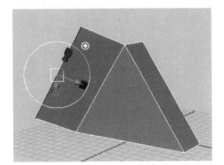

FIGURE 3.11   Polygon edge extruded.

Exercise: Modeling Starting from a Polygon Primitive

The second major method of polygon modeling is to start from a polygon primitive. This is most useful when the form you are trying to model is similar to an available primitive. You can see the available polygon primitives in Maya by selecting Create > Polygon Primitives.

1. Select File > New Scene.
2. Select the Maya Front view panel.
3. Select Create > Polygon Primitives and uncheck Interactive Creation. When this option is unchecked Maya creates the primitive at the origin (X = 0, Y = 0, Z = 0).
4. Select Create > Polygon Primitives > Cube.
5. In the Perspective view window, select Shading > Smooth Shade All or use the keyboard shortcut 5. You should see a gray cube.
6. In the Channel Box, enter the following values: Scale X = 5, Scale Y = 5, Scale Z = 5 (see Figure 3.12).

FIGURE 3.12   Channel Box scale values.

7. Right-click the cube and select Face.
8. Select the right and left faces.
9. Select Edit Mesh > Extrude. Three manipulators appear on the face. You should also see polyExtrudeFace1 in the Channel Box (see Figures 3.13 and 3.14).

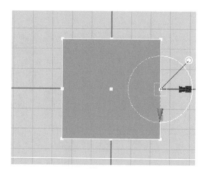

FIGURE 3.13   Extrude Face manipulators.

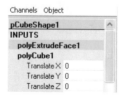

FIGURE 3.14   polyExtrudeFace1.

10. Scroll down in the Channel Box until you see the Local Translate and Local Scale attributes of polyExtrudeFace1.

11. Enter the following values: Local Translate Z = 4 (both faces should extrude four grid sizes simultaneously), Local Scale X = 0.2, Local Scale Y = 0.2 (both faces should scale simultaneously, as shown in Figure 3.15). You also can scale the extruded faces by clicking and dragging the Scale tool on the extrude manipulator as shown in Figure 3.16.

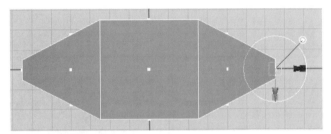

FIGURE 3.15   Cube faces extruded and scaled.

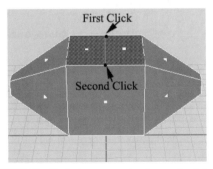

FIGURE 3.16   Scale icon on extrude manipulators.

12. Select Edit Mesh > Split Polygon Tool.

13. Click first in the middle of the back edge and second in the middle of the front edge of the cube's top face to split it.

14. Press Enter to finish the split polygon operation. Now you should have two faces on the top of the cube (see Figure 3.17).

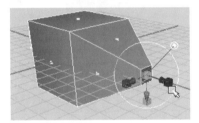

FIGURE 3.17   Scale icon on extrude manipulators.

15. Select Edit Mesh > Keep Faces Together. Make sure that the Keep Faces Together option is checked. When the Keep Faces Together option is checked, the edges of the extruded faces are merged. When Keep Faces is off, Maya creates separate edges for each extruded face. By default, this option is off.

16. Extrude and scale the new faces (see Figure 3.18).

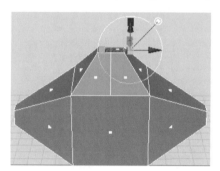

FIGURE 3.18   Cube top faces extruded and scaled.

17. Save your work.

You can toggle Keep Faces Together on and off by pressing and holding down the Ctrl+Shift+RMB key combination.

Exercise: Using Profile Curves for Polygonal Modeling

The third major polygon modeling method is similar to the way in which wooden boats were once constructed. You first create a set of cross sections, and then you fit a surface onto those sections. These sections are created with curves, also called splines. While the resulting geometry is polygonal, the construction cross sections can be either lines or NURBS curves. In this case, we will use NURBS circles as our cross sections, since the circle primitive is only available in NURBS form.

1. Select File > New Scene.
2. Select the Front view panel.
3. Select Create > NURBS Primitives > Circle.
4. In the Channel Box, enter the following values: Scale X = 3, Y = 3, Z = **3**; Rotate X = 90, Y = 0, Z = 0. You should see the circle as shown in Figure 3.19.

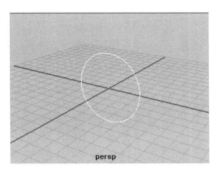

FIGURE 3.19   NURBS (Non-Uniform Rational B Spline) circle.

5. Select Edit > Duplicate Special Option Box, and enter these values: Number of Copies = 6, Translate Z = 3.
6. Click the Duplicate Special button. You should have six circles in a row, as shown in Figure 3.20.

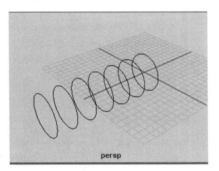

FIGURE 3.20   NURBS circle duplicated.

7. Click each circle from left to right.
8. Press F4 to go to the Surfaces menu set. Select Surfaces > Loft (see Figure 3.21).

FIGURE 3.21   Loft menu. Maya lofts the circles in the order in which they are selected. To have a smooth lofted surface, you must select the circles in sequence.

9. You should see a new surface called LoftSurface1 (see Figure 3.22). Save your work.

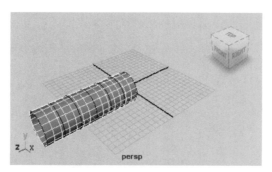

FIGURE 3.22   NURBS circles lofted.

If you have the Construction History feature enabled (which is Maya's default), then you can move, scale and rotate your construction curves even after an object has been created. For example, you could make a primitive worm by offsetting some of your NURBS circles slightly with the Move tool.

You can use any of these methods, and sometimes a combination of them, to model your characters. The method you choose depends on the object's overall shape, the shape of a subcomponent of the object, and your personal preference.

Smoothing Polygons

Polygon surfaces may have sharp edges, which make the object's shape angular. This is desirable for objects that really are angular, such as furniture, but not for more rounded organic shapes, such as the human body. Fortunately, you can model in two or more passes, first using sharp-edged polygons to approximate the overall form and then having Maya smooth the surface. Smoothing the surface comes at the cost of vastly multiplying the number of polygons, which can make a model harder to edit and slower to animate or render. As a result, smoothing is often applied as a last step, and animators often use an unsmoothed version of a model for setting poses and keys. To see how this process works, let's smooth out that most angular of forms, a cube.

1. Select File > New Scene.
2. Select Create > Polygon Primitives > Cube. Make sure Interactive Creation is unchecked.
3. With the cube still selected, press F3 to go to the Polygons menu and select Mesh > Smooth Option Box (see Figure 3.23).

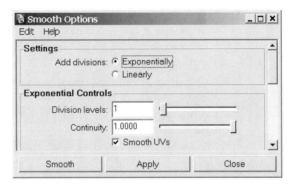

FIGURE 3.23   Polygon Smooth Options window.

4. In the Division Levels field, enter 2.
5. Click the Smooth button (see Figure 3.24).

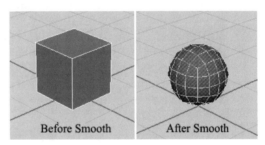

FIGURE 3.24   Cube before and after being smoothed.

6. Save your work.

With appropriate smoothing, the individual polygons of a model rapidly become indistinguishable from one another. However, as you will see shortly, to achieve good smoothing, you must have a clean base model to work from. Save your base model before using the smooth polygon function.

Maya allows you to preview the smoothed model by pressing the following hot keys on the keyboard.

- **1.** This displays the model with the smooth preview off.
- **2.** This displays the model with the smooth preview on plus the cage mode.
- **3.** This displays the model with the smooth display on and the cage mode off.
- **Page Up and Page Down.** These increase and decrease the number of division levels on the smooth preview.

MODELING STRATEGIES

When you are modeling with polygons, consider the following strategies.

• Working with symmetry
• Using image planes to bring in reference sketches or imagery
• Decomposing complex forms into simpler subcomponents, also known as *block modeling*
• Using four-sided polygons
• Maintaining polygons of relatively uniform size and aspect ratio

Working with Symmetry

Many natural and manmade objects are basically symmetrical. In computer modeling, you can easily "mirror" geometry. This saves time in initial construction and helps maintain the correct form when editing the geometry. For example, to model a human face, you should first model only one side of the face. When this is done, mirror that geometry to get the other side. As it happens, human faces are not entirely symmetrical, so after you are happy with the overall shape of the face, you might then make minor tweaks to each side. Recognizing symmetry, or near symmetry, in objects is an important observational skill that you can develop (see Figure 3.25).

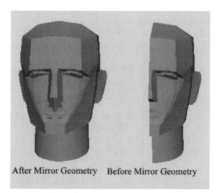

After Mirror Geometry   Before Mirror Geometry

FIGURE 3.25   A head before and after mirror geometry.
(Character design and modeling by Michael Melo.)

Understanding Mirroring and Merging Polygon Vertices

When you mirror a polygon surface, Maya duplicates and flips it on the axis chosen by you. The vertices in the center of your new surface will be duplicates positioned exactly on top of each other. Because this is not usually desirable, Maya provides an option to merge them automatically. Overlapped, non-merged vertices make the geometry heavier and more difficult to edit and light.

1. Open the file named circle_loft.mb in the MayaToolsFiles subfolder from the chapter3, MayaWorkingFiles folder on the CD-ROM.
2. Select LoftSurface1.
3. Select Mesh > Mirror Geometry Option Box.
4. In the Polygon Mirror Options window, select –Z, Merge with the Original, and Merge Vertices (see Figure 3.26).

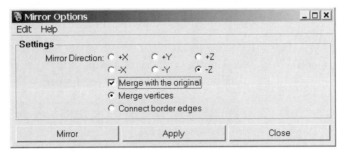

FIGURE 3.26   Polygon Mirror Options window.

5. Click the Mirror button. You should see the lofted geometry mirrored, as in Figure 3.27.

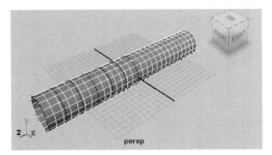

FIGURE 3.27   Loft geometry mirrored on –Z axis.

Using Image Planes to Bring in Reference Sketches or Imagery

In Maya, you can bring in 2D imagery to use as the basis for your 3D modeling. Depending on your level of traditional sketching skills and the availability of appropriate reference imagery, 2D imagery is often a good starting point. When taking photographs or creating sketches, you should try to get two images: one of the object head-on and the other in full profile. These are known as "orthogonal" images. Obtaining or creating this kind of view is important because Maya cannot correct perspective in images. (A three-quarter profile portrait might be artistically interesting, but would be almost useless for modeling reference because the figure's proportions would be difficult to determine given the perspective.) You can use Adobe Photoshop and other image-processing tools to remove small perspective distortions if necessary.

You can scan in images and save them to any standard format that Maya recognizes. When saving the images, note the aspect ratio (proportion of width to height) so that when you map the image to a plane in Maya you can scale the plane to the same aspect ratio and avoid distortion.

Importing an Image Plane in Maya

To import an image plane, follow these steps.

1. In the Front view panel, select View > Image Plane > Import Image.
2. Open the image_plane.jpg file from the chapter3, Image_Planes folder on the CD-ROM (see Figure 3.28).

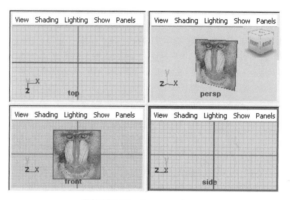

FIGURE 3.28   Image plane.

You can move and scale the image plane by changing the attribute's value in the Channel Box. Image plane attributes can also be accessed using the View > Image Plane > Image Plane Attributes menu

Block Modeling the Object or Character

The most efficient way to model a character is to block its shape first and add detail as necessary. For example, to model a human head, you create the overall shape of the head and then create the eye sockets, ears, lips, and so on (see Figure 3.29).

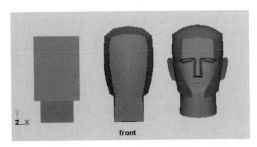

FIGURE 3.29   A head in different phases of the modeling process.
(Character design and modeling by Michael Melo.)

Keeping All Polygons Quads

Like most modeling packages, Maya enables you to create polygonal faces with any number of edges. However, limiting your polygons to four-sided ones, or *quads*, is good modeling practice. This is because Maya and other systems, when smoothing a polygon model, try to average the tension between corners of each face. With rectangular faces, the center point is obvious and always corresponds with the center of tension. With non-quadrangular faces, this behavior is not geometrically guaranteed, and this can lead to ugly smoothing behavior. Even when you are not planning on smoothing your model, keep in mind that under normal lighting models, renderers *tessellate* your surface to calculate lighting on subsections of a polygonal face. The process of tessellation is essentially the same as smoothing and thus can lead to similar problems with arbitrary *n*-sided polygons (see Figure 3.30).

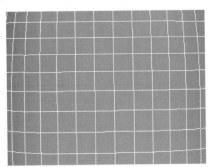

FIGURE 3.30   Polygon quads.

Polygon Shape and Size

Similar but less severe issues come up for polygon shape and size. Although you can mix very small and very large polygons in a model, this is generally not recommended in models designed for animation. Similarly, very long and skinny polygons are prone to causing problems in texture mapping and later in animation. There are no hard and fast rules here, but a good model typically has polygons varying in size by no more than a factor of three, and few with an aspect ratio of greater than 3:1.

Now that we've run through some of the basic techniques, strategies, and rules of thumb, let's consider a few more advanced topics. First, we'll look at two tools that you use to rapidly alter many polygons at once: the Sculpt Polygon tool and lattices. Then we'll look at Maya's powerful construction history system and learn how to manage it.

ADVANCED MODELING TECHNIQUES

Maya offers several advanced modeling tools. Here, we will explore a few of the most powerful and commonly used: deformations, editing by "painting," and manipulations of the editing history.

Lattice Deformer

One of the most useful tools for shaping an object is the *lattice*. A lattice in Maya is a 3D array of points that you use to control the deformation of objects. You can select the object or objects to be deformed and then specify the lattice resolution in X, Y, and Z. You then change the shape of the object by translating, scaling, or rotating one or more lattice points. With this technique, you can control the level of detail of the deformation based on the resolution of the lattice you specify. For example, a $2 \times 1 \times 1$ lattice enables you to deform all of the polygons on one side of an object without affecting those on the other side. You could also specify a $20 \times 20 \times 20$ lattice for the same object, yielding a much finer degree of control (see Figure 3.31).

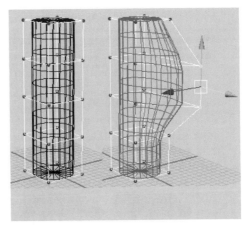

FIGURE 3.31   Object deformed by a lattice.

Sculpt Geometry Tool

You use the Sculpt Geometry tool to edit a surface by painting on it with brush strokes. Unlike a normal brush, which changes a surface's appearance, the Sculpt Geometry tool moves the object's vertices according to the characteristics of the brush. Because this tool understands the direction a surface is facing, you can use it to push and pull vertices relative to the surface, specifying a maximum displacement. You can also use the tool to smooth vertex displacements, a useful method when you've ended up with a surface that's too bumpy or an edge that's too sharp. You can specify the brush size interactively, so you can easily shape large areas and then focus on details (see Figure 3.32).

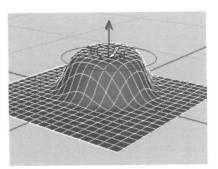

FIGURE 3.32   Surface sculpted with the Sculpt Geometry tool.

Understanding Construction History

When you are creating an object in Maya, the history of the modeling process is recorded. You can use Construction History at any point in the modeling process to revise an earlier decision. When you change the original parameters, the changes ripple through all the subsequent actions automatically. For example, imagine that you are making a stool with three legs. After attaching the legs to the seat, you realize that they look a little too short and thick. Rather than having to delete all three legs and start again, you can scale the legs appropriately while keeping their correct position.

Let's work through a simple example so you can see Construction History in practice. We'll use a single profile curve revolved around an axis to create a vase. Using the Construction History, you will be able to modify the profile curve even after the revolve operation has been conducted so that you can shape the vase in context.

1. Select Create > CV Curve Tool.
2. In the Front view panel, create a vase-shaped profile curve, as shown in Figure 3.33.

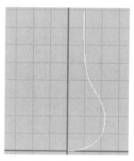

FIGURE 3.33   Vase-shaped profile curve.

3. Press F4 for the Surfaces menu and select Surface > Revolve Option Box (see Figure 3.34).
4. Make sure that Axis Preset Y is selected.
5. Click the Revolve button. You should see a new geometry, as shown in Figure 3.35.
6. Select the profile curve.
7. Right-click the profile curve and select Control Vertex.
8. Select any CVs (control vertices) and drag them to the left or right. The revolved geometry's shape should have updated automatically (see Figure 3.36).

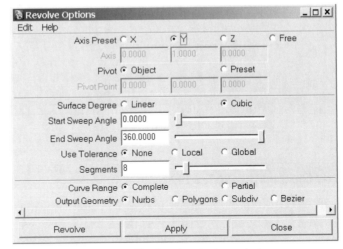

FIGURE 3.34   The Revolve Options window.

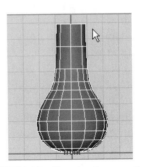

FIGURE 3.35   Revolved geometry.

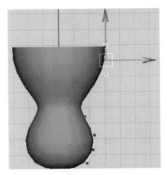

FIGURE 3.36   Shape modified with Construction History.

As useful and powerful as it is, Construction History has a couple of disadvantages. On large, complicated, multistep models with multiple deformers, construction history can introduce significant performance lag and bloat file sizes. Therefore, it is sometimes useful either to temporarily turn off Construction History or to delete it. You could keep a modeling version file for each major model and create a separate file version without Construction History for animation purposes. Later, in Tutorial 3.1, we will see how to delete Construction History after using lattice edit.

POLYGON UV COORDINATES AND TEXTURE MAPPING

When you apply textures to simple primitives, you don't need to place textures precisely because Maya defines sensible default texture mapping behaviors for those objects. When you create your own geometry, however, you will need to control this process.

When you apply textures to 3D surfaces, Maya must do something very similar to gift-wrapping a package. Maya must pick a point on the surface on which to apply one corner of the texture, and it must wrap the texture around the object in one direction or another. The texture must have a seam where it overlaps back on itself. Most likely, you want the seam to be in an inconspicuous place. You want the texture to be parallel to some portion of the object and not skewed. Finally, if you have a complex geometry to wrap, you might find it easier to use several pieces of wrapping paper, each covering a different portion of the whole.

In Maya, as in most modern 3D graphics packages, each vertex on a surface can carry additional information defining which part of a texture should be "stuck" to that vertex. This information is in the form of a pair of coordinates, called U and V, which range from 0.0 to 1.0. The U coordinate represents the distance along the horizontal dimension of the texture, and the V represents the distance along the vertical dimension. Texture application typically starts at the vertex with UV texture coordinates of 0.0, 0.0. This vertex gets the bottom-left corner of the texture. The mapping continues as the values of U and V increase, typically until the UV coordinates of 1.0, 1.0 are reached. These coordinates represent the top-right of the texture, as shown in Figure 3.37.

In the situation just described, a texture is mapped so that its full extent is visible on the portion of the object facing the camera (that is, if 2D Texture Placement Attributes Coverage values are less than 1.0). However, by specifying coverage values greater than 1.0 you can use only a portion of a texture. For example, if the texture coverage is set to 2.0 in both dimensions, then the texture size is effectively multiplied by 2, so that only a portion of the full texture is visible on the object, as shown in Figure 3.38.

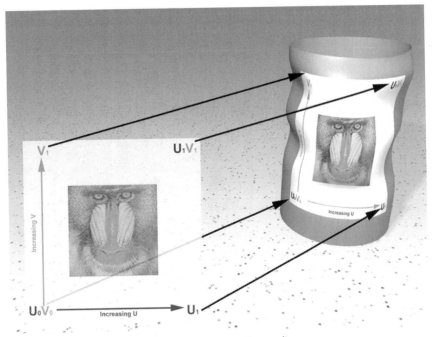

FIGURE 3.37   Texture coordinate diagram.

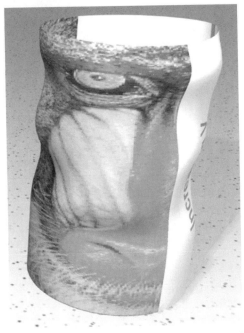

FIGURE 3.38   Using texture placement coverage attributes to magnify a surface texture.

Texture application always begins at the UV origin of the target object. In the case of texture magnification, the portion of the texture beyond the maximum UV value on the surface is simply clipped. You can see this by looking at the seam of the object. In most cases, you want to orient the seam to face away from the camera.

You can also repeat a texture many times across a surface, as shown in Figure 3.39.

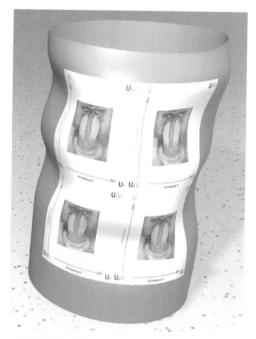

FIGURE 3.39   Texture repeated across a surface.

Projecting Texture Coordinates

Rather than manually specifying each texture coordinate, you can more conveniently project texture coordinates onto a surface. Imagine that your 3D object exists in the real world as a white painted surface and that you have a slide projector pointing toward it with your texture on the slide. For surfaces facing the projector, you get a relatively clean image. However, for surfaces facing away from the projector, you start to get distortion, as shown in Figure 3.40.

This method is essentially what the "planar projection" method in Maya does, and the limitations of the two methods are similar. Projecting texture coordinates works well for relatively flat objects but not for others.

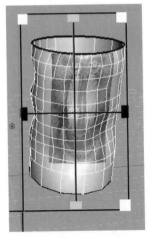

FIGURE 3.40   Texture planar projection with distortion.

Fortunately, several other methods are available, depending on the basic shape of your object. For example, cylindrical mapping obviously works well for cylinders but also for generally cylindrical forms such as limbs. Similarly, cubic mapping works well for things with distinct fronts, backs, and sides. Finally, an automatic mapping method is available, which is the best choice for complex objects, such as a human body. This method is like using multiple pieces of wrapping paper on a package. You specify the number of pieces, and the application tries to orient textures to minimize distortion (see Figure 3.41).

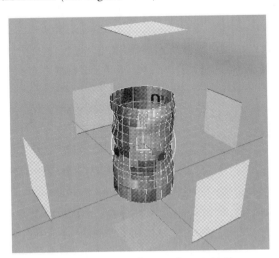

FIGURE 3.41   Automatic mapping projection.

Stitching Textures

When you end up with more than one texture mapped onto an object, you will find that you have less distortion—but more seams. For complex objects, multiple seams are unavoidable. The trick is to minimize them and place them where they are inconspicuous. This is such a common issue that Maya has an entire interface, known as the *Texture Editor*, for tweaking textures. You use the Texture Editor to see how your texture is being applied in UV space (see Figure 3.42).

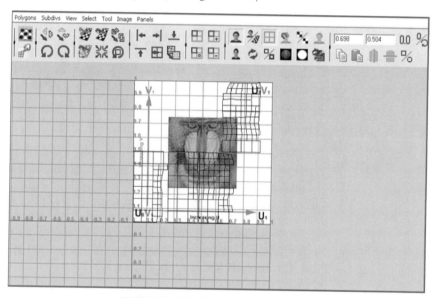

FIGURE 3.42   The Texture Editor window.

Getting Used to the Texture Editor

You use the Texture Editor to view and manipulate the UVs and the texture so that you can place textures precisely on objects. Follow these steps as a warm-up exercise.

1. Click the Maya Two Persp/Outliner layout button (see Figure 3.43).

FIGURE 3.43   Persp/Outliner button.

2. In the left panel (Outliner), select Panels > Panel > UV Texture Editor. Make both panels approximately the same size (see Figure 3.44).

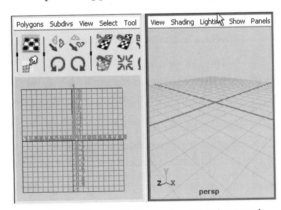

FIGURE 3.44   Texture Editor and perspective panels.

3. Select Create > Polygon Primitive > Cube. Make sure Interactive Creation is unchecked.
4. Move the cube to 0.5 on the Y axis. With the cube still selected, notice that you can see the cube in 2D in the UV Texture Editor, as shown in Figure 3.45.

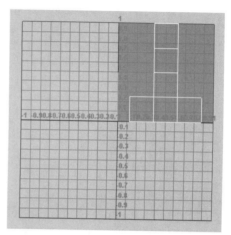

FIGURE 3.45   Cube in the 0–1 texture space.

Creating a Texture for the Cube in Adobe Photoshop

Although you can create textures in Maya, using an external image editor such as Adobe Photoshop is a more flexible and powerful technique. Although in this chapter, you will make only a simple demonstration texture, in real projects, multichannel textures are common. By using Photoshop layers for various types of texture image attributes, you can easily derive one channel from another and keep them in one file.

If Photoshop is not available to you, take the 3D Paint Tool tutorial in the Maya documentation.

1. Select the cube.
2. Right-click the cube and select Material > Assign New Material > Blinn, as shown in Figure 3.46. Materials (or shaders) are Maya's way of organizing the properties of surfaces, including textures and the rendering properties.
3. Name the new material cube_material. The cube should still be selected.
4. In the UV Texture Editor, select Image > Create PSD Network, as shown in Figure 3.47. The PSD Network creates a link between the Maya texture and Photoshop.

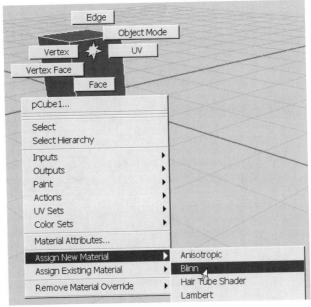

FIGURE 3.46   Assign New Material marking menus.

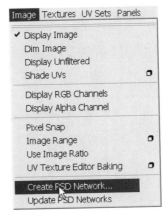

FIGURE 3.47   Create PSD Network Options menu.

5. In the Create PSD Network Options window, make sure that Open Adobe Photoshop and Include UV Snapshot are selected, as shown in Figure 3.48.

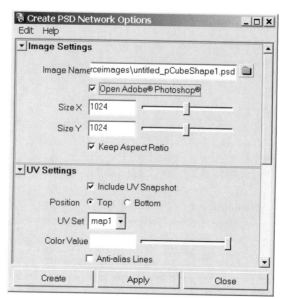

FIGURE 3.48   Create PSD Network Options window.

6. Scroll down in the Attributes Selection region of the PDS Network window until you see Blinn Shader.
7. Double-click the word "color" to move it to the Selected Attributes field as shown in Figure 3.49. By selecting the color attribute you are creating a connection between the Photoshop image and the Material color attribute.

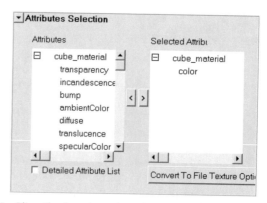

FIGURE 3.49   Blinn Shader selected attributes in the PSD Network window.

8. In the Image Name field under Image Settings, specify where you will put the image, name it, and click the Create button. You should see the UV snapshot in Photoshop.
9. Paint the image and save it.

Importing the Photoshop Texture into Maya

To import the Photoshop texture into Maya, follow these steps.

1. In Top view, select Panels > Panel > Hypershade. Double-click cube_material to open the Attribute Editor.
2. Go to the Common Material Attributes section and click the black-and-white button to the right of the color, as shown in Figure 3.50. The PSDFileText Attribute Editor should open.

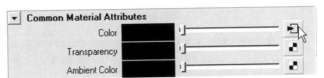

FIGURE 3.50   Material map color button.

3. In the PSDFileTexture Attribute Editor, File Attribute section, change Link to Layer Set to Composite, as shown in Figure 3.51. With this option selected, Maya supports Photoshop layers and text.

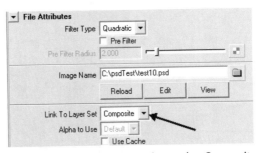

FIGURE 3.51   Link to Layer Set changed to Composite.

4. In the Hypershade, select the cube shader and select Graph > Input/Output Connections. The shader network opens. You should see your painting as part of the shader network, as shown in Figure 3.52.

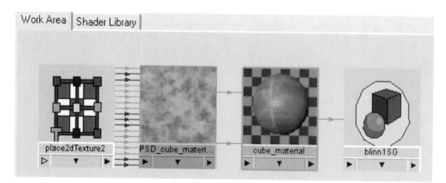

FIGURE 3.52   Snapshot painting as part of the shader network.

5. Select the cube.
6. Open the Texture Editor by selecting Panels > Panel > UV Texture Editor.
7. In the Texture Editor, right-click and select UV.
8. Select the UVs and then move and rotate them. Notice that the texture changes on the cube when you manipulate the UVs, as shown in Figure 3.53.

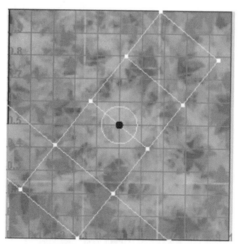

FIGURE 3.53   Cube's UVs rotated.

TUTORIAL 3.1: MODELING A SACK

By modeling and texturing a sack, you will become acquainted with basic Maya polygon modeling and texturing tools.

Modeling the Sack

To model the sack, follow these steps.

1. Create a new project and call it sack.
2. Press F3 to go into Polygons mode.
3. Select Panels > Saved Layouts > Four View.
4. You should find it helpful to see your model in Top, Front, Side, and Perspective views.
5. In Front view, select View > Image Plane > Import Image.
6. Open the file called sack_front.tif from the chapter3, Image_Planes folder on the CD-ROM (see Figure 3.54).

ON THE CD

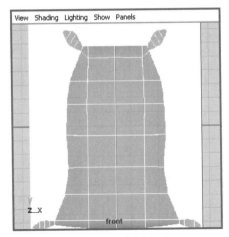

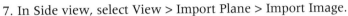

FIGURE 3.54   Sack image plane in the front view.

7. In Side view, select View > Import Plane > Import Image.

ON THE CD

8. Open the file sack_side.tif from the Image_Planes folder on the CD-ROM. Notice that the image planes are centered in the origin of the axes. You are going to move and scale them.
9. Select both image planes in the Perspective view.
10. In the Channel Box, scroll down until you see imagePlane under INPUTS.
11. Enter the following values: Offset X, Y = 0, 0, Center X = 0, Center Y = 7.6, Center Z = 0, Width = 15, Height = 15 (see Figure 3.55).

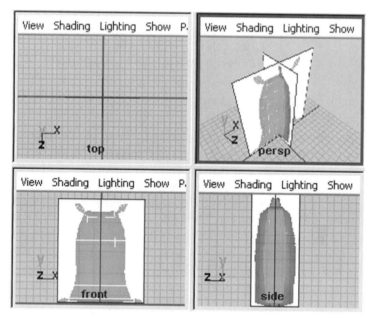

FIGURE 3.55   Image planes seen from all windows.

12. Select Create > Polygon Primitives > Cube. Make sure Interactive Creation is unchecked. Maya creates the cube at the origin.
13. In the Channel Box or the Hypergraph window, change the name of the cube to sack.
14. In the Channel Box, enter 0.5 in the Translate Y axis field. This moves the sack to ground level.
15. With the sack still selected, press the W key to change to the Move tool.
16. Press the Insert key to see to the sack's pivot point.
17. Holding down the X key on the keyboard, move the pivot point to the bottom of the sack, at the origin of the axes, as shown in Figure 3.56.

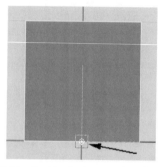

FIGURE 3.56   Sack's pivot moved to the origin.

18. Press the Insert key to close Pivot mode.
19. With the sack still selected, press the R key to change to the Scale tool.
20. In Front view, scale the sack in the X and Y axes to match the sack's size in the Image plane.
21. Press the 5 key to change the cube to Smooth Shade All mode, as shown in Figure 3.57.

FIGURE 3.57   Polygon sack scaled to match the reference image.

22. In the Front view, select Shading > X-Ray. This makes the cube transparent.
23. Select Edit Mesh > Cut Faces Tool.
24. In Front view, hold down the Shift key, press and hold the left mouse button, and drag to cut the sack. Cut the sack into four parts of equal size horizontally and six parts of equal size vertically (see Figure 3.58).

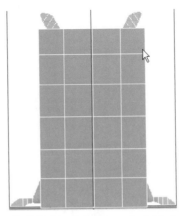

FIGURE 3.58   Polygon sack divided.

25. Press the Q key to change to the Selection tool.
26. Right-click the sack and select Face.
27. Select all the faces of the sack on the left side of the axis grid, as shown in Figure 3.59.

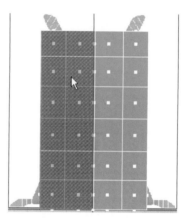

FIGURE 3.59   Selected faces of the sack on the left side of the grid.

28. Press the Delete key. You should have only half of the sack. Because the sack is symmetrical, you can work on half of the model, as shown in Figure 3.60 and later on in the modeling process mirror it,.

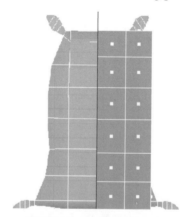

FIGURE 3.60   Half of the sack.

29. Right-click the sack and select Face.
30. In Side view, select the top face of the sack's side, as shown in Figure 3.61.

FIGURE 3.61   Top face of the sack's side selected.

31. Select Edit Mesh > Extrude Option Box.
32. Enter 3 in the Divisions field and click Extrude Face, as shown in Figure 3.62.

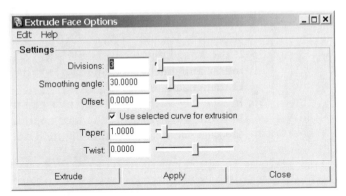

FIGURE 3.62   Extrude Face Options window.

33. In Top view, press and hold the left mouse button to select the blue handle and then drag to the right approximately three units to create the sack's arm, as shown in Figure 3.63.

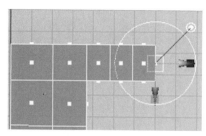

FIGURE 3.63 The sack's face extruded to create the sack's arm.

34. In Front view, drag the green handle approximately three units as shown in Figure 3.64.

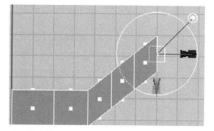

FIGURE 3.64 Extruded faces pulled up.

35. If the image plane covers the sack, select Show in the view panel menu and uncheck Cameras. This hides the image plane. (Select Camera again to see the plane.)
36. In Side view, select the bottom face of the sack's side.
37. In Front view, extrude the face approximately three units to create the sack's foot, as shown in Figure 3.65.

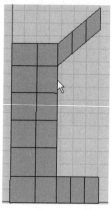

FIGURE 3.65 Bottom face of the sack's side extruded.

38. Press F2 to change Maya's mode to Animation.
39. Press F8 to change the mode to Object mode.
40. Select Deform > Create Lattice. You should see the lattice enveloping the sack, as shown in Figure 3.66.

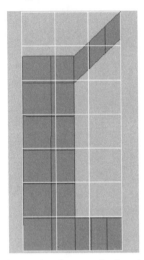

FIGURE 3.66   Lattice enveloping the sack.

41. In the Channel Box, under SHAPES, find a node called ffd1Lattice-Shape. You should see S, T, and U Divisions. These are the lattice space coordinates.
42. Enter the following division values: S Divisions = 4, T Divisions = 8, U Divisions = 2.
43. In Perspective view, right-click the lattice and select Lattice Point.
44. In Front view, click the lattice influence points in the two inner rows between the arm and the foot while holding down the Shift key. Make sure you have selected only the front points. Deselect any other lattice influence points (see Figure 3.67).

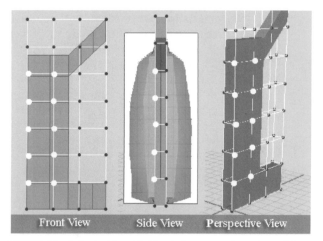

FIGURE 3.67   Selected front lattice influence points viewed from Front, Side, and Perspective views.

45. Make sure the view is in the Smooth Shade All mode. In Side view, select Shading > X-Ray. You should see the reference image behind the sack.
46. Press the W key and drag the selected lattice influence points to the left approximately two units on the Z axis. Drag the individual lattice points to the edge of the sack (see Figure 3.68).

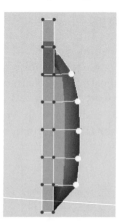

FIGURE 3.68   Points of the lattice adjusted to match the image plane.

47. In Perspective view, select the lattice influence points in the back of the sack by clicking on them. Make sure you select the two inner rows between the arm and the foot. Any other point should be deselected (see Figure 3.69).

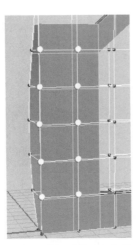

FIGURE 3.69   Selected back lattice influence points.

48. In Side view, drag the selected points approximately two units on the Z axis to match the other side of the sack, as shown in Figure 3.70.

FIGURE 3.70   Lattice influence points dragged on both sides of the sack.

49. Select the sack and then select Edit > Delete By Type > History. This deletes the lattice but preserves the sack deformation.
50. Make sure the cube is in shaded mode.
51. In Top view, select the two outer edges of the sack's top and move them a bit inward to narrow the top of the sack, as shown in Figure 3.71.

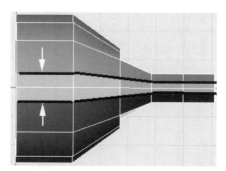

FIGURE 3.71   The sack's top outer edges moved inward.

52. Select the sack and then select Mesh > Mirror Geometry Option Box.
53. Click Mirror direction –X and make sure Merge with the Original and Merge Vertices are selected. Click the Mirror button.
54. Save your work.

Sack Artistic Features

At this point, you have a conventionally shaped sack. To give the sack a more artistic shape, use the Sculpt Geometry Tool to shape the polygon mesh. This tool allows you to modify the polygon's vertices by painting them with a brush. The Sculpt Geometry Tool pushes, pulls, and smoothes the vertices. To use the tool, follow these steps.

1. Select the sack and select Mesh > Sculpt Geometry Tool Option Box.
2. The tool Attribute Editor opens on the right side of the screen.
3. Position the mouse cursor on the sack. Notice that the cursor has a circle on it. This circle is the size of your brush, as shown in Figure 3.72.

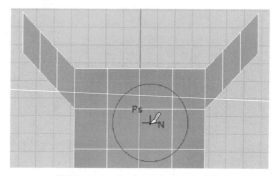

FIGURE 3.72   Sculpt Polygon brush.

4. Hold down the B key while pressing the middle mouse button and then drag the mouse to the right or left to adjust the brush size. You also can adjust the brush size numerically on the Sculpt Geometry Tool Brush settings.

5. In the Sculpt Parameter, check the operation push or pull and paint the sack to see the results. The control vertices should move when you paint the sack.

6. Continue to paint the sack to give it some character.

7. When you have finished sculpting, close the Sculpting tool.

8. Right-click the sack and select Edge.

9. Click the middle edge of the sack's right arm to select it, as shown in Figure 3.73.

FIGURE 3.73   Middle edge of the right arm selected.

10. Hold down the Ctrl key while right-clicking on the edge.

11. Select Edge Loop Utilities > To Edge Loop. This selects all the edges on that loop, as shown in Figure 3.74.

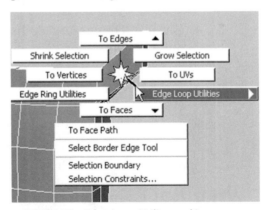

FIGURE 3.74   Edge Loop Utility marking menus.

12. Repeat the same procedure to select the middle edge loop of the left arm.

13. Press R to change to the Scale tool and scale the selected edge's loop a bit on the Y axis, as shown in Figure 3.75.

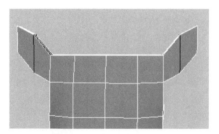

FIGURE 3.75   The arm's edge loops scaled.

14. Right-click the sack and select Face.
15. Select the face on the end of the right arm and scale it a bit, as shown in Figure 3.76.

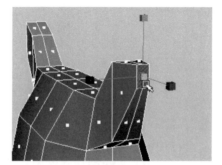

FIGURE 3.76   Front face of the right arm scaled.

16. Repeat steps 6 through 10 for the right and left legs.
17. Continue sculpting the sack until you have a pleasing shape.

Smoothing the Sack

To smooth the sack, follow these steps.

1. Select the sack.
2. Select Mesh > Smooth Option Box.
3. Make sure Add Divisions: Exponential is selected and Division Levels is 1, as shown in Figure 3.77.
4. Click the Smooth button. Notice that the sack now has a smoother surface.
5. In the Channel Box under INPUTS, look for PolySmoothFace1 and click it. You should see a series of attributes, including Divisions.
6. Type the value 0 in the Divisions field, as shown in Figure 3.78.

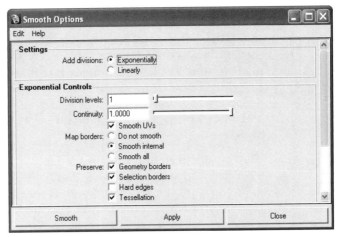

FIGURE 3.77 Polygon Smoothing Options window.

FIGURE 3.78 Polygon Smoothing Channel Box parameters.

Notice that the sack surface changed back to a nonsmooth surface. You can switch the surface to smooth and nonsmooth by changing the Divisions values. When the Divisions value is set to 0, the surface is in Nonsmooth mode, and when the Divisions value is set to 1, the surface is set to Smooth mode.

TUTORIAL 3.2: UV TEXTURING THE SACK

In this tutorial you will use a planar mapping strategy for UV texturing, as previously described in the "Polygon UV Coordinates and Texture Mapping" section. The basic technique is to manually select a number of faces that roughly constitute a plane, and then to create UV coordinates using a planar projection. Once the UVs are set, you will edit your textures in an external image editor, and finally apply the textures onto the 3D sack in Maya.

1. Press F3 to go into Polygons mode.
2. Select the sack and, in the Channel Box, look for PolySmoothFace1. Make sure the Divisions value is set to 0. To simplify texturing, the sack should be in the Nonsmooth mode.
3. In any view, select Panels > Saved Layouts > Persp/UV Texture Editor (see Figure 3.79).

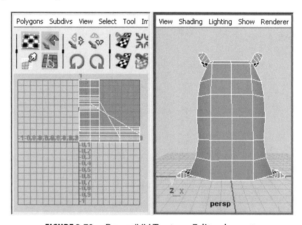

FIGURE 3.79 Persp/UV Texture Editor layout.

4. Middle-click the left (Persp) panel to make it active.
5. Press and hold down the spacebar, right- or left-click, and select Top View, as shown in Figure 3.80. Pressing the spacebar displays the hotbox, which is a quick way to access the Maya menus.
6. Select Edit > Paint Selection. This tool enables you to select polygon components by brushing over them.
7. In Top view, right-click the sack and select Face.
8. Paint the two rows of faces on top of the sack only. Make sure you paint the two faces on the side of the top and that no other face is painted, as shown in Figure 3.81. Hold the Ctrl key to deselect any accidental faces.

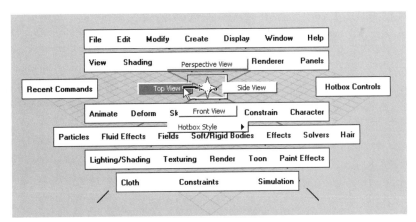

FIGURE 3.80   Making the Top view active.

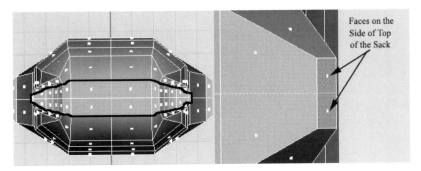

FIGURE 3.81   Top faces selected with the Paint Selection Tool.

9. Select Create UVs > Planar Mapping Option Box.
10. Select Edit > Reset Settings, and then click the camera option. This projects the UVs from the Camera view.
11. In the Polygon Planar Mapping Options window, click the Project button, as shown in Figure 3.82.

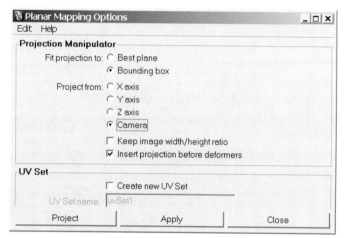

FIGURE 3.82   Planar mapping options window.

12. In Top view, click the green handle and then drag it upward to scale the projected UVs, as shown in Figure 3.83.

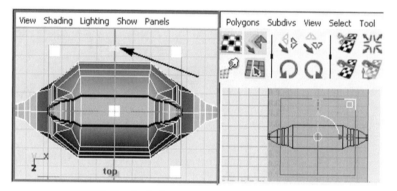

FIGURE 3.83   Scaled projected UVs with manipulator.

13. In the Texture Editor, right-click and select UV (see Figure 3.84).
14. In the Texture Editor, drag a rectangle to select all the projected UVs.
15. Press the W key to change to the Move tool.
16. Move the UVs to the left, out of the 0–1 gray texture grid, as shown in Figure 3.85. (This move is only to temporarily isolate the UV coordinates).
17. In Top view, select View > Predefined Bookmarks > Bottom, as shown in Figure 3.86.

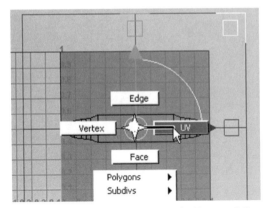

FIGURE 3.84   Selected UV option in the Texture Editor.

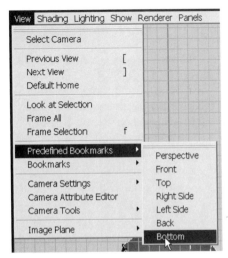

FIGURE 3.85   Moved UVs in the Texture Editor.

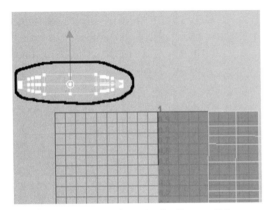

FIGURE 3.86   Bottom of Top view selected.

18. Paint-select the faces on the bottom of the sack, as shown in Figure 3.87.

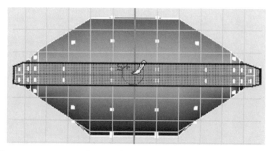

FIGURE 3.87   Bottom-selected faces using the Paint Selection Tool.

19. Repeat steps 9 through 12 to scale the UV projection and move the UV in the Texture Editor. Scale the UVs as needed.
20. Select the Front view and paint-select all the faces in the front of the sack, including the front faces of the arms and feet, as shown in Figure 3.88.

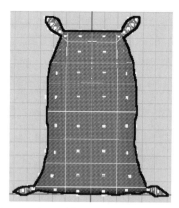

FIGURE 3.88   Front-selected faces using the Paint Selection Tool.

21. Select Create UVs > Planar Mapping (see Figure 3.89).
22. In Bottom view, select View > Predefined Bookmarks > Back.
23. Paint-select all the faces on the back of the sack, including the arms and feet.
24. Select Create UVs > Planar Mapping.
25. Select the UVs in the Texture Editor and move them out of the 0–1 gray texture grid.
26. Select View > Predefined Bookmarks > Right Side.
27. Paint-select the faces on the right side.
28. You may need to zoom in close to see the faces underneath the arms and on the foot (see Figure 3.90).

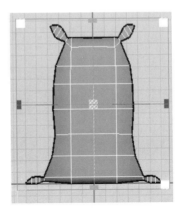

FIGURE 3.89   Planar mapping manipulator in Front view.

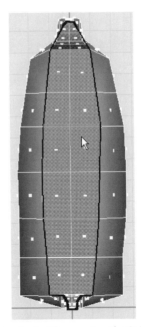

FIGURE 3.90   Right-selected faces using the Paint Selection tool.

29. Select Create UVs > Planar Mapping (see Figure 3.91).

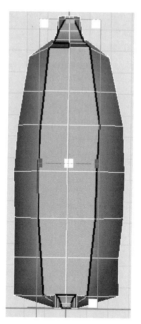

FIGURE 3.91   Planar mapping manipulator in Right view.

30. Select the red handle and then drag it to scale the UVs, as shown in Figure 3.92. Alternatively, you can scale the UVs in the Texture Editor.

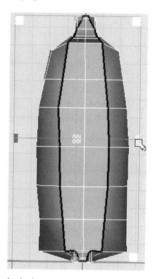

FIGURE 3.92   Scaled planar mapping manipulator in Right view.

31. Select the UVs in the Texture Editor and move them out of the 0–1 gray texture grid.
32. Select View > Predefined Bookmarks > Left Side.
33. Paint-select the faces on the left side of the sack using the same method you used for the right side.
34. Select Create UVs > Planar Mapping.
35. Drag the green square and, if necessary, the red square to scale the UVs.
36. Select the UVs in the Texture Editor and move them out of the gray texture grid. There should be no UVs in the dark gray box in the Texture Editor. If you see any UVs in the gray box, this means you missed a face when you select-painted. To fix this problem, select the UV in the Texture Editor to see where it is on the sack. Select-paint again the entire part of the sack to which the UV belongs and planar-map it again. For example, if the UV you missed belongs to the back of the sack, select-paint the entire back part of the sack and planar-map it again.
37. Right-click the Texture Editor and select UV.
38. Drag a square over all of the planar-mapped parts to select them all. Make sure you don't miss any UVs. Only selected UVs are affected by commands.
39. In the Texture Editor window, select Polygons > Normalize UVs Option Box. Normalizing UVs scales the U and V values to the range between 0 and 1.
40. In the Polygon Force UV Options window, make sure Collectively and Preserve Aspect Ratio are selected. Click the Apply and Close button, as shown in Figure 3.93.

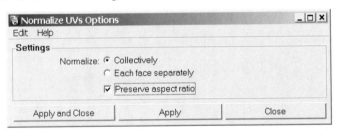

FIGURE 3.93   Updated settings in the Polygon Force UV Options window.

41. You should see all the parts inside the 0–1 gray box Texture Editor, as shown in Figure 3.94.

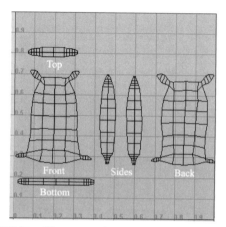

FIGURE 3.94 All parts inside the 0–1 Texture Editor grid.

42. Drag a square to select all the UVs again. Make sure you don't miss any UVs.

43. In the Texture Editor, select Polygons > Unfold UVs Option Box (see Figure 3.95).

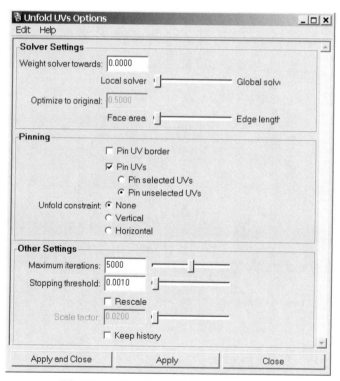

FIGURE 3.95 The Unfold UV Options window.

44. In the Unfold UV Options window, select Edit > Reset Settings and click the Apply and Close buttons. This should unwrap any UVs in the mesh that are overlapping.

Painting the Sack Texture in Photoshop

To paint the sack texture in Photoshop, follow these steps.

1. Right-click the sack and select Materials > Apply New Material > Lambert, as shown in Figure 3.96. *Lambert* is a material with a dull finish that does not reflect light. The Attribute Editor for the Lambert material should open.

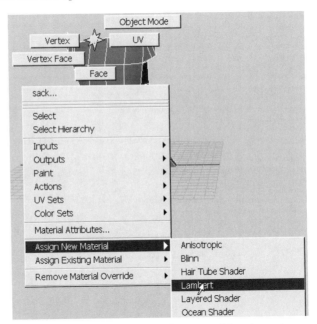

FIGURE 3.96   Assigning a Lambert material to the sack.

2. Name the material sack_material.
3. Select the sack. In the Texture Editor panel, select Image > Create PSD Network.
4. Name the UVsnapShot and make sure Open Adobe® Photoshop® and Include UV Snapshot are selected, as shown in Figure 3.97.

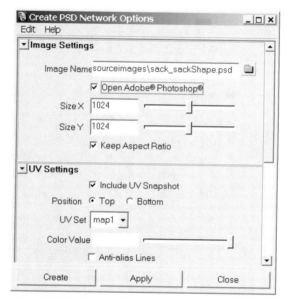

FIGURE 3.97 Updated Create PSD Network options.

5. In the Create PSD Network Options window, double-click the word "color" under sack_material1. The word "color" should move to the Selected Attributes area, as shown in Figure 3.98.

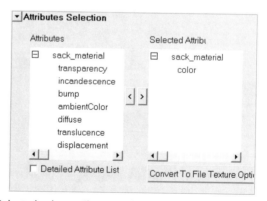

FIGURE 3.98 Selected color attribute on the Create PSD Network Options window.

6. Click the Create button. Photoshop should open and show your image. The Photoshop image should have three layers: background, sack_materialcolor, and UVSnapshot.

7. Create a new layer for the image and call it burlapTexture.

8. Open the file burlap.psd from the chapter3 Texture folder on the CD-ROM.

9. Copy and paste the file burlap.psd in the new burlapTexture layer. Alternatively, you can create your own burlap texture.

10. Using the UV snapshot as a reference, type the word decaf three times on the front of the sack, as shown in Figure 3.99.

FIGURE 3.99   Sack front UV snapshot with "decaf" text.

11. Hide the snapshot layer and save the file in PSD format. You should not see the UV snapshot when you save the image.

Importing the Photoshop file Into Maya

To import the Photoshop file into Maya, follow these steps.

1. In any of the Maya views, select Panels > Layouts > Three Panes Split Left, as shown in Figure 3.100.

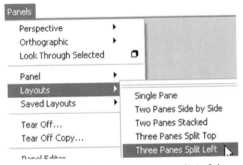

FIGURE 3.100   Choosing Three Panes Split Left layout.

2. Select the three panels as follows: In the top-left panel, select Panels > Panel > UV Texture Editor. Set the bottom-left panel to Hypershade. Set the right side to Perspective.
3. Double-click sack_material to open the Attribute Editor.
4. Click the black-and-white button of the color attribute, as shown in Figure 3.101. The PSDFileText Attribute Editor opens.

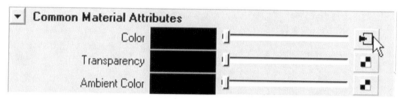

FIGURE 3.101   Color attribute texture box.

5. In the PSDFileText Attribute Editor, File Attributes section, change Link to Layer Set to Composite.
6. Open the UVsnapShot.psd file.
7. You should see the Photoshop file attached to the Lambert material.
8. Apply the Lambert material to the sack by either middle-mouse dragging it onto the sack or selecting the sack, right-clicking on the material, and selecting Assign Material to Selection.
9. If the burlap pattern is scaled differently in the different parts of the sack, scale the UVs in the Texture Editor until the burlap pattern scale looks the same on all parts of the sack.
10. If the burlap pattern does not follow the direction of the arms, select all the arms' UVs and rotate them until the texture aligns with the arms (see Figure 3.102). Rotating the UVs doesn't rotate the geometry, only how the texture is applied.
11. Save your work.

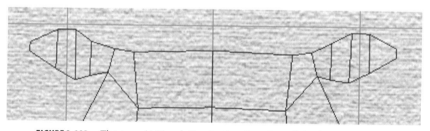

FIGURE 3.102   The arms' UVs relative to the direction of the burlap texture.

SUMMARY

In this chapter, you have seen the major methods and strategies for 3D polygon modeling in Maya. You have had a chance to use both basic tools for manipulating a single polygon component at a time and more advanced tools that operate on a portion of the surface or even the model as a whole. You have also learned how textures are mapped to polygons using UV coordinates, how to establish these relationships using projection methods, and how to adjust them in the Texture Editor. With these skills in place, you have the fundamental techniques for modeling almost any object.

In the next chapter, you will learn how to start bringing your models to life by "rigging" them with skeletons and posing them.

CHALLENGE ASSIGNMENTS

1. Model a Cell Phone

Use the techniques you learned in this chapter to model a cell phone using polygons. Find a photograph or photographs to use as reference and make the cell phone as specific as possible. Use either textures or geometry to model the details of the phone (your choice).

2. Model a Piece of Furniture

Find a reference photograph of a piece of furniture, and model the furniture using polygons. Texture your model and render a still image of it.

4

RIGGING AND ANIMATING A SIMPLE CHARACTER

In This Chapter

- Understanding Rigging
- Basic Rigging Process

*R*igging is the process of creating skeletons and attaching them to a character. In this chapter, you will learn how to create a simple rig and attach it to the geometry of the sack that you modeled in Chapter 3. Attaching a skeleton to geometry is called *binding* or *skinning*. You will also learn how to establish character poses to guide the rigging design process and test the skeleton.

Understanding Rigging

Unlike real-world creatures, 3D characters have simplified skeletons and anatomy. Rigging design changes according to your character's anatomy and motion. Before you start rigging, you must study the character's shape and movement so you can create and test the appropriate rig.

In production, a single character might have multiple rigs. For example, one rig might be designed only for full-body shots, and a second rig might be designed for the detailed finger movements required in a single shot or series of shots.

Shot Storyboard

The process of rigging begins by analyzing the storyboard of a shot or a set of shots. Study the action of the character and identify characteristic body postures, especially those representing extremes of motion or emotion. In this process, it is often useful to consult reference footage.

Let's start with some rough sketches for a simple shot. Figure 4.1 shows the preliminary drawings that you are going to use to pose the coffee sack character.

FIGURE 4.1   Sack jump shot storyboard. (Courtesy of Brittney Lee.)

You practiced animating a bouncing ball in Chapter 2, so you may be tempted to use just three poses to show the sack jumping.

- The sack at rest
- The sack at the highest point of the jump
- The sack on landing

These poses, however, would probably not result in a convincing animation. Animated characters, unlike simple mechanical objects, are both self-propelled and intelligent. Animated characters have two key characteristics: *anticipation* and *follow-through*. Anticipation also has two important aspects. The first is mental. A character must have a moment to think before starting an action, and this moment must be long enough for the audience to "see the character thinking." The second aspect of anticipation is physical. The character "winds up" before moving, much as a baseball pitcher winds up for a pitch. The character positions his body to move in one direction. Essentially, he is orienting his body so that muscle tension and gravity will propel him in the desired direction.

Now consider the sack trying to jump to his left. What is his first move (after perhaps pausing to think)? He backs up onto his right foot, lifts his pelvis, rotates it backwards, bends the right knee, and twists his spine back. All these can be seen in Figure 4.1. The sack is all coiled up in anticipation of a jump to the left.

Jumping, then, consists of flexing the muscles in the right leg to push off, pivoting the pelvis over the left foot, and straightening the pelvis and spine. This is evident in the second pose.

Because the jump is intentional, the character does not land like a rock. As he makes contact with a firm surface, he reacts by using his joints to absorb the shock. You will need separate keys for the moment of contact, the maximum reaction, and then the resumption of a normal stance.

Anticipation and follow-through are fundamental to the way we judge if something is alive or dead. If you consider these principles when animating an object, you will create the illusion of life. Your audience will believe that even a normally inanimate object such as a coffee sack is alive and has emotions.

Rigging Design

The first goal of rigging is to give a character enough of a skeleton that it can bend and move as required. In the case of a sack, it is not entirely clear from the raw geometric model how the skeleton should work. Much of this understanding must come from the shot storyboard or reference footage.

The shot storyboard of the sack shows that it behaves like a human being. Therefore, some equivalent of feet, legs, arms, and spine should be included in the rigging, even though some of these features are not explicit in the geometry of the model. In particular, the corners of the sack have to behave like feet, even though the sack does not have feet. You can decide to simplify the skeleton by not including fingers or toes. You need to create an abstracted biped skeleton for the sack to move as it is shown in the shot storyboard.

BASIC RIGGING PROCESS

Rigging involves the following basic steps.

1. Create the skeleton appropriate to your model and its motion.
2. Add inverse kinematics (IK) chain handles to the skeleton.
3. Create object constraints.
4. Bind the skeleton to the geometry.
5. Test and adjust the skeleton and binding parameters to work for the character's poses.
6. Create skeleton controls that facilitate posing the character.

Creating a Skeleton

A skeleton is a hierarchy of joints. When you create two joints, Maya automatically creates a bone linking the two joints, as shown in Figure 4.2.

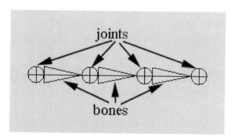

FIGURE 4.2   Joint hierarchy.

For predictable joint behavior, you should first snap the joint to the grid to align the joint's local axis. To snap the joints to the grid, press and hold down the X key on the keyboard while clicking the mouse to create the joints. After snapping the joints to the grid, you can move their pivot position to move the joints to their final location. To see a joint's pivot, press W to change to the Move tool, select the joint, and press the Insert key on the keyboard.

Joints have a local axis. To see a joint's local axis, select the joint, change to Component mode by pressing F8, and click the question mark icon in the Status Line, as shown in Figure 4.3.

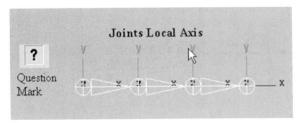

FIGURE 4.3   Joints showing local coordinates.

The local and global coordinates can be modified with the Rotation tool.

Adding Kinematics

When you animate or pose a character, you specify the translation and rotation of the skeleton joints to create motion. This process is called *kinematics*. There are two types of kinematics: forward and inverse.

Forward kinematics (FK) is the process of animation in which the animator animates the joints individually. FK is useful in animating broad motions such as arm swings and waving hands. However, with FK, an animator has no direct control of the position of child joints—they can only be positioned by rotating their parents. For example, the elbow position is based on the shoulder rotation. If the exact position of the child joints is important, this process can be relatively time-consuming and requires intense reasoning and observation. For example, when you move your hand, you usually don't think how much the elbow and shoulder joint rotate. When you animate with FK, you must consider these rotations individually and how they accumulate, as shown in Figure 4.4.

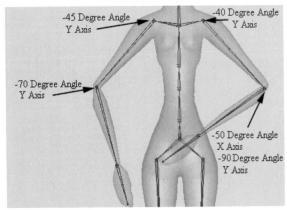

FIGURE 4.4   Arm joints animated with FK.

Let's create a simple joint and animate it by using FK.

1. Press F2 to change to Animation mode.
2. Select Skeleton > Joint Tool.
3. In the Front view, press and hold down the X key and position the mouse cursor approximately in the middle of the screen. Click three times on a straight line from left to right and then press the Enter key to finish creating joints. You should see three joints and two bones in a row, as shown in Figure 4.5.

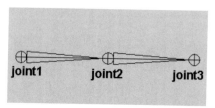

FIGURE 4.5   Three joints connected by bones.

4. Click on joint1 to select it, as shown in Figure 4.6. Notice that the joints below are also selected.

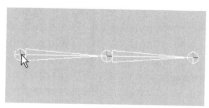

FIGURE 4.6   Joint1 selected.

5. Press the E key on the keyboard to change to the Rotation tool.
6. Rotate the joint 45 degrees on the Z axis. You can do this by dragging the Rotate tool blue handle, as shown in Figure 4.7, or by typing 45 in the Rotate Z channel of the Channel Box. Observe that the joints below follow along.
7. Select joint2 and rotate it 45 degrees in the Z axis. You should see the joints rotated as shown in Figure 4.8. In this case, notice that joint2 has no effect on joint1.

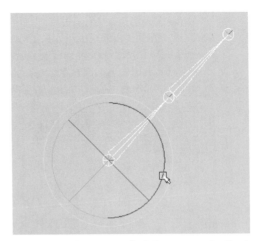

FIGURE 4.7   Joint1 rotated 45 degrees on the Z axis.

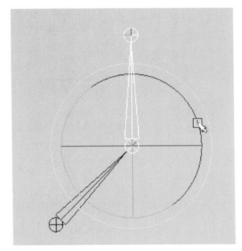

FIGURE 4.8   Joint2 rotated 45 degrees on the Z axis.

Inverse Kinematics

IK is the process of animating joints indirectly by specifying the desired end point of a portion of the skeleton. For example, you can position a wrist joint, and the elbow and shoulder joints will follow. To do this, you use an IK handle, which connects the joints in a chain. By moving the last joint of the chain, you move all the joints above it. An IK handle has a start point, an end point, and an end effector, which is located at the last joint of the IK chain. When you drag the IK handle, it pushes the IK chain, and the joints are automatically translated and rotated by an algorithm called IK Solver (see Figure 4.9).

The effector is represented in Maya's views as a 3D cross, and IK chains by lines that connect the start and end joints. However, depending on the camera angle, end effectors can be difficult to see and to select. Later, you will see how rigging controls can be used to make end-effector selection easier. Meanwhile, note that effectors can always be seen and selected in the Hypergraph and in the Outliner.

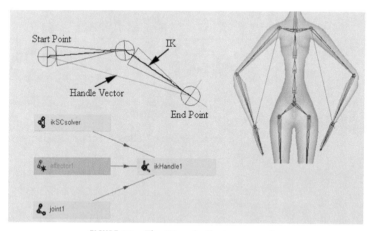

FIGURE 4.9   The IK end effector moved.

1. Select Skeleton > Joint Tool.
2. In Front view, press and hold down the X key on the keyboard and position the mouse cursor approximately in the middle of the screen. Click three times in a straight line to create three joints in a row and then press the Enter key to finish creating joints.
3. Click on joint2 to select it and rotate it approximately 20 degrees in the Z axis, as shown in Figure 4.10.

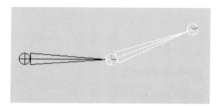

FIGURE 4.10   Joint2 rotated 20 degrees in the Z axis.

4. Select Skeleton > Set Preferred Angle. This indicates the preferred (i.e. default) rotation of the joint and helps it to behave predictably when rotated by an IK system.
5. Rotate joint2 back to 0 degrees by typing 0 in the Rotate Z field of the Channel Box.
6. Select Skeleton > IK Handle Tool.

7. Click first on joint1 and then on joint3. You should see the IK handle.
8. Click and drag the red handle of the Move tool to the left. Joint2 and joint3 should move with the IK handle, as shown in Figure 4.11.

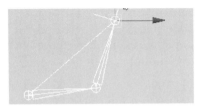

FIGURE 4.11   Joint1 and joint2 moved with the IK.

With the IK system, Maya uses two main methods to pick the intermediate joint positions. These methods are the IK Single Chain Solver and the Rotate Plane Solver (see Figure 4.12).

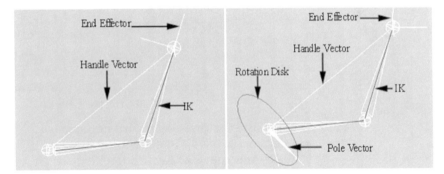

FIGURE 4.12   Single Chain and Rotate Plane IK System.

With the IK Single Chain Solver, you can translate and rotate the skeleton by translating and rotating the end effector. With the IK Rotate Plane Solver, you can translate the skeleton only by translating the solver. This solver has a separate channel called Twist to rotate the skeleton. These solvers are like the brain of the IK chain. When you move a joint chain to a particular position by dragging the IK handle, the solvers decide how much to rotate the joints to achieve that position. The Rotate Plane Solver has a pole vector, which can be moved to change the orientation of the plane. The pole vector can only be moved when constrained to another object with a pole vector constraint.

Using a Rotate Plane Solver requires more work during animation, but also gives more control. In some cases, the Single Chain Solver can suddenly flip around the rotation of a joint unexpectedly during animation. If you run into this problem, try changing the Single Chain Solver to a Rotate Plane Solver.

IK/FK Blend

Using an IK chain is a practical way to animate a character, but some motions created with IK don't look natural. For example, it is hard to animate arcs using IK because you cannot directly control the intermediate joints' positions and rotations. To create a convincing motion, sometimes you need to use both IK and FK. Maya offers you the option of blending IK and FK.

1. Make sure Maya is set to the Animation mode by pressing F2.

ON THE CD

2. Open a file called IK_FK.mb from the chapter4, IKFK folder on the CD-ROM (see Figure 4.13.)

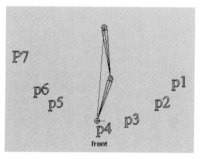

FIGURE 4.13   IK/FK.mb.

3. Make sure the Time Slider current frame is 1.
4. Select the IK handle and move it to p1.
5. Select Animate > Set Key Option Box.
6. In the options window, select Edit > Reset Settings.
7. Click on the Set Key button.
8. Advance the current frame to 15. You can do this by typing the number in the Set the Current Time field.
9. Move the IK handle to p2.
10. With the IK handle still active, select Animate > IK/FK Keys > Set IK/FK Key (see Figure 4.14). This sets keys for the joints and IK handle. The IK Blend will blend from enable to disable from frame 15 to 20. At frame 20, the IK is disabled, and you can animate the joints in FK mode.

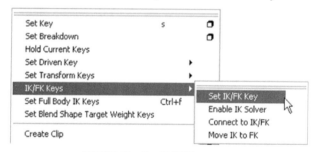

FIGURE 4.14   Set IK/FK Key menu.

11. Advance the Time Slider to frame 20.
12. Move the IK handle to p3.
13. Select Animate > IK/FK Keys > Set IK/FK Key.
14. Still in frame 20, change the IK Blend value to 0 in the Channel Box.
15. Right-click on the IK Blend and select Key Selected.
16. Advance the Time Slider to frame 30.
17. Select the shoulder and rotate it approximately –20 in the Rotate Z channel.
18. Select the elbow and rotate it approximately –35 in the Rotate Z channel. The arm should be hanging down at p4, as shown in Figure 4.15.

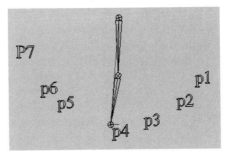

FIGURE 4.15   Arm in position at p4.

19. Select the shoulder and elbow joints.
20. Press S to set a key for the joints on frame 30.
21. Advance the Time Slider to frame 45.
22. Rotate the shoulder and the elbow until the hand joint reaches p5. Make sure the elbow is a bit bent.
23. Select the IK handle.
24. Select Animate > IK/FK Keys > Set IK/FK ey.
25. Advance the Time Slider to frame 50.
26. Rotate the shoulder until the hand reaches p6.
27. Select the IK handle.
28. Select Animate > IK/FK Keys > Set IK/FK Key.
29. Change the IK Blend value to 1 in the Channel Box.
30. Right-click on IK Blend and select Key Selected.
31. Advance the Time Slider to frame 60.
32. Move the IK handle to p7.
33. Press S to set a key for the IK handle.
34. Play the animation.
35. Save your work.

Notice that on frames 20 and 50, you first set an IK/FK key, and then you set a key for the IK Blend in the Channel Box. The inverse procedure may cause undesirable results.

Bind Skin

Binding skin is the process of attaching a deformable object such as a lattice or geometry to joints or a skeleton. When a deformable object is bound to a skeleton, Maya attaches the points of the geometry to the joint in a hierarchy. Points are NURBS control vertices (CVs), polygon vertex, or lattice points.

Maya has two skin bind types: smooth and rigid. In a *smooth bind*, more than one joint influences each point. This causes a smooth geometry deformation when you bend the joints, as shown in Figure 4.16.

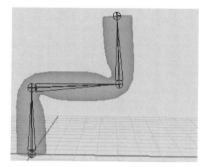

FIGURE 4.16   Smooth binding.

Smooth Bind

Maya offers two smooth bind methods. You can choose to attach the points to the closest joint in the hierarchy or closest in distance. When you choose the Closest in Hierarchy option, Maya determines which joints in the hierarchy are closest to each point and assigns point weights that control the influence of the joints on each point. When you choose the Closest Distance option, Maya ignores the joints hierarchy and assigns point weights based on closeness. This method may cause undesirable geometry deformation. For example, when a hand skeleton is bound to the geometry, the vertices of the finger geometry may be influenced by the joints of two fingers, as shown in Figure 4.17. This occurs because the finger joints of adjacent fingers are closer to each other than they are to their parent joint.

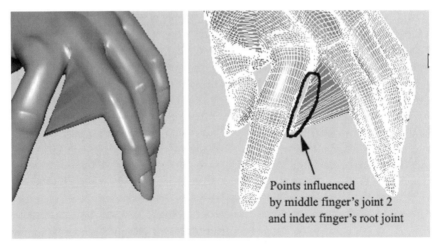

Points influenced
by middle finger's joint 2
and index finger's root joint

FIGURE 4.17   Vertex of the middle finger's geometry
influenced by the index finger root joint.

The Closest Distance option is useful in situations where the joint hierarchy does not allow Maya to determine the next logical parent or child joint to consider in binding. In complex rigs, there can be multiple grouping nodes and control objects between separate sub-skeletons. In these cases, the Closest in Hierarchy option will fail to assign some joints and thus the Closest Distance option is more appropriate. Note that while you cannot use more than one bind method simultaneously on the same geometry, you can use different methods on different portions of a character. For example, the torso might be bound using Closest Distance and the arms using Closest in Hierarchy.

Let's create a simple example to see how smooth bind works in practice.

1. Select File > New Scene.
2. Select Create > Polygon Primitives and uncheck Interactive Creation.
3. Select Create > Polygon Primitives > Cylinder Option Box.
4. Select Edit > Reset Settings.
5. In the Height divisions field of the Polygon Cylinder Options window, type 20 and then click the Create button, as shown in Figure 4.18. To avoid ugly creasing, it is important that a skin mesh have sufficient density to deform smoothly as the bones move.

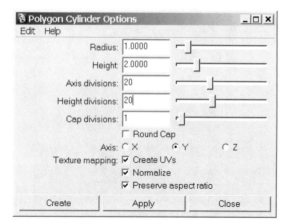

FIGURE 4.18   The Polygon Cylinder Options window.

6. In the Channel Box, type 10 in the Scale Y field.
7. Select Skeleton Joint Tool.
8. In Front view, press and hold down the X key on the keyboard, and click three times to create three joints: joint1 at the bottom of the cylinder, joint2 at the middle of the cylinder, and joint3 at the top of the cylinder, as shown in Figure 4.19.

FIGURE 4.19   Three joints created in the cylinder.

9. Click on joint1, press and hold down the Shift key on the keyboard, and click on the cylinder. Make sure joint1 and the cylinder are selected.

10. Select Skin > Bind Skin > Smooth Bind Option Box.
11. In the Smooth Bind Options window, make sure the Bind To field is set to Joint Hierarchy and the Bind Method field is set to Closest in Hierarchy, as shown in Figure 4.20.

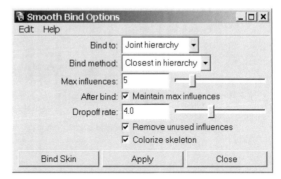

FIGURE 4.20   The Smooth Bind Options window.

12. Click the Bind Skin button.
13. In Front view select Shading > X-Ray Joints. You should see all joints.
14. Select joint2, and in the Channel Box, type 90 in the Rotate Z field.
15. Press 5 on the keyboard to see the cylinder in Smooth Shader All mode. Notice that the geometry bends smoothly around joint2, as shown in Figure 4.21.

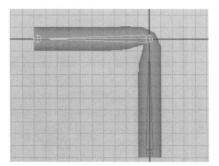

FIGURE 4.21   Cylinder bound with the smooth binding.

Rigid Bind Alternative

Unlike the smooth bind, in a *rigid bind*, each point is only influenced by a single joint. This causes rigid deformation when the joints bend. Rigid binding isn't used much except in special cases—for example, for insects or robots where surface stiffness is appropriate.

Now let's modify our previous smooth bind example and see how rigid binding compares.

1. Repeat steps 1 through 6 from the previous exercise.
2. Select Skin > Bind Skin > Rigid Bind Option Box.
3. In the Rigid Bind Skin Options window, make sure the Bind To field is set to Complete Skeleton and then click on the Bind Skin button (see Figure 4.22).

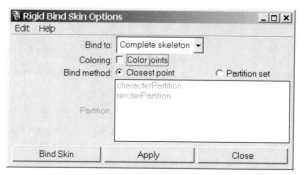

FIGURE 4.22   The Rigid Bind Skin Options window.

4. Press 4 on the keyboard to see the cylinder in Wireframe mode.
5. Click on joint2 and, in the Channel Box, type 90 in the Rotate Z field.
6. Press 5 on the keyboard to see the cylinder in Smooth Shader All mode. Notice that the cylinder bends rigidly at joint2, as shown in Figure 4.23.

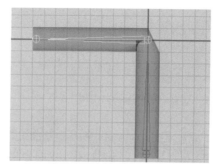

FIGURE 4.23   Cylinder bound with rigid binding.

Smooth Bind Challenges

When you bind a character by using the smooth bind method, the point weights that Maya automatically assigns often do not deform the geometry properly. In this case, you must edit the point weights manually by using the Paint Skin Weight tool.

The points have weight values from 0 to 1, and these values are represented by the colors black and white. Black has a value of 0, and white has a value of 1. With the Paint Skin Weight tool, you can change the points' values to any weight between 0 and 1 to adjust the geometry deformation properly.

1. Select File > New Scene.
2. Select Create > Polygon Primitive and uncheck Interactive Creation.
3. Select Create > Polygon Primitive > Cylinder Option Box. In the Subdivisions Along Height field of the Polygon Cylinder Options window, type 20 and then click the Create button.
4. Scale the cylinder 10 units on the Y axis.
5. Create three joints: joint1 at the bottom of the cylinder, joint2 at the middle of the cylinder, and joint3 at the top of the cylinder.
6. Select joint1, joint2, and the cylinder.
7. Select Skin > Bind Skin > Smooth Bind Option Box.
8. In the Bind To field, select Selected Joints and click on the Bind Skin button.
9. Rotate joint2 90 degrees on the Z axis.
10. Select the cylinder. Select Skin > Edit Smooth Skin > Paint Skin Weights Tool Option Box, as shown in Figure 4.24. The tool settings appear on the right side of the screen.

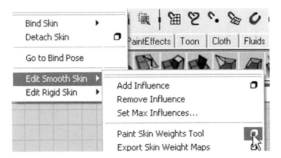

FIGURE 4.24   Paint Skin Weights Tool options box selection.

11. In the Influence section, click on joint1. Notice that the gradient starts with white at joint1 and extends past joint2, as shown in Figure 4.25. This is because the Max Influences value, which specifies the number of joints that can have influence on each point, defaults to 5 (joints) and Dropoff to 4.0. The dropoff rate determines the influence decrease of each joint on the skin points.

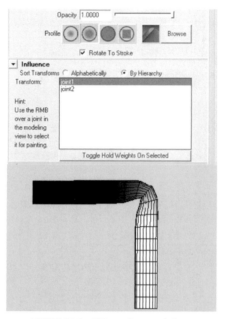

FIGURE 4.25   Skin points weights.

Visualize the Direction of Bind Influence

One of the hardest things about smooth-bound joints is visualizing the direction in which the points are being pulled. The CVs are not pushed or pulled relative to the surface; instead, they are pushed or pulled relative to the joints influencing them. The best way to get a feeling for this is with a contrived example.

1. Select joint1 and enter 1.0 in the Paint Weights Value field.
2. Click on the Flood button. You should see something like Figure 4.26.

When you have a set of joints, the CV weights must add up to 1.0. If you flood the CV weights on one joint to 1.0, as in this example, the other joint (or joints) gets automatically set to 0. If all CVs have a weight of 1.0 on joint1 and 0 on joint2, the CVs are influenced only by joint1. Because joint1 starts out pointing straight up, the CVs line up this way.

Now try flooding the points of joint1 to 0. This effectively reverses the situation, so that only joint2 has influence. The points migrate to the current rotation of joint2, which in this case is horizontal.

Finally, consider what would happen if you flood joint 1 to 0.5. The result of a 0.5 weight on every CV of joint1 is that every point of joint2 also gets a 0.5 weight (0.5 + 0.5 = 1). Because each point is influenced equally by the rotational position of joint1 and joint2, the points move as if rotated halfway between the joints, as shown in Figure 4.27.

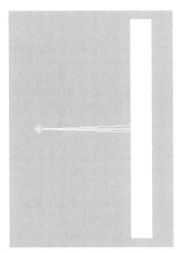

FIGURE 4.26   Skin weights flood with value 1.

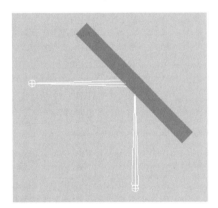

FIGURE 4.27   Skin weights flood with value 0.5.

Now try to paint the weights so that the "elbow" does not appear to lose mass when it bends. The process of painting skin weights can be tedious, but it also provides the fine degree of artistic control needed for moving complex joints.

Understanding Constraints

When you are creating rigs, it is often useful to specify that two things move or rotate together. Sometimes this can be accomplished by using hierarchical relationships. When this is not possible, you can use constraint relationships to make things move and rotate in sync. A constrained object rotates, translates, scales, or follows another object called the target object. Maya offers many types of constraints. The constraints most commonly used for rigging are point, orient, parent, and pole constraints.

Point Constraints

A *point constraint* is like a magnet point attaching the constrained object to the target object. When the target object moves, the constrained object moves with it. Both objects maintain their global position. When the target object is rotated or scaled, it does not affect the constrained object. This is unlike the parent-child relationships discussed earlier, in which rotation and scaling transformations are inherited. In general, constraints are very useful for simulating temporary physical contact between discrete objects. This is because constraints can be animated and don't change the scene hierarchy.

Typically, parenting is used for more permanent relationships such as parts of the same object. For example, you might point-constrain a hand to a doorknob while the character is opening the door, and then release the constraint by animating it. The relationship between the doorknob and the door is more permanent and would more likely be done using parenting or grouping.

You can point-constrain one object to another with or without distance offset. When the Maintain Offset option is used, the objects maintain the same distance from each other when the target object is moved. Without distance offset, the constrained object's pivot jumps on top of the target object. You can constrain a specific axis or all objects' axes.

To point-constrain two objects, first click on the target object and then on the constrained object. Let's see how this works in practice

1. Select File > New Scene.
2. Press F2 to change to Animation mode.
3. Select Create > Polygon Primitives and uncheck Interactive Creation.
4. Select Create > Polygon Primitives > Sphere.
5. In the Channel Box, type 5 in the Translate X field.
6. Select Create > Polygon Primitives > Cone.
7. Deselect the sphere and the cone.
8. Click on the sphere as the target object, press and hold down the Shift key, and click on the cone as the constrained object.
9. Select Constrain > Point Constrain Option Box.
10. Make sure Maintain Offset is selected and click on the Add button.
11. Select the sphere and, in the Channel Box, type 12 in the Translate X field. The cone should move with it and should be translated seven units.
12. Rotate the sphere. The cone should not be affected.
13. Scale the sphere. The cone should not be affected.
14. Repeat the same exercise with the Maintain Offset option cleared.

Orient Constraint

An *orient constraint* makes the orientation of one object follow the orientation of another object. It is useful for orienting a joint's axis to an object direction and having two or more objects oriented synchronously. Let's create a simple example to see how this works.

1. Select Create > Polygon Primitives > Cube.
2. Select the cube and, in the Channel Box, enter 5 in the Translate X field and 3 in the Translate Y field.
3. Select Create > Polygon Primitive > Cone.
4. In the Channel Box, enter 3 in the Translate Y field.
5. Select the cube first and then select the cone.
6. Select Constrain > Orient.
7. Select the cube. Press the E key to change to the Rotation tool.
8. Drag the red handle of the Rotation tool up and down to rotate the cube in the X axis. The cube should rotate, and the cone should follow the cube's rotation.
9. Select Create > Polygon Primitives > Torus.
10. Select the cube first and then the torus. Select Constrain > Orient.
11. Now rotate the cube again in the X axis. The cone and the torus should follow the cube orientation.

Parent Constraints

Parent constraints work almost like parenting, which was discussed in Chapter 2. When the target object moves, the constrained object moves with it. When the target object rotates, the constrained object rotates with it and maintains the same global rotation as the target. For example:

1. Choose File > New Scene.
2. Select Create > Polygon Primitives and uncheck Interactive Creation.
3. Select Create > Polygon Primitives > Sphere.
4. In the Channel Box, type 5 in the Translate X channel.
5. Select Create > Polygon Primitives > Cone.
6. Deselect both objects.
7. Click on the sphere first as the target object and then click on the cone as the constrained object.
8. Select Constrain > Parent Constraint Option Box. Make sure Maintain Offset is selected and click on the Add button.
9. Select the sphere only.
10. In the Channel Box, type –45 in the Rotate Z field.
11. Click on the cone and check that its Z rotation is –45, just as it is for the sphere.

Pole Vector Constraint

You use the pole vector constraint to control the rotation of the Twist channel of the Rotate Plane IK handle. This constraint is usually used for controlling the position of elbows and knees.

1. Select File > New Scene.
2. Create three joints as shown in Figure 4.28.

FIGURE 4.28   Three joints.

3. Select Skeleton > IK Handle Tool Option Box.
4. Make sure the Current Solver field is set to IKRPSolver.
5. Click first on joint1 and then on joint3. You should see the IK handle with a rotation disk, as shown in Figure 4.29.

FIGURE 4.29   IK handle with a rotation disk.

6. Select Create > Locator. *Locators* are special objects in Maya that are visible during interactive use of the program but that do not render. They are often used as components of rigging controls.

7. In Front view, move the locator onto joint1.
8. In the Channel Box, type 5 in the Translate Z field.
9. Select Modify > Freeze Transformations. Notice that the translation and rotation of the locator were reset to 0. This allows you to move the locator back simply by typing 0 in its transformation channels.
10. Click first on the locator to select it as a target object and then click on the IK handle.
11. Select Constrain > Pole Vector. You should see a vector connecting the IK handle to the locator.
12. In Perspective view, move the locator to the right and left to see the skeleton twist.

Using Constraints to Develop Rigging Controls

When rigging, you can create controls to quick-pick IK handles and other parts of the rig to adjust the skeleton. Controls are usually created with CV curves and are not rendered.

For example, as mentioned earlier, IK end effectors are very difficult to select in the normal Maya interface. A good rig provides easy-to-grab controls with which you can move the end effector. These control objects are usually visually distinct from the character and in the form of graphical symbols such as cubes, circle, and arrows. The control objects are usually point-constrained or parented to the rigging hierarchy.

In the following tutorial, you will learn how to integrate these techniques to create a simple character rig.

TUTORIAL 4.1: RIGGING THE SACK

Now that you've seen the principal elements used in rigging, let's put these pieces together in a practical context by rigging the sack modeled previously. First you are going to create the sack's spine.

Creating the Spine

To create the spine, follow these steps.

ON THE CD

1. Open the file called sack_modeling_done.mb in the Sack_Modeling subfolder in the chapter3, MayaWorkingFiles folder on the CD-ROM.
2. Make sure you are in Animation mode.
3. In Perspective view, select Panels > Saved Layouts > Four View.
4. In all four views, select Shading > Smooth Shade All (shortcut 5) and X-Ray. The sack should be transparent.
5. Create a layer and add the sack to the new layer. Name the layer body.

6. Click on the middle column of the layer until you see an R. This protects the model from accidental editing (see Figure 4.30).

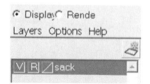

FIGURE 4.30   Reference layer setting.

7. Select Skeleton > Joint Tool Option Box, as shown in Figure 4.31.

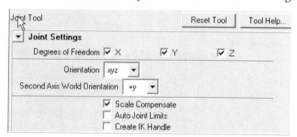

FIGURE 4.31   The Joint Tool options window.

8. Click on the Reset Tool button. Notice that the joint is going to be created as a ball joint. *Ball joints* have freedom on X, Y, and Z. You can adjust the joint's rotation constraints using the Attribute Editor later in the rigging process. For now, create the joints using the defaults.
9. In Front view, hold down the X key and click once at four grids above the bottom of the sack over the origin. Release the X key and click for the second time just above the root to create Joint2. Hold down the X key again, and click seven times to create Joint3, Joint4, Joint5, Joint6, Joint7, Joint8, and Joint9. Press the Enter key to finalize the create joints operation (see Figure 4.32).

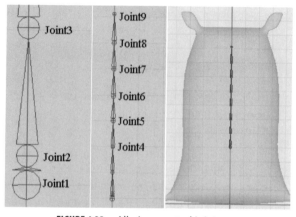

FIGURE 4.32   All nine created joints.

10. Select Window > Hypergraph Scene Hierarchy. The Hypergraph opens unattached to the panels. This way you have all four views available to see the rigging. In the Hypergraph, name each joint as follows: Joint1 = root, Joint2 = spine1, Joint3 = spine2, Joint4 = spine3, Joint5 = spine4, Joint6 = spine5, Joint7 = spine6, Joint8 = spine7, and Joint9 = spine8 (see Figure 4.33).

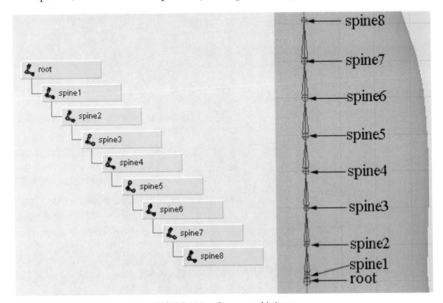

FIGURE 4.33   Renamed joints.

 You can rename the joints using the Quick Rename tool. Click on the black arrow next to the Rendering Settings Window icon on the Status Line and select Quick Rename. Type the joint name on the Rename the Selected Object field.

Creating the Arms

To create the arms, follow these steps.

1. Select the Joint tool. Consider that the sack is facing you. Holding down the X key, click four times in a straight line toward the left of the sack to create the left arm (see Figure 4.34).

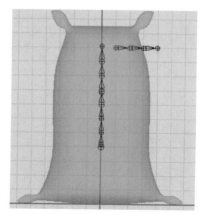

FIGURE 4.34 Left arm of sack created.

2. Name the joints LtClavicle, LtShoulder, LtElbow, and LtHand.
3. Press W, select LtClavicle, and press the Insert key. You should see the joint's pivot.
4. Move the pivot of LtClavicle to position the joint.
5. Still in the Pivot mode, click on LtShoulder, LtElbow, and LtHand one at a time and position the joints as shown in Figure 4.35.

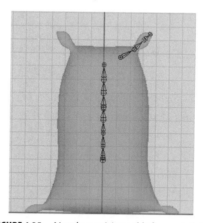

FIGURE 4.35 Newly positioned left arm joints.

6. Press the Insert key again to turn off the Pivot mode.
7. Select LtClavicle.
8. Select Skeleton > Orient Joint Option Box.
9. In the options window, select XYZ. This orients all the chain joints' local axes uniformly. The X axis will be pointing to the next joint following the bone orientation. Orienting joints ensure that the joints rotate in the same direction.
10. Select LtClavicle and then select Skeleton > Mirror Joint Option Box.

11. Select Skeleton > Mirror Joint Option Box.
12. Check the options: Mirror Across = YZ and Mirror Function = Behavior. In the Replacement names for duplicate joints fields, type Search for = Lt and Replace With = Rt. This will mirror all the joints and will rename them with Rt. Click the Mirror button (see Figure 4.36).

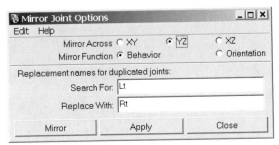

FIGURE 4.36   The Updated Mirror Joint Options window.

Creating the Legs

To create the legs, follow these steps.

1. Hold down the X key and, in the lower-right side of the sack, click five times in a straight line downward to create the left leg (see Figure 4.37).

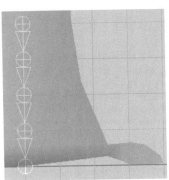

FIGURE 4.37   Five left leg joints.

2. Name the joints LtHip, LtKnee, LtAnkle, LtBall, and LtToe.
3. Press W, select LtHip, press the Insert key to see the joint's pivot, and then move it a bit upward. Move all the joints of the left leg as shown in Figure 4.38.

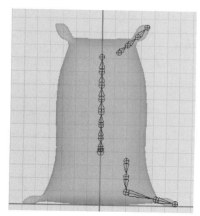

FIGURE 4.38   Newly positioned left leg joints.

4. In Side view, move LtKnee joint's pivot approximately $1/4$ of a unit forward to position it a little bit bent forward. This will help the joint bend with the IK later in the rigging process (see Figure 4.39).

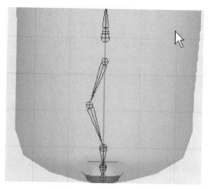

FIGURE 4.39   Left knee joint bent.

5. Select LtHip joint and select Skeleton > Orient Joint. In the options window, make sure Orientation is set to XYZ.
6. Select LtHip and mirror the joints. At this point, you should have the joints as shown in Figure 4.40.

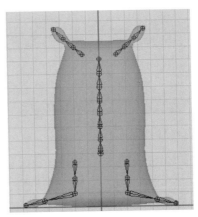

FIGURE 4.40 Complete view of all joints.

Parenting the Arms and Legs to the Torso

Now you have the sack's spine, arms, and legs, but they are unattached. You need to attach them to create a one-piece skeleton. For this task, you will use the previously mentioned process called parenting.

First, you need to decide which joint is going to be the child and which joint is going to be the parent. The best thing is to study your own body. If you stretch out your arms in a cross position and move your spine to the left and right, you will notice that your shoulders move along with your spine. So, you can see that the shoulder is the child of the spine.

Parenting the Arms to the Torso

To parent the arms to the torso, follow these steps.

1. In the Front view, select LtClavicle as the child, select spine8 as the parent, and press P. You also can parent the joints by selecting Edit > Parent. Notice that Maya creates a new bone between the child and the parent, as shown in Figure 4.41.

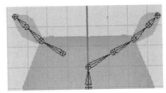

FIGURE 4.41 Left arm parented to the spine.

2. Repeat the same procedure for RtClavicle (see Figure 4.42).

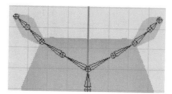

FIGURE 4.42 Both arms parented to the spine.

Parenting the Legs to the Torso

To parent the legs to the torso, follow these steps.

1. Select LtHip joint as the child, select the root as the parent, and press P.
2. Repeat the same procedure for RtHip. Now you should have both arms and legs attached to the torso, as shown in Figure 4.43.

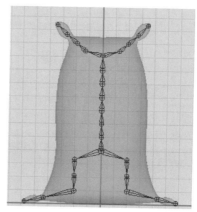

FIGURE 4.43 Attached arm, leg, and torso joints.

Creating the Rib Cage

To create the rib cage, follow these steps.

1. Select Skeleton > Joint Tool. In the Front view, click once approximately three units to the right of spine3. Call the new joint LtRib1 (see Figure 4.44).
2. Create a rib joint on the side of joints 4, 5, 6, and 7. Call them LtRib2, LtRib3, LtRib4, and LtRib5 (see Figure 4.45).
3. Now you need to parent the ribs to the spine. Select LtRib1 (as the child), then select spine3 (as the parent), and press P (see Figure 4.46).

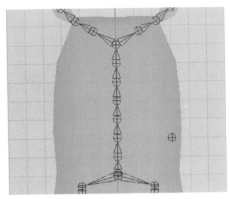

FIGURE 4.44   New rib joint to the right of spine3.

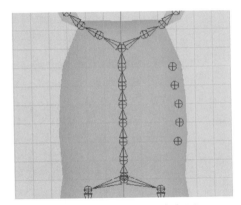

FIGURE 4.45   All five created rib joints.

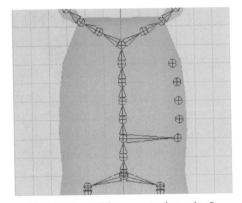

FIGURE 4.46   LtRib1 parented to spine3.

4. Repeat the parenting process and parent all left ribs to the spine (see Figure 4.47).

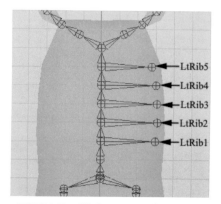

FIGURE 4.47 All ribs parented to spine.

5. Click on the ribs one by one and move them a little bit upwards (see Figure 4.48).

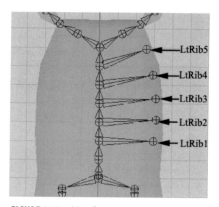

FIGURE 4.48 Newly positioned rib joints.

6. Select LtRib1.
7. Select Skeleton > Mirror Joint Option Box. In the Mirror Joint Options window, make sure Mirror Across YZ is checked, the Search For field has the letters Lt typed in, and the Replace With field has the letters Rt typed in.
8. Click on the Apply button.
9. Repeat steps 7 and 8 to mirror LtRib2, LtRib3, LtRib4, and LtRib5 (see Figure 4.49).

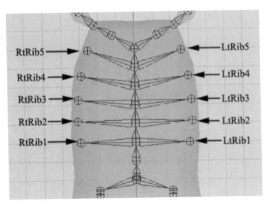

FIGURE 4.49   Ribs mirrored.

After you mirror LtRib1, you can use the shortcut key G (repeat the last command) to mirror the other rib joints.

Creating the IK Handles for the Legs

You will use a single chain IK handle for the sack's legs. This is mainly to illustrate the IK Single Chain Solver, but also because the sack's legs motion will not require hip and knee rotation. They will move in a single plane orientation.

To create the IK handles for the legs, follow these steps.

1. Select all of the leg joints, one by one, and make sure all joints have rotation 0 in the XYZ axes in the Channel Box so the joints rotate properly.
2. Select Skeleton > IK Handle Tool Option Box.
3. In the Current Solver drop-down menu, select ikSCsolver, which means IK Single Chain Solver (see Figure 4.50).

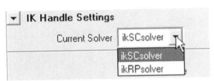

FIGURE 4.50   Selecting ikSCsolver from the Current Solver menu.

4. Click on LtHip to place the root of the IK handle and click on LtAnkle to place the end of the IK handle (see Figure 4.51).

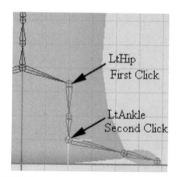

FIGURE 4.51 Connected left leg IK handle.

5. In the Hypergraph, name the IK handle LtLegIK.
6. Repeat steps 1 through 5 for the right leg. Name the IK handle RtLegIK.

Creating the IK Handles for the Arms

This time you will use a rotate plane IK handle. This is because this option will allow you to control the rotation of the sack's shoulders and elbows properly by using a pole vector constrain.

To create the IK handles for the arms, follow these steps:

1. Make sure all the joints of the left arm have 0 rotation on XYZ axes in the Channel Box.
2. Select LtElbow and rotate it 45 degrees on Z (see Figure 4.52).

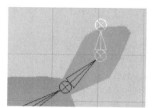

FIGURE 4.52 The LtElbow joint rotated 45 degrees on Z.

3. Select Skeleton > Set Preferred Angle Option Box (see Figure 4.53).

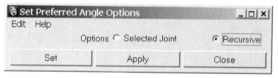

FIGURE 4.53 The Set Preferred Angle Options window.

4. Make sure Recursive is checked and click on the Set button. This will help the joint rotate correctly.
5. Rotate LtElbow back to 0 degrees on Z.
6. Select Skeleton > IK Handle Tool Option Box. This time, select ikRP-solver, which means Rotate Plane Solver (see Figure 4.54).

FIGURE 4.54   The IK Handle Tool options window.

7. Click on LtShoulder and then on LtHand. Notice that the IK handle has a rotation plane at the shoulder (see Figure 4.55).

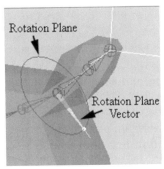

FIGURE 4.55   Connected ikRPsolver left arm IK handle.

8. Name the IK handle LtArmIK.
9. Repeat steps 1 through 8 for the right arm. Name the right arm IK handle RtArmIK.

Creating the IK Spline Handle for the Spine

IK spline handles are used for hierarchies with more than one joint between the root and the end effector of the handle. The IK spline handle is commonly used to animate spines and tails. Spline IK handles work almost like the regular IK handles in that they have a root, an end effector, and a CV curve. However, the IK spline handle is animated by the curve and not by the end effector.

1. Select all the spine joints (one by one) and make sure their rotations have a value of 0 on the X, Y, and Z axes.
2. Select Skeleton > IK Spline Handle Tool Option Box. Click on Reset Tool and uncheck Auto Parent Curve (see Figure 4.56).

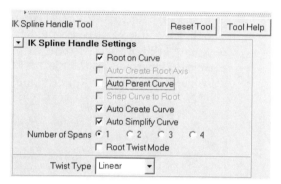

FIGURE 4.56 The IK Spline Handle Tool options window.

3. Click on spine1 and then on spine8 (see Figure 4.57).

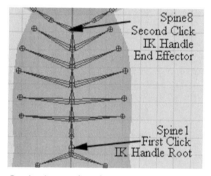

FIGURE 4.57 Beginning and end positions of the IK spline handle.

4. In the Hypergraph, you should see ikHandle1 and curve1. Name the IK spline handle sackSpineIK and name curve1 splineCurve.
5. In the Maya Status Line, click on the black arrow and select All Objects Off, as shown in Figure 4.58.

FIGURE 4.58 Selecting All Objects Off under the Object Selection Mask menu.

6. Click on the backward "S" icon on the Maya Status Line. This allows you to pick only splineCurve (see Figure 4.59). Alternatively, you can open the Outliner by selecting Panels > Panel > Outliner to select splineCurve. You also can select the curve in the Hypergraph.

FIGURE 4.59   Activating Curves under Object Selection Mask options.

7. In Perspective view, zoom in to the sackSpline IK handle until you see the curve, as shown in Figure 4.60.

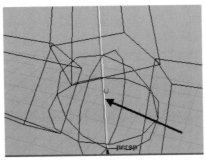

FIGURE 4.60   Zoomed in view of the IK handle's curve.

8. Right-click on the curve and select Control Vertex. Notice that the curve has four CVs, as shown in Figure 4.61. These CVs on splineCurve may be in slightly different positions than shown in the figure. They will be used to animate the spine. Because they are not easy to pick, we are going to create cluster handles to be more efficient. A *cluster* is one or more CVs grouped and is designated by the letter C. When you move a cluster, all CVs of that cluster move together.

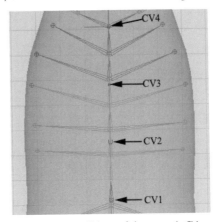

FIGURE 4.61   All four of the curve's CVs.

9. Select the first CV (CV1). Select Deform > Create Cluster Option Box. Select Edit > Reset Settings and click Create. Notice that a letter C is created on top of the CV, as shown in Figure 4.62.

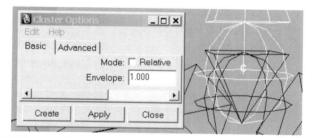

FIGURE 4.62 The Cluster Options window and resulting letter C.

10. Name the cluster X.
11. Select the second and the third control vertices (CV2 and CV3) and create another cluster.
12. Name the cluster Y.
13. Select the fourth control vertex (CV4) and create another cluster.
14. Name this cluster Z.
15. In the Maya Status Line, click on the black arrow and select All Objects On, as shown in Figure 4.63.

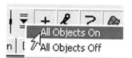

FIGURE 4.63 Selecting All Objects On under the Object Selection Mask menu.

If you create an IK spline handle and delete it, make sure you also delete the curve that is part of it. When you delete the IK handle, Maya does not delete the curve by default. It is sometimes confusing because you end up with more than one IK spline handle curve.

Creating Cluster Handles

Even though the clusters are visible, they are difficult to select. You want to make each cluster as easy as possible to select, so you need to create handles for the clusters.

1. Select Create > Text Option Box.
2. Select Edit > Reset Settings and select the Curves option (see Figure 4.64).

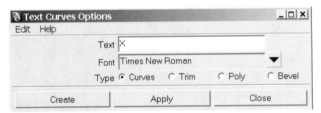

FIGURE 4.64   The Text Curves Options window.

3. Type the letter X in the Text field and click on the Create button. By default, the Text field shows the word Maya.
4. Create two other letters: Y and Z. The letters are created one on top of the other at the origin (0, 0, 0).
5. You should see the X, Y, and Z group nodes in the Hypergraph (see Figure 4.65).

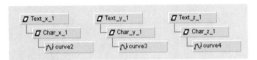

FIGURE 4.65   Text Curves X, Y, and Z group nodes in the Hypergraph.

6. Middle-click on the curve node of X and drag it out of the group.
7. Repeat step 6 to separate curve2 and curve3 from their respective groups.
8. Name the curves as follows: curve1 = clusterX_handle, curve2 = clusterY_handle, and curve3 = clusterZ_handle.
9. Delete the text_X_1, text_Y_1, text_Z_1, char_X_1, char_Y_1, and char_Z_1 group nodes.
10. In the Front view panel, move clusterX_handle on top of clusterX, clusterY_handle on top of clusterY, and clusterZ_handle on top of clusterZ (see Figure 4.66).
11. Select the three cluster handles and type -6 for Translate Z in the Channel Box. This will move the handles six units behind the sack (see Figure 4.67).

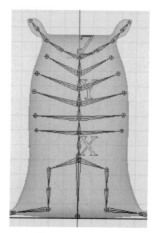

FIGURE 4.66 Cluster handles positioned over cluster counterparts.

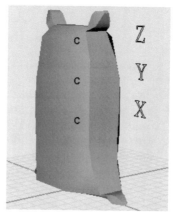

FIGURE 4.67 Perspective view of cluster handles six units behind the sack.

12. Select clusterX_handle, clusterY_handle, and clusterZ_handle. In the Channel Box, type Scale X = 0.5, Scale Y = 0.5, and Scale Z = 0.5.
13. Select clusterX_handle. Press the Insert key to see the handle's pivot.
14. Hold down the V key while you move and snap clusterX_handle's pivot on top of the root joint, as in Figure 4.68. This way the point of rotation of clusterX_handle is on the root joint.
15. Select clusterY_handle and snap its pivot to clusterY.
16. Select clusterZ_handle and snap its pivot to clusterZ.
17. Select clusterX_handle, clusterY_handle, and clusterZ_handle.
18. Select Modify > Freeze Transformations Option Box. Make sure Translate, Rotate, and Scale are checked, as shown in Figure 4.69. Freezing the transformation of the clusters' handles resets the handles' transformations to 0. This helps you translate and rotate them accurately.

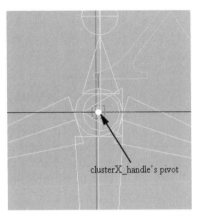

FIGURE 4.68   clusterX_handle's pivot on top of the root joint.

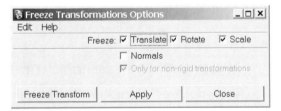

FIGURE 4.69   The Freeze Transformations Options window.

19. Click on the Freeze Transform button. Notice that the handle Translate and Rotate values are all set to 0, and the Scale is set to 1.

Creating a Constraint for the Cluster Handles

To create a constraint for the cluster handles, follow these steps.

1. Select clusterY_handle and then select clusterY.
2. Select Constrain > Point Constraint Option Box. Make sure the Maintain Offset checkbox and the Constraint Axes All checkbox are checked. Click on the Add button (see Figure 4.70).

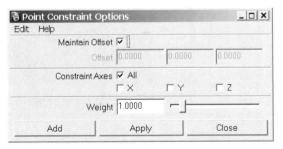

FIGURE 4.70   The Point Constraint Options window and updated settings.

3. Repeat steps 1 and 2 to point-constrain clusterZ to clusterZ_handle.
4. Select clusterX_handle and then select clusterX.
5. Select Constraints > Parent Constraint Option Box. Make sure Maintain Offset is checked.
6. Click on the Add button.
7. Moving clusterX will create an inappropriate effect for the hips. To solve this problem, constrain the rotation of the root joint to the clusterX_handle. Delete the parent constraint you just created. Select clusterX_handle and then select the root joint.
8. Select Constrain > Parent Option Box. Make sure the Maintain Offset checkbox and the Rotate All checkbox are checked. Uncheck Translate All.
9. Click on the Add button.
10. Check all the cluster handles. Select clusterY_handle and clusterZ_handle, one at time, and move them. The clusters should move with them.
11. Select clusterX_handle and rotate it. The hip joints should rotate with it.

Creating a Pole Vector Constraint for the Arms

If you move the arms' IK handles, you will notice that the arms can flip. You need to create a pole vector constraint to control the shoulder rotation. You will use a locator as the controller of the IK Pole Vector.

1. Select Create > Locator. Do this again (or press G) so that two locators are created. The locators are created at the origin, and they are called locator1 and locator2.
2. Name locator1 LtArmPVC (pole vector constraint) and locator2 RtArmPVC.
3. Select LtArmPVC.
4. Hold down the V key and drag LtArmPVC on the LtElbow joint. Make sure the locator snaps on the elbow joint (see Figure 4.71).

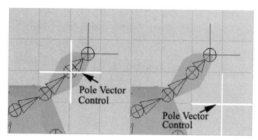

FIGURE 4.71   The LtArmPVC locator snapped to the LtElbow joint.

5. With LtArmPVC still selected, type –6 in the Translate Z attribute in the Channel Box. This will move the locators behind the arm six units.
6. With LtArmPVC still selected, select Modify > Freeze Transformations. Notice that the Translate and Rotate values of LtArmPVC are 0, 0, and 0 for XYZ.
7. Select LtArmPVC, hold down the Shift key, and select the LtArmIK.
8. Select Constrain > Pole Vector. You should see a line constraining LtArmIK to LtArmPVC (see Figure 4.72).

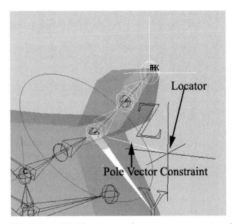

FIGURE 4.72   The LtArmPVC locator pole vector constrained to LtArmIK.

9. Repeat steps 3 through 8 for the RtArmIK.

Creating the Leg and Arm Controls

The arm and leg controls help you select the IK handles easily for animation. They should be created with NURBS curves so that they are not visible in the rendered images.

1. Make sure you have the sack on Smooth Shade All and X-Ray mode. The sack needs to be transparent for you to see the cube.
2. Import a control called leg_control.mb from the chapter4, Rigging_Controls folder on the CD-ROM.
3. Name the cube LtLegControl.
4. In Front view, snap LtLegControl on top of the LtAnkle joint (see Figure 4.73).

ON THE CD

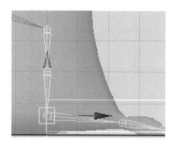

FIGURE 4.73   Snapping LtLegControl onto the LtAnkle joint.

5. With LtLegControl still selected, select Modify > Freeze Transformations.
6. Select Edit > Duplicate Special Option Box (see Figure 4.74).

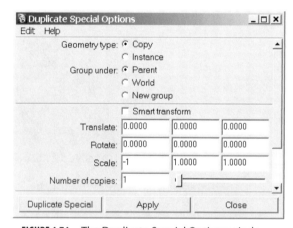

FIGURE 4.74   The Duplicate Special Options window.

7. In the Duplicate Special Options window, select Edit > Reset Settings. Set Scale to –1, 1, and 1 for X, Y, and Z, respectively.
8. Click on the Duplicate Special button.
9. Call the duplicated cube RtLegControl.
10. Snap RtLegControl to the RtAnkle joint.
11. Select Modify > Freeze Transformations.

Constraining the Controls to the Legs

To constrain the controls to the legs, follow these steps.

1. Open the Hypergraph.
2. In the Hypergraph, click on LtLegControl first, hold the Shift key, and click on LtLegIK.
3. Select Constrain > Point Option Box.

4. In the option window, make sure that Maintain Offset is not checked and that Constraint Axes All is checked. Click on the Add button (see Figure 4.75).

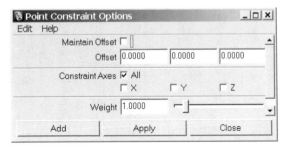

FIGURE 4.75 Updated Point Constraint Options settings.

5. Click on LtLegControl and move it. The entire leg should move with it as shown in Figure 4.76.

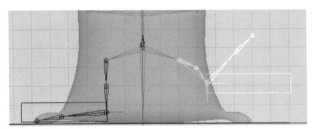

FIGURE 4.76 Leg influenced by the LtLegControl cube's movement.

6. The LtBall and LtToe joints move in a different direction than LtLegControl because LtAnkle is being rotated by the IK, and the control is not affected by the IK. To fix that, you need to orient LtAnkle to the control. Select LtLegControl first and then select LtAnkle.
7. Select Constrain > Orient Option Box.
8. Make sure both Maintain Offset and Constraint Axes All are checked. Click on the Add button.
9. Move LtLegControl again. The foot should follow the same orientation as LtLegControl, as shown in Figure 4.77.
10. Repeat steps 2 through 8 to constrain RtLegIK to the RtLegControl.

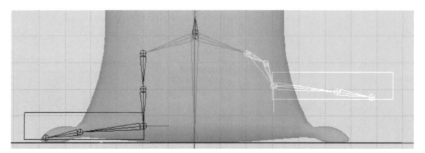

FIGURE 4.77   Foot influenced by the LtLegControl cube's movement.

Constraining the Controls to the Arms

To constrain the controls to the arms, follow these steps.

1. Import the cube.mb file from the chapter4, Rigging_Controls folder on the CD-ROM. Name the cube LtArmControl.
2. In Front view, move the cube on top of the LtHand joint (see Figure 4.78).

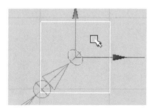

FIGURE 4.78   Cube on top of the LtHand joint in Front view.

3. In the Channel Box, set a value of 1.5 for the Scale X, Y, and Z attributes.
4. Select Modify > Freeze Transformations.
5. Duplicate the cube and move it on top of the RtHand joint.
6. Select Modify > Freeze Transformations.
7. In the Hypergraph, click on LtArmControl first, hold the Shift key, and click on LtArmIK.
8. Select Constrain > Point.
9. Click on LtArmControl and move it. The entire arm should move with it.
10. Repeat steps 6, 7, and 8 to constrain RtHandIK to RtArmControl.

Creating a Local Control

At this point in the rigging process, the spine and the cluster controls are not moving with the root joint, so you cannot move the character in one piece. You need to create a local control to parent the cluster handles under it. This way, the entire skeleton will move together.

1. Select Create > NURBS Primitives Circle.
2. Name the circle local_control.
3. In the Channel Box, set a value of 6 for the Scale X, Y, and Z attributes.
4. Move and snap it to the root joint.
5. Select Modify > Freeze Transformations.
6. Select Edit > Delete by Type > History.
7. Open the Hypergraph, middle-click on clusterX_handle, and drag it on top of local_control.
8. Repeat step 7 to parent clusterY_handle and clusterZ_handle under local_control.

Creating a Global Control

A global control is a control at the top level of the skeleton hierarchy. Unlike a local control, which moves part of the skeleton, a global control allows you to place your entire character in different places in the scene by moving the global control.

To create a global control:

1. Select Create > NURBS Primitives Circle.
2. Name the circle global_control.
3. In the Channel Box, set a value of 8 for the Scale X, Y, and Z attributes.
4. Select Modify > Freeze Transformations.
5. Select Edit > Delete by Type > History.
6. In the Hypergraph, middle-click on local_control and drag it on top of the global_control.
7. Middle-click on LtArmPVC and drag it on top of global_control.
8. Repeat step 7 for RtArmPVC, LtArmControl, RtArmControl, LtLegControl, RtLegControl, LtLegIK, RtLegIK, and root.

Organizing the Rigging Nodes in the Hypergraph

A typical Maya scene can have from dozens to hundreds of nodes. In order to find things quickly, it helps to keep them logically organized. The freeform node layout gives you full control of the nodes' location in the Hypergraph. This allows you to organize them as you feel appropriate for your scene.

To organize the rigging nodes:

1. In the Hypergraph, select Options > Layout > Freeform Layout. This layout allows you to organize the rigging nodes in a customized way (see Figure 4.79).

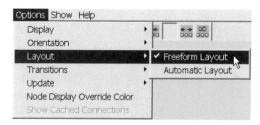

FIGURE 4.79   Selecting Freeform Layout under Hypergraph Options.

2. Rearrange all of the nodes as shown in Figure 4.80 and 4.81.

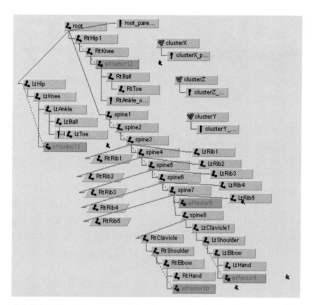

FIGURE 4.80   Rearranged rigging nodes in the Hypergraph.

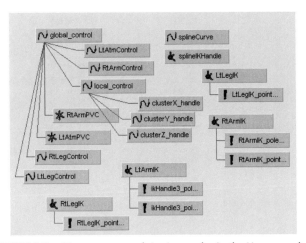

FIGURE 4.81   More rearranged rigging nodes in the Hypergraph.

Hiding Objects

When you rig a character, you should lock and hide attributes that you don't need to animate. This facilitates the animation process, because it prevents you from picking the wrong attribute accidentally.

1. Select all of the following IK handles: LtArmIK, RtArmIK, LtLegIK, RtLegIK, and sackSplineIK.
2. Create a new layer and call it non_touchables.
3. Add all the IK handles and clusters (C) to the non_touchables layer.
4. Hide the visibility of the IKs by clicking on the V in the first box of the layer.

Locking and Hiding Attributes

To lock and hide attributes:

1. Select LtArmControl, RtArmControl, LtArmPVC, and RtArmPVC.
2. In the Channel Box, hold down the Shift key, and click-drag on Rotation X, Y, Z; Scale X, Y, Z; and Visibility channels to select all of them (see Figure 4.82).
3. Right-click on the selected channels and select Lock and Hide Selected (see Figure 4.83).

FIGURE 4.82   Multiple attributes selected in the Channel Box.

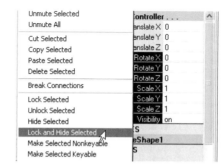

FIGURE 4.83   Lock and Hide Selected option in Channel Box.

4. Repeat steps 1 through 3 for the cluster handles Y and Z.
5. Select clusterX_handle. Lock and Hide the Translate X, Y, Z; Scale X, Y, Z; and Visibility channels.
6. Select LtLegControl, RtLegControl, local_control, and global_control. Lock and hide Scale X, Y, Z, and Visibility channels.

TUTORIAL 4.2: SKINNING THE SACK

At this point, you have a model and a skeleton, but the two are still completely independent. The next step in the process is to make sure your model is appropriately smoothed and then to use the smooth bind operation so that the skeleton position will drive the model.

1. Select the sack and, in the Channel Box, find the polySmoothFace1 attribute and click on it. Remember that you smoothed the sack in Chapter 3.
2. Scroll down in the Channel Box until you see the polySmooth attribute called Divisions.
3. Make sure Divisions is set to 1 (see Figure 4.84).

FIGURE 4.84   Divisions attribute under polySmooth command.

4. Press F2 to change into Animation mode.
5. Select the root joint of the skeleton.
6. Holding down the Shift key, select the sack geometry.
7. Select Skin > Bind Skin > Smooth Bind (see Figure 4.85).

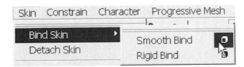

FIGURE 4.85   Selecting Smooth Bind under the Skin menu.

8. Select LtLegControl and move it up and down. Notice that the geometry moves with it.
9. Save your work. Call the file sack_smooth_bind.mb.

TUTORIAL 4.3: ANIMATING THE SACK

Posing a coffee sack is a classic animation exercise. Because a sack lacks physical details, you must concentrate on conveying emotion through body language. Before you start setting keyframes for the sack skeleton, you need to create a character set. A character set is a method of automatically setting keyframes for multiple objects' attributes. When you create a character set, you specify all the objects you want to be in the set; when you set a keyframe, Maya keyframes all of the attributes of all objects in the set. Because Maya automatically keyframes the attributes, you end up with many unnecessary keyframes. This is not such a problem considering that it facilitates the animation process, and you can delete the extra keyframes later.

ON THE CD

1. Open a file called jump_shot.tif from the shot_storyboard subfolder in the chapter4 folder on the CD-ROM and try to create three poses to match the drawings.
2. Open your sack_smooth_bind.mb file or the one in the chapter4, MayaWorkingFiles folder on the CD-ROM.
3. Press F2 to change Maya to Animation mode.
4. Select both arm controls, both pole vector controls, both leg controls, all clusters' handle controls, the local control, and the global control.
5. Select Character > Create Character Set Option Box.

6. In the Name field, type sackCharacter and click on Create Character Set. You should see the character set on the right of the red arrow in the Command Line, as shown in Figure 4.86.

FIGURE 4.86   Character set seen in the Command Line.

Creating the Sack's First Pose

To create the sack's first pose:

1. Make sure you are in frame 1 and the sackCharacter is visible in the Command Line.
2. Press S to set a key for sackCharacter in bind pose.
3. Advance to frame 15.
4. Pose the sack as shown in the first drawing of the jump shot image by dragging LtLegcontrol up a bit, moving clusterY_handle to the right of the sack, and rotating clusterX_handle.
5. The sack's first pose should be approximately as shown in Figure 4.87.

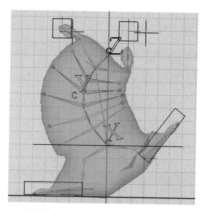

FIGURE 4.87   The sack's first pose.

6. Press S to set a key. Note that the controls do not have to be selected to set a key. After they are members of the character set, they will be keyed without being selected.

7. Move back to frame 1 to have the sack in bind pose.

Creating the Sack's Second Pose

To create the sack's second pose:

1. Advance to frame 30.
2. Select global_control and move it 12 units in X and 5 in Y. You also can move global_control by typing 12 in the Translate X channel and 5 in the Translate Y channel in the Channel Box.
3. Push, pull, and rotate the handles and controls to pose the sack approximately as shown in Figure 4.88.

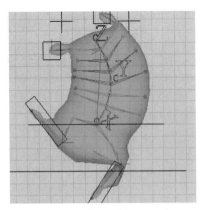

FIGURE 4.88   The sack's second pose.

4. Press S to set a key.
5. Move back to frame 1 to have the sack in bind pose.

Creating the Sack's Third Pose

To create the third pose:

1. Advance to frame 45.
2. Translate global_control 20 units in X and 0 in Y.
3. Select local_control and drag it down approximately –0.8 units in Y. This will squash the sack's body to absorb the impact of landing.
4. Push, pull, and rotate the handles and controls to pose the sack in the landing position. The pose should be approximately like the one shown in Figure 4.89.
5. Set a key.

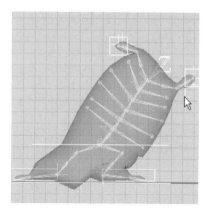

FIGURE 4.89   The sack's third pose.

Creating the Follow-Through Pose

To create the follow-through pose:

1. Advance to frame 55.
2. Without moving the sack, drag local_control to the left and position it approximately –1.3 units in Translate X and 0 in Translate Y. Drag clusterY_handle to the left about –1.7 units in Translate X and 0 in Translate Y. You should have a pose as shown in Figure 4.90.

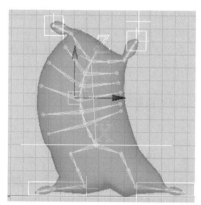

FIGURE 4.0   The sack's follow-through pose.

3. Advance to frame 65.
4. Pose the sack in the bind pose and set another key. You can do this by typing 0 in the Translate and Rotate boxes of the controls in the Channel Box.
5. Play back the animation.

SUMMARY

Congratulations! You have completed your first character animation using anticipation and follow through.

In this chapter, you have learned how to rig, bind, and animate a simple character. You also have learned how to use IK systems and constraints to facilitate the animation process. Now you understand the difference between forward kinematics and inverse kinematics and how to blend them to create realistic motion. With this set of skills, you can create more complex riggings and keyframe animations.

In the next chapter, you will learn how to model a character with NURBS and animate it using path animation.

CHALLENGE ASSIGNMENTS

1. Draw the Sack Walking or Running

Draw a storyboard of a scene that illustrates the sack starting to walk or run across the computer screen. The shot should include anticipation and follow through. Create a 5- to 10-second pose-to-pose animation of the shot.

2. Draw the Sack Lifting and Throwing

Sketch a storyboard for a scene in which the sack must lift and throw a heavy object. Use the principles discussed in the "Newton's Laws" section in Chapter 2 to help convey the weight to the viewer. Use cinematography to emphasize the physical struggle of the character against the weight. Include physical anticipation as the sack prepares to lift the weight. Create a 5- to 15-second pose-to-pose animation of the scene.

5

NURBS MODELING AND PATH ANIMATION WITH DYNAMICS

In This Chapter

- NURBS Curves
- NURBS Modeling Tools
- Motion Path Animation
- Hair Curves as Deformers

*N*URBS stands for *non-uniform rational B spline*. Fortunately, you don't need to understand the name to take advantage of this highly useful modeling method. NURBS modeling allows you to specify smooth curves using a small number of controls. These curves can be used to build up complex organic surfaces. NURBS is commonly used for modeling cars, animals, and human bodies. Because NURBS retains detail when scaled up, it is often used in motion picture production. In this chapter, you will use Maya's NURBS tools to model a fish.

You will then learn two new animation techniques to animate the fish: path animation and dynamics. In *path animation*, you first draw a curve representing a desired movement over time and then attach an object or character to the path. The process works much like direct keyframing, except that all in-between positions are constrained to the path.

Dynamics is Maya's built-in module that simulates real-world physics. Dynamic simulations are very useful for secondary motion (motion that is a consequence of the direct intentional movements of a character). In this case, you will use dynamics to simulate the motion of the fish's fins and tail through the water. A second important use of dynamics is to connect a character to the surrounding environment. Here, you will use dynamics to simulate water movement, including the wake and splashing "caused" by the fish.

NURBS CURVES

NURBS curves form the basis upon which NURBS surfaces are built.

NURBS Terminology

NURBS modeling introduces a number of technical terms that may not be familiar to you. Most of these elements have a distinct visual representation in Maya's interface. A single continuous NURBS curve is usually composed of multiple segments, known as *spans*.

NURBS curves contain two kinds of points: edit points and control vertices.

- **Edit points (EPs).** EPs are markers on the NURBS curve itself that indicate the extent of a span. In Maya, an edit point is represented by an x on the curve.
- **Control vertices (CVs).** CVs are points that control the position of the curve between the EPs. CVs are not necessarily on the curve itself.

NURBS Display Preferences

Depending on your preferences, Maya can automatically display some or all of the components discussed here as you draw your NURBS curves. One additional component that you may find useful is the hull. *Hulls* are straight lines that connect CV points. They can't be individually manipulated, but they do make it easier to differentiate between CVs and EPs.

To ensure that you have all components displayed, bring up Maya's main preferences window by following these steps.

1. Select Window > Setting/Preferences > Preferences.
2. Under the Categories section on the left, select Display > NURBS.
3. In the NURBS, Display Settings for New NURBS Objects section, find the New Curves entry.
4. Select the checkboxes for Edit Points, Hulls, and CVs (see Figure 5.1).

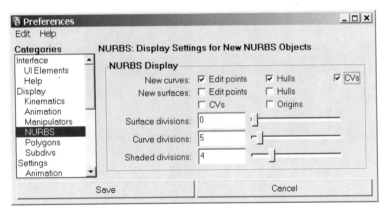

FIGURE 5.1   The Preferences window.

NURBS Curve Tools

Maya provides two separate tools for creating NURBS curves: the Edit Point (EP) Curve tool and the Control Vertex (CV) Curve tool. Both tools create NURBS curves with equivalent properties containing both EPs and CVs. However, with the EP Curve tool, you place edit points, and Maya automatically creates CVs. With the CV Curve tool, you directly place the CVs, and Maya automatically creates EPs. The difference between the two usually comes down to personal preference. The EP Curve tool is more straightforward to use, but the CV Curve tool gives slightly more interactive control over the curve shape.

Try experimenting with both tools.

1. Make sure Edit Points, Hulls, and CVs are checked in the Preferences window.
2. Select Create > EP Curve Tool.
3. Hold down the X key to snap to your grid.
4. Click alternating grid corners one grid cell apart, as shown in Figure 5.2. When done, press Enter to complete the curve. The result should be a continuous curve that goes through each location clicked.

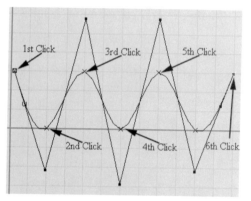

FIGURE 5.2   EP Curve tool clicking positions.

5. Repeat the same pattern of click locations but use the CV Curve tool (also under the Create menu). In this case, you will also get a continuous curve, but with a distinctly different shape. Note that the overall curve is much flatter, undulating up and down toward the clicked CV locations but never reaching them (see Figure 5.3).

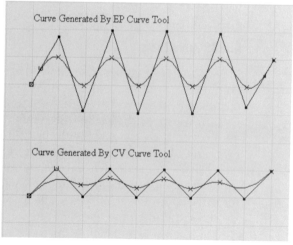

FIGURE 5.3   EP and CV NURBS Curve tools.

A Matter of Degree

As you may have noted in the NURBS curve creation tool options, NURBS curves have an important property known as the "degree" of the curve. First-degree curves are linear and thus run flat between EPs. Maya defaults to creating third-degree curves, which is usually what you'll want. You can also create curves of higher degree. This has the advantage of allowing twistier interpolation between EPs but the significant disadvantage that it becomes harder to get local control of the curve.

Summary of NURBS Components

In summary, here are the basic components of NURBS curves.

- **Spans.** Segments of a NURBS curve bounded by EPs
- **Edit points (EPs).** Points on a NURBS curve
- **Control vertices (CVs).** Points not on the NURBS curve itself but that control the curvature between edit points
- **Hulls.** Display lines that connect the CVs (see Figure 5.4)

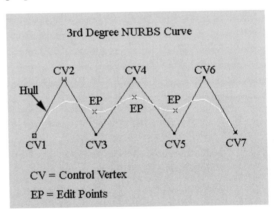

FIGURE 5.4   Summary of NURBS components.

Curve Directions

NURBS curves have a distinct beginning and end. The first CV is represented by a square box, and the second one is represented by the letter U, indicating the curve direction, as shown in Figure 5.5. Curve directions become very important when using curves to generate surface geometry, as will be described momentarily.

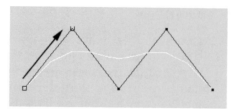

FIGURE 5.5   Letter U indicating the curve direction.

Attaching, Snapping, and Detaching Curves

To conveniently create the profile of a complex object, it is sometimes necessary to use multiple NURBS curves. Fortunately, NURBS curves can be attached and detached as necessary.

1. Press Ctrl+N to create a new scene.
2. Press F4 to go to the Surfaces menus.
3. Select Create > CV Curve Tool.
4. In Front view, click eight times anywhere on the screen to create a curve as shown in Figure 5.6.

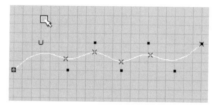

FIGURE 5.6   CV curve created with the CV Curve tool.

5. Right-click the curve and select Edit Points.
6. Click the third EP to select it, as shown in Figure 5.7.

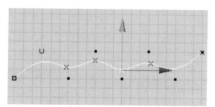

FIGURE 5.7   Curve's third EP.

7. Select Edit Curves > Detach Curves Option Box.
8. In the option box, make sure Keep Original is not checked.
9. Click the Detach button. Notice that you have two curves now, as shown in Figure 5.8.

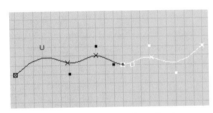

FIGURE 5.8   Curve detached.

Attach Curves

To attach curves, follow these steps.

1. Hold down the Shift key and click both curves to select them.
2. Select Edit Curves > Attach Curves Option Box.
3. In the Attach Curves Option window make sure Attach Method Blend is checked and Keep Originals is unchecked, as shown in Figure 5.9.

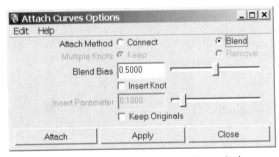

FIGURE 5.9   The Attach Curves Options window.

4. Click the Attach button. You should have only one curve now.

Cut Curve

NURBS curves can also be cut at the intersection of two curves.

1. Select File > New Scene.
2. Select Create > CV Curve Tool. In Front view, click approximately in the middle of the screen eight times and press Enter to create a horizontal curve.
3. Press G to go to the last tool, which in this case is the Create CV Curve tool.
4. Click four times from top to bottom and press Enter. You should have curve1 horizontally and curve2 vertically, as shown in Figure 5.10.

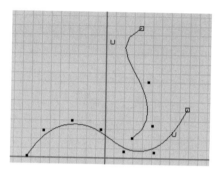

FIGURE 5.10   Two CV curves.

5. Press W to change to the Move tool.
6. Right-click curve2 and select Control Vertex.
7. Click the last CV of curve2.
8. Hold down the C key. Notice that the Move tool's yellow square changes to a circle. That indicates that you are in the Snap on Curve mode.
9. Holding down the C key, middle-click-drag approximately in the middle of curve1. The selected CV should snap to curve2, as shown in Figure 5.11.

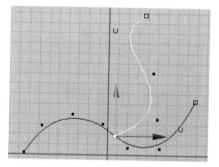

FIGURE 5.11   Curve snapped.

10. Deselect both curves.
11. Click curve1 and Shift-click curve2.
12. Select Edit Curves > Cut Curve. Notice that curve1 was cut at the intersection with curve2 (see Figure 5.12).
13. Select and delete the left part of curve1.

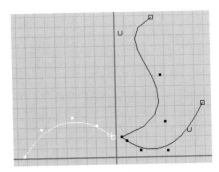

FIGURE 5.12   CV curve cut.

Rebuild Curves

NURBS curves can also be rebuilt. The Rebuild Curve function is useful to match the topology of another curve, increase or decrease spans, or simply to make the spans uniform.

1. Select File > New Scene.
2. Select Create > CV Curve Tool.
3. In Front view, click eight times approximately in the middle of the screen and press Enter.
4. With the curve still selected, right-click the curve and select curve1. The Attribute Editor should open.
5. In the Attribute Editor, open the NURBS Curve History tab. Look at the Spans field, and notice that the curve has five spans.
6. With the curve still selected, select Edit Curves > Rebuild Curve Option Box.
7. In the options window, select Edit > Reset Setting.
8. In the Number of Spans field, type 10. This means the curve will be rebuilt with 10 spans, as shown in Figure 5.13.

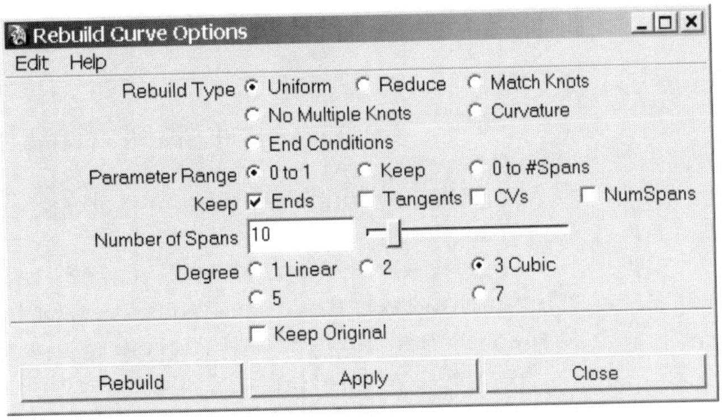

FIGURE 5.13   The Rebuild Curve Options window.

9. Click the Rebuild button. Look again in the curve Attribute Editor and notice that the spans are set to 10.
10. Right-click the curve and select Edit Points. Notice that the spans are uniformly sized.

NURBS curves do not normally render in Maya. Usually, they are used as construction curves in creating renderable NURBS geometry, commonly known as patches.

NURBS Patch

A NURBS *patch* is a piece of geometry created with two or more curves. A NURBS patch has all of the elements of the component curves used to create it. It also has a new component known as an isoparm. An *isoparm* is a line connecting two or more editing points. Isoparms allow you to visualize a NURBS surface, even when rendered interactively in a wireframe model. The number of isoparms on a surface can be adjusted to show more or less surface detail.

When you create a NURBS patch, Maya automatically establishes a 2D coordinate system on that surface. The coordinate system has two directions, called U and V (see Figure 5.14). These U and V coordinates are used to texture map surfaces.

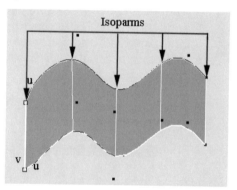

FIGURE 5.14   NURBS patch showing U and V directions.

The UV directions are used to manage surface continuity and for texture placement.

Like NURBS curves, NURBS patches can be detached, attached, and rebuilt. However, there are two important factors to consider. The first is that a NURBS patch can only have one continuous set of isoparms. If you try to attach two surfaces with an unequal numbers of isoparms, Maya will complete the operation but will add isoparms to the portion of the surface that had fewer of them. The second factor to consider is that Maya performs all NURBS patch operations based on the UV directions of the input surfaces and not based on proximity. Thus, if you try to attach two NURBS surfaces oriented with opposing UVs, Maya will attach them by "reaching around the back" of one surface—usually not the expected result. As shown in the following sets of steps, both types of problems can be avoided by paying attention to UV directions and isoparms while you model and by rebuilding surfaces when needed.

To detach a NURBS surface follow these steps.

1. Create a new scene.
2. Select Create > NURBS Primitives > Plane Option Box.
3. In the options window, type 10 in the U and V Patches fields, as shown in Figure 5.15.

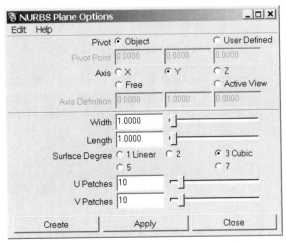

FIGURE 5.15   The NURBS Plane Options window.

4. Click the Create button.
5. In the Top view, right-click the plane and select Isoparm.
6. Click the fourth horizontal isoparm from bottom to top as shown in Figure 5.16. The isoparm color changes to red indicating that it is selected.

FIGURE 5.16   Isoparm selected.

7. Select Edit NURBS > Detach Surfaces Option Box.
8. In the options window, make sure that Keep Original is not checked.
9. Click the Detach button.
10. Click any isoparm, and notice that you have two surfaces.

When Maya detaches a surface, a new detached surface is created. If the Keep Original option is unchecked, Maya automatically deletes the original surface, leaving only the detached one. If the Keep Original option is checked, Maya creates the new detached surface on top of the original and leaves both available.

Attach NURBS Surfaces

When attaching two NURBS surfaces, their topology is a consideration.

Both surfaces must have the same topology to result in a new uniform surface, as shown in Figure 5.17. Surfaces are topologically equivalent if they have the same NURBS structure in terms of the number of isoparms, spans, CVs, and degree. This can be true even if they do not have the same shape or size,

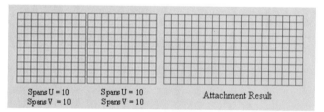

FIGURE 5.17   The attachment of two surfaces with the same topology.

If you attach two surfaces with different topologies, Maya tries to match the isoparms of both surfaces, and the attachment can have an undesirable result (see Figure 5.18).

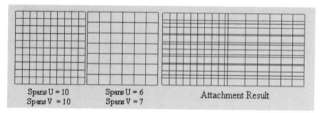

FIGURE 5.18   The attachment surfaces with different parameterizations.

Rebuild Surface

The rebuild surfaces function is useful for changing a surface topology or just to make it uniform.

1. Create a new scene.
2. Select Create > NURBS Primitives > Plane Option Box.
3. In the options window, type 5 in the U Patch field and type 5 in the V Patch field.
4. Click the Create button.
5. With the plane still selected, select Edit NURBS > Rebuild Surfaces Option Box.
6. In the Rebuild Surfaces Options window, select Edit > Reset Settings.
7. In the Number of Spans U field, type 10; in the Number of Spans V field, type 10 and make sure that Keep Original is not checked as shown in Figure 5.19.

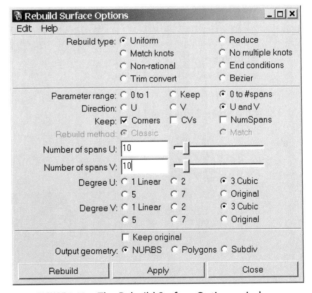

FIGURE 5.19   The Rebuild Surface Options window.

8. Click the Rebuild button. The surface should have 10 spans in U and V directions as shown in Figure 5.20.

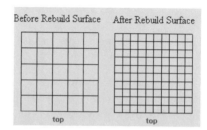

FIGURE 5.20   Surface before and after being rebuilt.

NURBS Modeling Tools

Maya offers several NURBS modeling tools. Among the most commonly used are the Birail and the Boundary tools.

Understanding the Birail Tool

The Birail tool allows you to create a surface based on three or more curves. This tool sweeps one or more profile curves along two birail curves (path curves).

This tool has three options:

- **Biral 1 tool.** This requires two birail curves and one profile curve (see Figure 5.21).

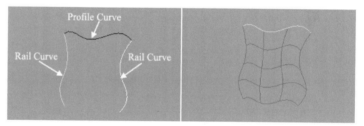

FIGURE 5.21   Birail 1 rail and profile curves

- **Birail 2 tool.** This requires two birail curves and two profile curves (see Figure 5.22).

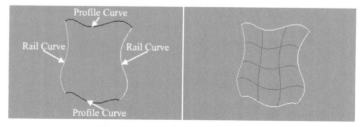

FIGURE 5.22   Birail 2 rail and profile curves

- **Birail 3+ tool.** This requires three birail curves and two profile curves (see Figure 5.23).

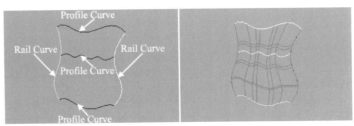

FIGURE 5.23   Birail 3+ rail and profile curves

To create a birail geometry, you need to create three or more curves that must intersect.

1. Open a new scene.
2. Select Create > CV Curve Tool.
3. In the Front view, create three curves as shown in Figure 5.24.

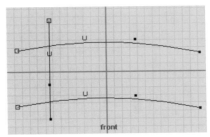

FIGURE 5.24   Three curves to create a birail surface.

4. Look at the curves in the perspective, and make sure that the vertical curve intersects with the two horizontal ones.
5. Select Surfaces > Birail > Birail 1 Tool as shown in Figure 5.25. The mouse cursor should change to an arrow.

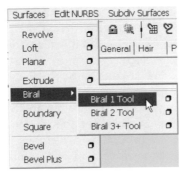

FIGURE 5.25   Birail menu.

6. Click first on the vertical curve to select it as the profile curve. Second, click the bottom horizontal curve, and third click the top horizontal curve. The horizontal curves are the rail curves (see Figure 5.26).

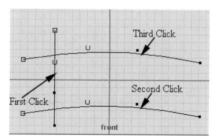

FIGURE 5.26   Birail tool click sequence.

7. Press F5 to change to the Smooth Shade All mode, and you should see the Birail geometry as shown in Figure 5.27.

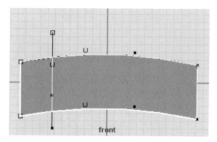

FIGURE 5.27   Birail surface.

If you don't see the birail geometry, it is because the profile curve is not intersecting with the rail curves. An easy way to make sure that the curves are intersecting is to snap the parameterization CV of the vertical curve to the horizontal ones.

Understanding the Boundary Tool

The Boundary tool creates a surface within boundary curves. This tool has two options that decide how the surface is created: Automatically and As Selected.

When you choose the Automatically option, Maya decides how to create the boundary surface. When you choose As Selected, the order in which you pick the curves alters the boundary surface. You also have to choose a common end point option. If you choose Optional, the boundary surface is created even if the curves' end points don't match. If you choose Required, the curves common end points must match. The best way to match the curves and end points is using the curve snap feature previously discussed.

1. Open a new scene.
2. In the Front view, create four CV curves as shown in Figure 5.28. Notice that the two vertical curves were created from top to bottom, and the two horizontal curves were created from left to right.

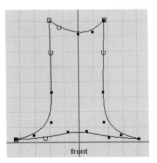

FIGURE 5.28   Four curves to create a boundary surface.

3. Name the curves as follows (see Figure 5.29):

- Left vertical curve: curve_left
- Right vertical curve: curve_right
- Bottom horizontal curve: curve_bottom
- Top horizontal curve: curve_top

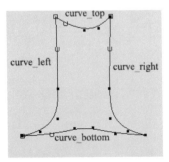

FIGURE 5.29   Named curves for the Boundary tool.

4. Select Surfaces > Boundary Option Box.
5. In the Boundary Options window, click Curve Ordering Automatically, as shown in Figure 5.30.

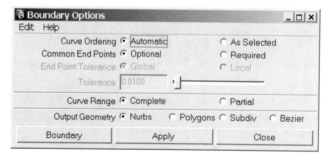

FIGURE 5.30 The Boundary Options window.

6. Select the four curves by clicking on them one by one in any order. The order in which you select the curves does not matter.
7. Click the Apply button. The Boundary Options window should stay on, and a new boundary surface should be created as shown in Figure 5.31.

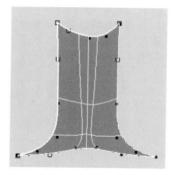

FIGURE 5.31 Automatic boundary surface generation options.

8. Delete the new boundary surface. You should see just the four boundary curves.
9. Select Surfaces > Boundary Option Box.
10. In the Boundary Options window, click As Selected.
11. Click first on curve_left, second on curve_bottom, third on curve_right, and fourth on curve_top.
12. Click the Apply bottom.
13. You should see a boundary geometry just like the one created previously with the Automatically option.
14. Delete the boundary surface you just created.
15. Select Surface > Boundary Option Box.
16. Now, click first on curve_left, second on curve_right, third on curve_bottom, and fourth on curve_top. Click the Apply button. You should see a different boundary surface as shown in Figure 5.32.The geometry was created between different curves; this resulted in a different shape.

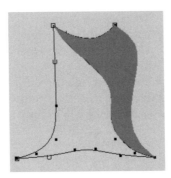

FIGURE 5.32   As Selected boundary surface.

MOTION PATH ANIMATION

Motion path animation refers to an object or character that is animated on a curve path. This is useful for animating creatures such as fish or snakes. It is also commonly used for rapidly generating *blocking animation*—the preliminary positioning of characters in a scene, and subsequent camera adjustments. Path animation can also be used to control camera motion itself, a method that directly mimics the physical camera tracks used in live-action film production.

By default, a motion path object moves continuously and evenly along the given path. However, you can adjust this as needed using keyframes to specify location along the path at a particular time.

1. Create a new scene.
2. Press F4 to change Maya to Surfaces mode.
3. Select Create > CV Curve Tool.
4. In the Top view, click several times from right to left to create a loop curve as shown in Figure 5.33.

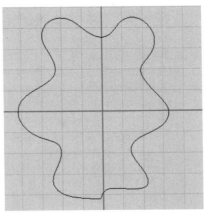

FIGURE 5.33   CV curve for motion path.

5. Select the curve's last CV. Holding down the V key, move and snap the CV to the curve's first CV.
6. Select Edit Curve > Open/Close Curve to make a continuous curve. A closed curve is a loop with the first and last edit points coinciding. In this case, you want a closed curve so that your motion path is continuous.
7. Select Edit Curve > Rebuild Curve Option Box.
8. In the options window, make sure that Rebuild Type Uniform is selected, Keep CVs is checked, and Keep Original is unchecked (see Figure 5.34).

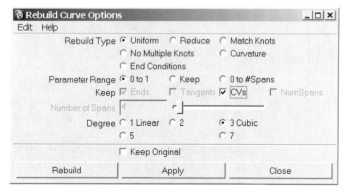

FIGURE 5.34   The Rebuild Curve Options window.

9. Click the Rebuild button. This distributes the CVs to uniformly create a smooth curve. Objects animated on smooth curves have smooth motion.
10. Select Create > NURBS Primitives > Sphere.
11. Press F2 to change Maya to Animation mode.
12. With the sphere still selected, Shift-click the curve to select it.
13. Select Animate > Motion Paths > Attach to Motion Path Option Box.
14. In the options window, check Time Range Start/End. Type 1 in the Start Time field, and type 500 in the End Time field. Check the Follow, Front Axis Z, and Up Axis Y options. In the World Up Type drop-down list, choose Scene Up (see Figure 5.35). Scene Up means that the Up vector of the object on the path tries to align with the scene up axis specified in the preferences. Maya defaults the scene up to positive Y.
15. Click the Attach button.
16. Make sure that the end time of the animation playback range is set to 500.
17. Play the animation. You should see the sphere moving along the curve.

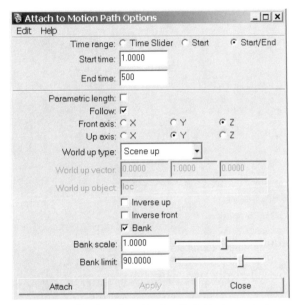

FIGURE 5.35   The Attach to Motion Path Options window.

Setting Motion Path Markers

Motion path markers allow you to control the speed of your object. The object speed decelerates between close markers, and accelerates between widely spaced markers.

To set a motion path marker, follow these steps:

1. Drag the Time slider to frame 200.
2. Select the motion path curve.
3. In the Channel Box under OUTPUTS, look for MotionPath1.
4. Click MotionPath1. You should see U value.
5. Click the U value to select it.
6. Right-click the U value and select Key Selected. A yellow marker with the number 200 should appear in the curve path.
7. Select the frame 200 marker, and in the Top view, move it close to the horizontal grid axis as shown in Figure 5.36.
8. Drag the time line to 300.
9. Repeat steps 3 to 6 to set another key on the U value.

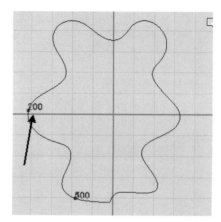

FIGURE 5.36   Marker 200 moved close to the horizontal grid axis.

Changing the Marker Time

To change the marker time, follow these steps:
1. Drag the time line to frame 400.
2. Set a key for the U value.
3. Select the marker 400 and open its Attribute Editor.
4. Under Position Marker Attributes, type 350 in the Time field as shown in Figure 5.37. The marker number should change to 350.

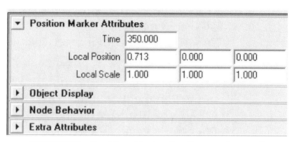

FIGURE 5.37   Position Marker Attributes changed.

5. Play the animation. Notice that the sphere moves according to the time set on the markers.

HAIR CURVES AS DEFORMERS

As the name implies, hair curves in Maya were originally designed to facilitate the creation and animation of hair. However, hair curves can also be used as deformers for a variety of flabby or floppy surfaces. Just like real hair, hair curves are attached at one end to an object called the *follicle* and have a degree of flex and bounce. Unlike real hair, hair curves in Maya can be attached to large objects and used to move them around.

To create a hair curve, you first create a normal NURBS curve and then convert it to a dynamic curve.

1. Create a new scene.
2. Select Create > NURBS Primitives Sphere.
3. In the Side view, hold down the X key and click once to start the curve on the very top of the sphere. Then release the X key and click 10 times to create a curve as shown in Figure 5.38.

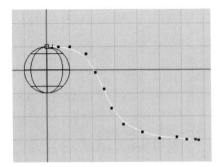

FIGURE 5.38   A curve created from the very top of the sphere.

4. Press Enter to finish the curve. By default, it is called curve1.
5. Press F5 to change Maya to Dynamics mode.
6. Select curve1.
7. Select Hair > Make Selected Curves Dynamic. Notice that Maya created another curve called curve2.
8. Open the Hypergraph, and you should see the hair nodes as in Figure 5.39.

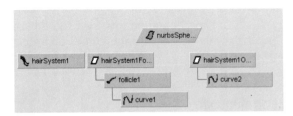

FIGURE 5.39   Hypergraph window showing the hair nodes.

9. Select follicle1, and open its Attribute Editor.
10. Under the Follicle Attributes tab, change the Point Lock to Base.
11. Parent HairSystem1Follicles under the nurbsSphere1.
12. Parent hairSystem1 under the curve2 (see Figure 5.40).

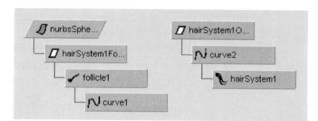

FIGURE 5.40   The hairSystem1 node parented under the curve2 node.

13. Press F2 to change to Animation mode.
14. Make sure that the Time slider is in frame 1.
15. Select nurbsSphere1, and press S to set a keyframe.
16. Drag the Time slider to frame 30.
17. In the Channel Box, type 8 in the Translate Y channel.
18. Press S to set another keyframe.
19. Drag the Time slider to frame 60.
20. In the Channel Box, type 0 in the Translate Y channel.
21. Press S to set another keyframe.
22. Press F5 to go to the Dynamics menu. With nurbsSphere1 still selected, select Hair > Display > Current Position (see Figure 5.41).

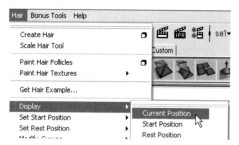

FIGURE 5.41   The Hair > Display Current > Position menu command.

23. Play the animation. You should see the dynamic curve moving flexibly when the sphere goes up and down.

TUTORIAL 5.1: FISH MODELING

Fish are great subjects for NURBS modeling. They are very curvy and come in an amazing variety of shapes. You will start by modeling a Japanese koi.

Creating the Fish Body

To create the fish body:

1. Open the CD > chapter5 > ImagePlanes folder on the CD-ROM.
2. Copy koi_side.jpg and koi_bottom.jpg onto your hard drive.
3. Select File > Project > New.
4. Name it koi.
5. Click the Use Defaults button, and then click Accept.
6. Select File > New Scene.
7. Choose Surfaces by pressing F4 or from the drop-down box.
8. Click the Four View button in the bottom-left area of the screen, as shown in Figure 5.42.

FIGURE 5.42   The Four View button.

9. In the Side view, select View > Image Plane > Import Image.
10. Import koi_side.jpeg.
11. In the Channel Box, you should see ImagePlane1. In the Image-Plane1, Center Y channel, type 6.5. This will bring the image plane up to the horizontal central axis of the Side view.
12. In the Top view, select View > Image Plane > Import Image.
13. Import koi_bottom. Although this is a little confusing because you are importing the bottom of the fish in the Top view, you need to see the bottom of the fish to create the fins.
14. In the Channel Box, in the Center Y channel, type 1 to move up the image plane a bit.
15. You should see the top and side image planes as shown in Figure 5.43.

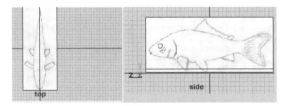

FIGURE 5.43   Top and side image planes.

16. In Side view, select Create > NURBS Primitives > Circle. Maya calls it circle1.

17. In the Channel Box, in the Rotate X channel, type 90.
18. Move circle1 to the mouth of the fish, as shown in Figure 5.44.

FIGURE 5.44   Circle1 at fish's mouth.

19. Select Edit > Duplicate Special Option Box. In the options window, select Edit > Reset Settings. In the Translate Z field, type –2; in the Number of Copies field, type 12, as shown in Figure 5.45.

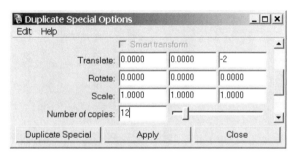

FIGURE 5.45   The Duplicate Special Options window.

20. Click the Duplicate Special button.
21. In the Side view, move and scale the circles on the Z axis across the koi body as in Figure 5.46.

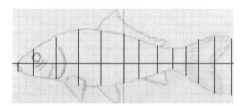

FIGURE 5.46   Circles arranged and scaled in the Side view.

22. In the Top view, scale the circles along the X axis as in Figure 5.47.
23. In the Side view, select all circles by clicking on them one by one, starting on circle1 through circle13.
24. Select Surfaces > Loft > Option Box.
25. In the options box window, select Edit > Reset Settings. Notice that Maya defaults the Output Geometry to NURBS, as shown in Figure 5.48.

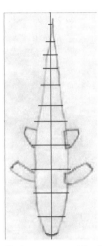

FIGURE 5.47   Circles arranged in the Top view.

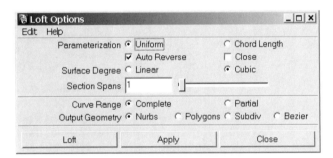

FIGURE 5.48   The Loft Options window.

26. Click the Loft button.
27. Name the new loft surface body.
28. In Side view, select circle1, right-click it, and select Control Vertex. Make sure that you see the CVs of circle1 only and not the loft surface.
29. Select circle1's middle CVs and pull them backward on the Z axis to create the mouth shape as shown in Figure 5.49. Notice that the loft surface updates automatically when you pull circle1's CVs because circle1 has construction history.

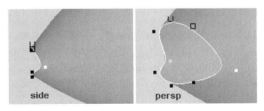

FIGURE 5.49   Circle1's CVs pulled back on the Z axis to create the mouth shape.

30. Select circle13, right-click it, and select Control Vertex.
31. Select the middle CVs, and pull them on Z axis (toward the head) to create the tail shape as shown in Figure 5.50.

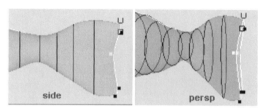

FIGURE 5.50   Circle13's CVs pulled forward on the Z axis to create the tail shape.

32. Select circle13. In the Channel Box, in the Scale X channel, type 0. This closes the tail gap as shown in Figure 5.51.

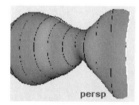

FIGURE 5.51   Circle13's Scale X set to 0, closing the tail gap.

33. Select the body, and then select Edit > Delete by Type > History. Deleting the body history breaks the connection between the circles and the body geometry. Deleting geometry history usually is done when the model is completely finished and will be used in another important phase of the production such as texturing, rigging, or animating.
34. Delete all profile circles.

Moving the Loft Seam

The fish's body geometry has a seam on the fish's back. This can create a visually obvious discontinuity in surface textures. Moving the seam to the belly of the fish will make it less visible from typical camera angles.

To move the loft seam:

1. Notice that the seam of the loft is on top of the fish. The seam is represented by a thicker line than the isoparms.
2. Using the Side and Perspective views, right-click the fish's body and select Isoparm. Click the thicker isoparm first, and then click the isoparm in the bottom of the body (without the Shift key) as shown in Figure 5.52. Only one isoparm should be selected for the Move Seam command.

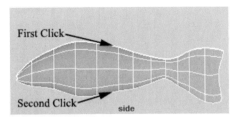

FIGURE 5.52   Selection order of isoparms on the body.

3. Select Edit NURBS > Move Seam. The seam should move to the bottom of the body.
4. Right-click the body, and then select Object Mode. Reselect the body.
5. Select Edit NURBS > Rebuild Surfaces > Option Box.
6. In the options window, select Edit > Reset Settings. Type 10 in the Number of Spans U field, and type 17 in the Number of Spans V field as shown in Figure 5.53.

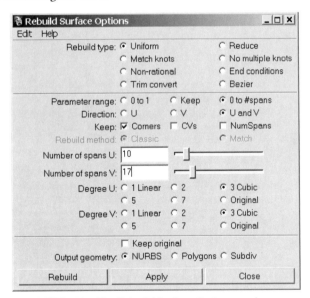

FIGURE 5.53   The Rebuild Surface Options wndow.

7. Click the Rebuild button. This increases the geometry's detail and creates a smooth surface.

Working with Symmetrical Shapes

The fish shape is symmetrical. That means both sides are mirror images of each other. For modeling efficiency, you can work on one half of the fish's body and, when finished, use Maya's mirroring functionality to generate the other half.

Since you are starting with a full fish body, you first need to split it in two. This can be done using the Detach command and then deleting the unneeded half.

Detaching a Surface

As mentioned, the first step is to detach the surface. Here's how:

1. Right-click the fish's body and select Isoparm.
2. Click the isoparm running down the fish's back, as shown in Figure 5.54.

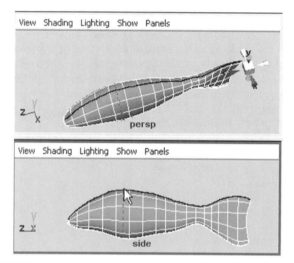

FIGURE 5.54   Selecting the isoparm in the middle of the fish's back.

3. Click the isoparm running the length of the fish's belly as shown in Figure 5.55. Note that you may need to zoom in substantially in the Perspective view to click the correct isoparms.
4. Select Edit NURBS > Detach Surfaces > Option Box.
5. In the options window, make sure that Keep Original is not checked as shown in Figure 5.56.

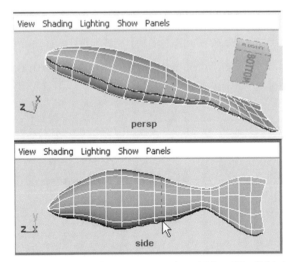

FIGURE 5.55   Selecting the isoparm in the middle of the fish's belly.

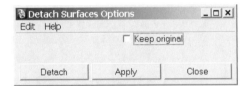

FIGURE 5.56   The Detach Surfaces Options window with Keep Original unchecked.

6. Click the Detach button. The fish's body should be detached in two half parts.
7. In the Front view, select the left side of the body, and delete it. You should have the body's right side only as shown in Figure 5.57.

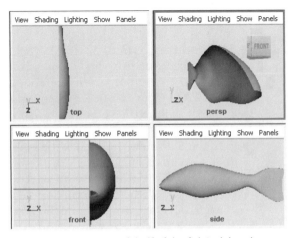

FIGURE 5.57   Left half of the fish is deleted.

Shaping the Fish's Head

Next, shape the fish's head. Do the following:

1. In the Side view, click the fourth isoparm from the mouth and drag it a bit to the right as shown in Figure 5.58.

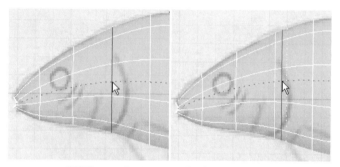

FIGURE 5.58   Positioning the fourth isoparm.

2. Release the isoparm, and you should see a dotted line.
3. Select Edit NURBS > Insert Isoparms Option Box.
4. In the options window, select Edit > Reset Settings. Note that Insert Location is At Selection by default as shown in Figure 5.59.

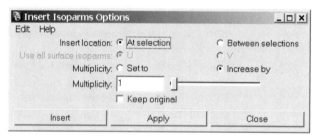

FIGURE 5.59   The Insert Isoparms Options window.

5. Click the Insert button.
6. Right-click the fish's body, and select Isoparm again.
7. Click the newly inserted isoparm, and drag it a bit to the right as shown in Figure 5.60. This is to form the gills.
8. Select Edit NURBS > Insert Isoparms. You should have three isoparms very close to each other as shown in Figure 5.61.
9. In the Side view, right-click the body, and select Control Vertex.
10. Press W to change to the Move tool.
11. In the Top view, click-drag a selection box around the third, fourth, fifth, and sixth CVs from top to bottom of the first duplicated isoparm, as shown in Figure 5.62.

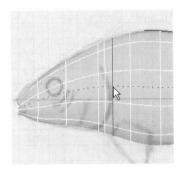

FIGURE 5.60   New isoparms now on the fish's body.

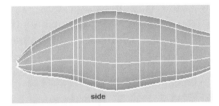

FIGURE 5.61   New isoparms now on the fish's body.

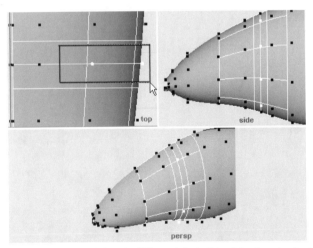

FIGURE 5.62   Selecting the third, fourth, fifth, and sixth CVs of the first duplicated isoparm.

12. The isoparm should have two CVs on the upper side and two CVs on the lower side unselected. To see the unselected CVs, rotate the camera in the Perspective view. In the Top view, move the CVs a bit on the X and Z axis as shown in Figure 5.63.

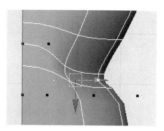

FIGURE 5.63 Repositioned CVs.

13. Adjust individual CVs to get the desired effect. The two CVs at the beginning and end of the isoparm shown in Figure 5.64 should not be moved along the X axis. Moving these CVs will cause geometry gap or overlap when the geometry is mirrored. At this point, you should have a fish head shape similar to the one shown in Figure 5.65.

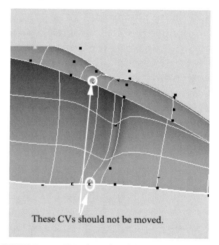

These CVs should not be moved.

FIGURE 5.64 CVs that should not be moved.

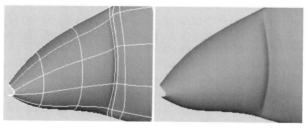

FIGURE 5.65 Fish head taking shape.

Mirroring the Body

To mirror the body, do the following:

1. In the Front view, snap all the CVs from the back and belly edges on the vertical grid axis as shown in Figure 5.66. Make sure that all CVs are correctly snapped to the grid. If any of the CVs are not snapped correctly, you may have undesirable results such as geometry gaps and overlap. You may have to snap the CVs individually to ensure accuracy.

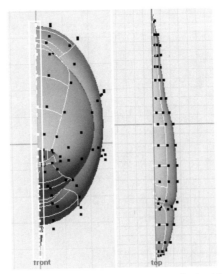

FIGURE 5.66   Snap CVs to the center vertical grid axis.

2. Select the fish's body.
3. Select Edit > Duplicate Special Option Box.
4. In the options window, select Edit > Reset Settings. Type –1 in the Scale X box as shown in Figure 5.67. This will mirror the selected geometry.

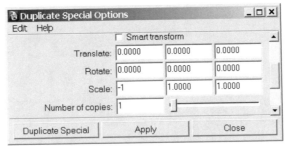

FIGURE 5.67   Setting Scale X to -1 in the Duplicate Special Options window.

5. Click the Duplicate Special button.
6. In the Perspective view, check if the mirrored geometry is aligned correctly with the original. If you see a gap or overlap, delete the mirrored geometry, and adjust the edge CVs of the original in the Front and Top views as discussed in step 1.
7. Click the original geometry, hold down the Shift key, and click the mirrored geometry. Both geometries must be selected.
8. Select Edit NURBS > Attach Surfaces Option Box.
9. In the options window, make sure that Attach Method Blend is checked and Keep Originals is unchecked, as shown in Figure 5.68.

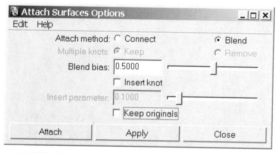

FIGURE 5.68   The Attach Surfaces Options window.

10. Click the Attach button.
11. Click the body. It should be one piece without gaps or overlapped geometry.
12. Select the body.
13. Select Edit NURBS > Rebuild Surfaces > Option Box.
14. In the options window, select Edit > Reset Settings. Select the Keep option button and the CVs checkbox as shown in Figure 5.69. This will rebuild the surface and will keep the same number of CVs in U and V directions. Click Rebuild.

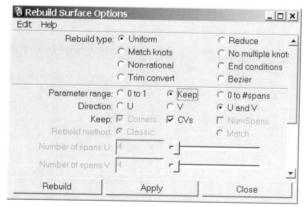

FIGURE 5.69   The Rebuild Surface Options window.

15. With the surface still selected, select Edit > Delete by Type > History. You should have geometry similar to the one shown in Figure 5.70.

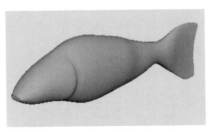

FIGURE 5.70   The fish body so far.

Creating the Top Fin

To create the top fin, do the following:

1. In the Perspective view, right-click the body and select Isoparm.
2. Click the isoparm along the back of the body as shown in Figure 5.71.

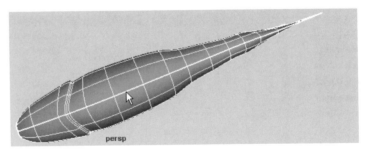

FIGURE 5.71   Selecting the isoparm on the back of the fish's body.

3. Select Edit Curves > Duplicate Surface Curves to create a new curve.
4. In the Side view, create three CV curves framing the fin as shown in Figure 5.72.

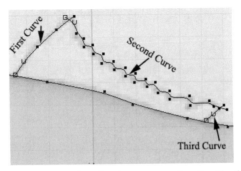

FIGURE 5.72   Creating the three curves framing the fin.

5. Name the curves as shown in Figure 5.73.

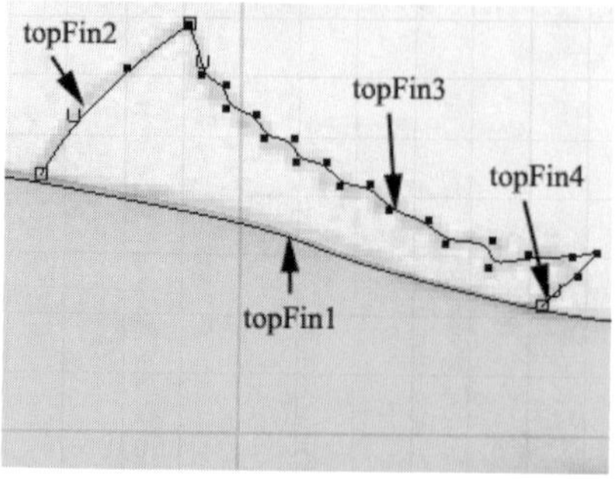

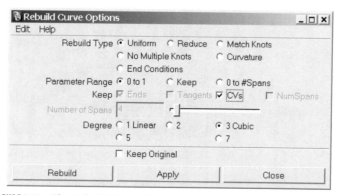

FIGURE 5.73   Renaming curves.

6. In the Side view, select topFin1.
7. Select Edit Curves > Rebuild Curve Option Box.
8. In the options window, select Edit > Reset Setting. Check Keep CVs as shown in Figure 5.74.

FIGURE 5.74   The Rebuild Curve Options window with Keep CVs selected.

9. Click the Apply button
10. Repeat steps 6 through 9 to rebuild topFin2, topFin3, and topFin4.

Intersecting the Curves

To intersect the curves:

1. In Side view, select Show and uncheck NURBS Surfaces. This will hide the fish's body. You will see the curves only.
2. Press W to change to the Move tool. Right-click topFin2, and select Control Vertex. Select the square box at the start of the topFin2 as shown in Figure 5.75.

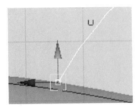

FIGURE 5.75   Selecting the first CV on topFin2.

3. Hold down the C key. Notice that the yellow square on the Move tool changes to a circle. The yellow circle means that you are in the Snap on Curve mode.

4. Holding down the C key, middle-click-drag anywhere on topFin1, and move the square box CV to topFin1 of the fin as shown in Figure 5.76. The square box CV of topFin2 should be snapped on topFin1.

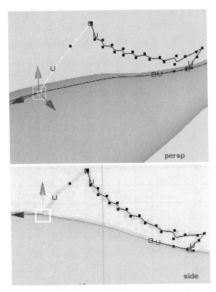

FIGURE 5.76   topFin2's first CV now snapped to topFin1.

5. Repeat steps 2 through 4 to snap topFin3 on topFin2, topFin3 on topFin4, and topFin4 on topFin1. You should have all the curves snapped at this point.

6. Click first on topFin1, hold down the Shift key, click second on topFin2, and click third on topFin3.

7. Select Edit Curve > Cut Curve. TopFin1 should be cut at the intersection with topFin2 and topFin4.

8. Select the extra curve on the left of topFin2 and on the right of topFin4 and delete them as shown in Figure 5.77. You should have four curves framing the fin only.

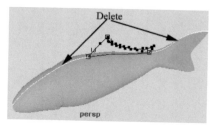

FIGURE 5.77 Delete the extra curves after cutting topFin1.

Using the Birail Tool to Create the Fin Surface

To create the fin surface with the Birail tool, follow these steps:

1. Select Surfaces > Birail > Birail 2 tool. The mouse cursor should change to an arrow shape.
2. In the Perspective view, click first on topFin2, second on topFin4, third on topFin1, and fourth on topFin3 as shown in Figure 5.78. Note that you may need to zoom in on topFin1 to be able to click it (see Figure 5.79). You should see the birail surface as shown in Figure 5.80. TopFin2 and topFin4 are the two profile curves. TopFin1 and topFin3 are the rail curves.

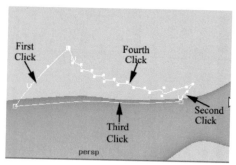

FIGURE 5.78 Proper selection order for the Birail 2 tool.

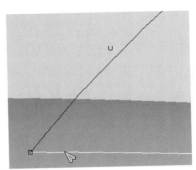

FIGURE 5.79   Zooming in and selecting topFin1.

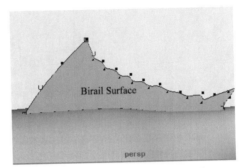

FIGURE 5.80   Properly made birail surface.

5. Name the new surface top_fin.
6. Select Edit NURBS > Rebuild Surfaces Option Box.
7. In the options window, select Keep NumSpans, and click the Rebuild button.
8. In the Side view, select Show, and check NURBS Surfaces to see the fish's body.
9. Delete topFin1, topFin2, topFin3, and topFin4.

Creating the Side Fins

To create the side fins:

1. In the Top view, select the body, and click the Make Live button icon on the Status Line (see Figure 5.81). The Make Live function allows you to create a curve on the object surface. This special curve is attached to the object's geometry UVs, which do not have coordinates X, Y, and Z.

FIGURE 5.81   Location of the Make Live button.

2. Select Create > CV Curve Tool, and then click four times from front to back, where the side fin meets the body, to create a curve on surface as shown in Figure 5.82.

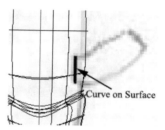

FIGURE 5.82   Creating a new curve where the side fin meets the body.

3. Rename the new curve on the surface to sideFin1. You need to name the curve in the Channel Box because a curve on the surface does not appear in either the Hypergraph or the Outliner.

4. Make sure that sideFin1 (the curve on the surface) is in the right place on the fish's body in Top, Side, and Perspective views as shown in Figure 5.83.

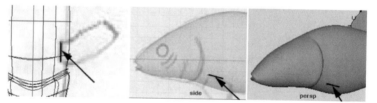

FIGURE 5.83   Proper position of sideFin1 in Top, Side, and Perspective views.

5. Make the fish not live by clicking the Make Live button again (refer to Figure 5.81).

6. Create three more curves to frame the fin and name them sideFin2, sideFin3, and sideFin4, as shown in Figure 5.84. Make sure that your curves have the same direction as the ones in Figure 5.84.

7. Click the black arrow on the Status Line and select All Objects Off as shown in Figure 5.85.

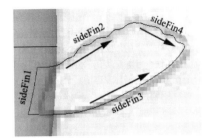

FIGURE 5.84   The four curves of the side fin.

FIGURE 5.85   Select All Objects Off.

8. Click the backward S, as shown in Figure 5.86, to be able to pick the sideFin1.

FIGURE 5.86   Turning on the NURBS selection mask.

9. Right-click sideFin2, and select Control Vertex.
10. Select the square box at the beginning of the curve, hold down the C key, and middle-click and drag on the curve on sideFin1. To make sure that sideFin2 is snapped on sideFin1, while holding down the C key, middle-drag the square box of sideFin2 to the first CV of the sideFin1. SideFin2 should not go beyond the first CV on sideFin1 if snapped.
11. Repeat steps 9 and 10 to snap sideFin3 to sideFin1, and snap sideFin4 to sideFin2 and sideFin3 (one on each end) as shown in Figure 5.87.

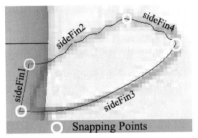

FIGURE 5.87   Curve end points properly aligned.

12. Select Surfaces > Birail > Birail 2 Tool.
13. In Top or Perspective view, click first on sideFin1, second on sideFin4, third on sideFin2, and fourth on sideFin3, as shown in Figure 5.88.

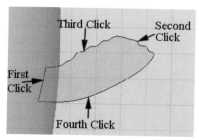

FIGURE 5.88   Selection order for the Birail 2 tool.

14. Name the new surface side_fin1.
15. Repeat steps 1 to 13 to create the second side fin. You should have the second fin as shown in Figure 5.89. Rename the second fin side_fin2.

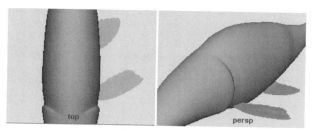

FIGURE 5.89   The fish with front and middle side fins.

16. Delete sideFin1, sideFin2, sideFin3, and sideFin4.
17. Click the black arrow in the Status Line, and select All Objects On.

Creating the Bottom Fin

To create the bottom fin:

1. Right-click the fish's body, and select Isoparm.
2. Select the isoparm in the middle of the fish's belly as shown in Figure 5.90.

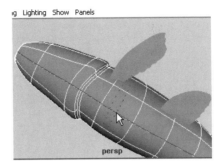

FIGURE 5.90   Select the isoparm in the middle of the fish's belly.

3. Select Edit Curves > Duplicate Surface Curves.
4. Name the duplicated curve bellyFin1.
5. Click the black arrow in the Status Line and select All Objects Off. Select the backward S again to turn the curves selection mask back on.
6. Select Create > CV Curve Tool.
7. Create two curves to frame the bottom fin. Start the curves close to the body going down away from the body. Name them bellyFin2 and bellyFin3 as shown in Figure 5.91.

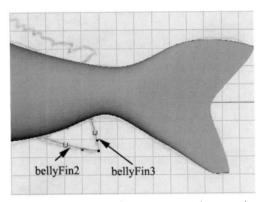

FIGURE 5.91   Bottom fin curves properly created.

8. Right-click bellyFin2 and select CV.
9. Snap the first CV of bellyFin2 on bellyFin1.
10. Right-click bellyFin3, and select CV.
11. Snap the first CV of bellyFin3 to bellyFin1.
12. Snap the last CV of bellyFin3 to bellyFin2.
13. Select all curves by clicking first on bellyFin1, second on bellyFin2, and third on bellyFin3.
14. Select Edit Curves > Cut Curve.
15. Delete the extra pieces of bellyFin1 (see Figure 5.92).

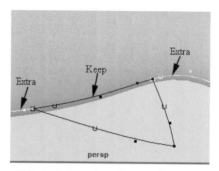

FIGURE 5.92   The three bottom fin curves.

16. Click bellyFin2 first, bellyFin3 second, and bellyFin1 third.
17. Select Surfaces > Boundary Option Box.
18. In the options window, select Edit > Reset Settings. Notice that Curve Ordering Automatic is selected by default as shown in Figure 5.93.

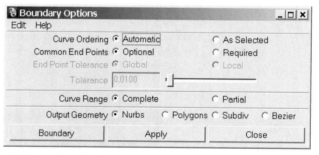

FIGURE 5.93   The Boundary Options window with Curve Ordering Automatic selected.

19. Click the Boundary button.
20. You should have a boundary geometry as shown in Figure 5.94. Rename the boundary surface bottom_fin.

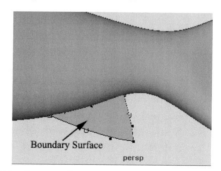

FIGURE 5.94   Bottom_fin is created out of a boundary surface.

21. Click the black arrow on the Status Line and select All Objects On.

Creating the Eye

To create the eye:

1. Select Create > NURBS Primitives > Circle.
2. Rotate the circle 90 degrees on the Z axis.
3. In the Side view, place the circle in front of the fish's eye as shown in Figure 5.95.

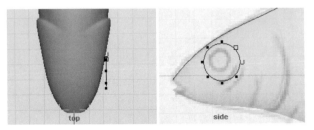

FIGURE 5.95   NURBS circle placed over the fish's eye.

4. Scale the circle to fit the fish's eye, as shown in Figure 5.96.

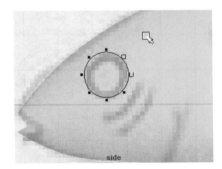

FIGURE 5.96   Scale the circle to fit the fish's eye.

5. In the Top view, move the circle a bit off of the fish's body, as shown in Figure 5.97.

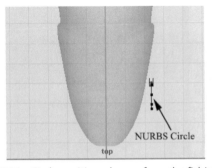

FIGURE 5.97   Circle positioned away from the fish's body.

6. In the Side view, click anywhere in the window to make it active.
7. Click the circle to select it, hold the Shift key, and click the fish's body to select it also.
8. Select Edit NURBS > Project Curve On Surface Option Box. This creates a curve attached to the surface.
9. In the options window, make sure that Active View is selected as shown in Figure 5.98.

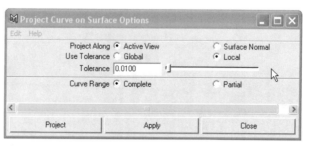

FIGURE 5.98   The Project Curve on Surface Options window with Active View selected.

10. Click the Project button. The circle will be projected, and a new circle on the surface appears on both sides of the fish's head as shown in Figure 5.99.

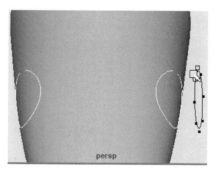

FIGURE 5.99   Circles projected onto the fish's body representing the location of the eyes.

11. With the new circle on the surface still selected, select Edit > Delete All by Type > History.
12. In the Side view, scale the original circle approximately half its size, and project it again. You should have two projected circles on both sides of the head as shown in Figure 5.100.

FIGURE 5.100   Inner circles now projected onto the fish body.

13. With the new circle on the surface still selected, select Edit > Delete All by Type > History.
14. On the Status Line, select All Objects Off, and click the Select by Object Type: Curves button (backward S).
15. Hold down the Shift key and click both circles on the surface on the left side of the fish's head.
16. Select Surfaces > Loft Option Box. Make sure that Geometry Output NURBS is checked in the options window.
17. Click the Loft button.
18. Name the loft surface LtEye_surface.
19. Select All Objects On in the Status Line.
20. Move the LtEye_surface geometry a bit outward as shown in Figure 5.101.

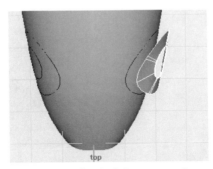

FIGURE 5.101   Lofted geometry for the left eye moved away from the body.

21. Right-click LtEye_surface and select Isoparm.
22. Select LtEye_surface's outer isoparm and the first projected circle as shown in Figure 5.102.

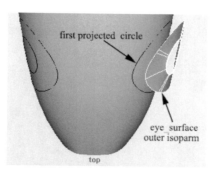

FIGURE 5.102   Select first the outer isoparm on the LtEye_surface
and the first projected circle.

23. Select Surface > Loft.
24. Select LtEye_surface.
25. Select Modify > Center Pivot. This moves the surface pivot to its center.
26. Move LtEye_surface on the X axis. Notice that the second loft surface updates because it still has construction history.
27. Adjust the loft surfaces to create a bulging eye.
28. Select Create > NURBS Primitives > Sphere.
29. With the sphere still selected, type 90 in the Rotate Z channel.
30. Scale the sphere and place it on the center of the fish's eye. You should have an eye similar to the one shown in Figure 5.103.

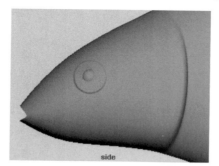

FIGURE 5.103   Fish head with eye.

31. Repeat steps 14 through 30 to create the right eye.
32. Select all curves on the surface and geometry, and delete the history.
33. Delete all curves on the surface. Deleting the curves should not affect the eye geometry. If the eye surface is deleted when you delete the curves on surface, it may be because the curves or geometry still have construction history. Select them one by one and delete the history again.
34. Select the front fin geometry and select Edit NURBS > Rebuild Surfaces Option Box.
35. In the Rebuild Surfaces Options window, make sure that NumSpans is checked. Click the Rebuild button.

36. Select Edit > Duplicate or press Ctrl+D.
37. With the duplicated geometry still selected, type -1 in the Scale X channel in the Channel Box. This will mirror the fin.
38. Repeat steps 34 to 37 to rebuild and mirror the middle fin. At this point, you should have a fish similar to the one shown in Figure 5.104.

FIGURE 5.104   Fish with the fins and eyes done.

39. Delete the history on any surfaces that still have curves affecting them, and delete the rest of the curves.

When mirroring an object symmetrically, make sure that the pivot of the object is at the origin (0,0,0).

Creating the Whiskers

To create the whiskers, you use a command called Extrude. This creates surfaces by sweeping a profile curve along a path curve. In this case, you will use a circle as the profile curve for the whiskers, so they will have a circular cross section. You will use a CV curve as the path curve defining where the whiskers point.

To create the whiskers, follow these steps:

1. Select Create > NURBS Primitives > Circle.
2. In the Side view, place the circle close to the mouth; rotate it 90 degrees on the Z axis; scale it on X, Y, and Z axes to 0.070; and offset it from the body as shown in Figure 5.105.

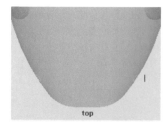

FIGURE 5.105   Circle placed near mouth.

3. Select the NURBS circle and the fish's body.
4. Make the Side view active.
5. Select Edit NURBS > Project Curve On Surface Option Box.
6. In the options window, make sure that Project along Active View is checked.
7. Click the Project button.
8. Select Create > CV Curve.
9. In the Front view, create a whisker profile curve. Start the curve close to the body.
10. Adjust the curve placement in Front, Side, and Perspective views as shown in Figure 5.106. Make sure that the beginning of the curve is in the center of the circle.

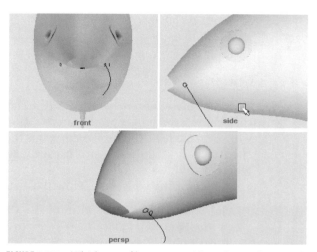

FIGURE 5.106   Whisker profile curve positioned near the mouth.

11. Select All Objects Off and click the Select by Object Type: Curves button.
12. Click first on the circle on the surface, and then click the whisker profile curve.
13. Select Surfaces > Extrude Option Box.

14. In the options window select the following parameters (see Figure 5.107):

- **Style:** Tube
- **Result Position:** At Profile
- **Pivot:** Closest End Point
- **Orientation:** Path Direction
- **Curve Range:** Complete
- **Output Geometry:** NURBS

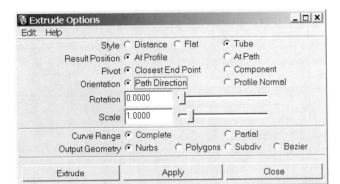

FIGURE 5.107   The Extrude Options window with Orientation set to Path Direction.

15. Click the Extrude button. You should see the extruded surface with the curve shape as shown in Figure 5.108.

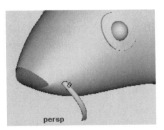

FIGURE 5.108   Whisker extruded along curve.

16. With the extruded surface still selected, look for extrude1 under IN-PUTS in the Channel Box.
17. Click extrude1 and scroll down the window until you see its Scale channel (see Figure 5.109).

FIGURE 5.109   Extrude1 selected in the INPUTS portion of the Channel Box.

18. Type 0.01 in the Scale channel. Notice that the end of the extruded surface becomes pointy as shown in Figure 5.110.

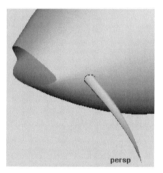

FIGURE 5.110   Extrusion scaled to create a pointy whisker.

19. Select the original circle and delete the history.
20. Select the whisker profile curve and delete the history.
21. Delete the circle and the curve.
22. Select All Objects On.
23. Select the extruded surface and then select Edit > Duplicate Special Option Box.
24. In the options window, type −1 in the Scale X channel.
25. Click the Duplicate button. The whisker should be mirrored and placed on the other side of the fish's head.

Keeping All Pieces Together

At this point, the fish body, fins, and whiskers are separate objects and move independently of each other. Grouping these parts of the fish will allow the pieces to move together.

To group together the fish's body, do the following:

1. Delete any extra profile curve still left on the file.
2. Open the Hypergraph window.
3. In the Hypergraph, select all of the fish's parts. Make sure not to miss any.
4. Press Ctrl+G to group all parts. Alternatively, you can select Edit > Group.
5. Save the file as fish.mb.

Rigging the Fish

Now that you have a good fish model, think for a moment about how a fish moves (consult some reference footage if necessary). What are the key movement characteristics of the body and of the fins? Various fish have differing degrees of spinal flexibility, as well as somewhat different fins; the koi is very flexible in its side-to-side motion along a central spine and shows almost no flex up and down on the spine. Meanwhile, its fins are quite stiff for most of their length but then very floppy for the rest of their length.

Based on these observations, the first rigging strategy is to use spline IK for the spine, animating it along a path that is twistier from side to side than up and down. The second strategy is to use Maya hair with dynamics to animate secondary (floppy) motion on both the tail and the fins.

TUTORIAL 5.2: CREATING THE FISH SKELETON

To create the fish skeleton, you first create the spine joints and then the fin joints. When the joints are in place you will create a spline IK handle, which will be used to animate the fish on a motion path curve.

Creating the Spine

To create the spine, follow these steps:

1. Open your fish.mb file.
2. Select Animation from the drop-down box.
3. Select Skeleton > Joint Tool.
4. In the Side view, hold down the X key to create 12 joints for the spine of the fish. The first joint should be at the fish's mouth, and the last joint at the fish's tail as shown in Figure 5.111. Notice that the joints are much closer on the tail. This is to give more flexibility to the tail bend motion.

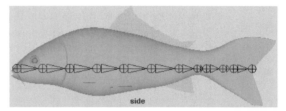

FIGURE 5.111 Proper joint layout for the fish.

5. Name the joints spine1 through spine12.

Creating the Joints for the Fins

To create the fin joints:

1. In the Top view, create four joints for the front fin. The joint should be created toward the extremity of the fin as shown in Figure 5.112.

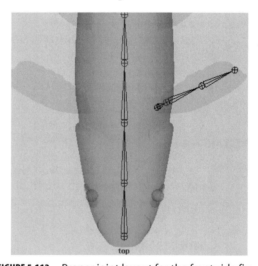

FIGURE 5.112 Proper joint layout for the front side fin.

2. Name the joints LtFrontFin1, LtFrontFin2, LtFrontFin3, and Lt-FrontFin4.
3. In the Side view, select LtFrontFin1 and move it down a bit.
4. Select LtFrontFin2 and move it down, touching the front fin geometry.
5. Look in all views to make sure that the placement of the joints is correct.
6. Select LtFrontFin1, and then select Skeleton > Mirror Joint > Options Box. In the options window, make sure that Mirror Across YZ and Mirror Function Behavior are checked.
7. In the Search For field, type Lt; in the Replace With field, type Rt (see Figure 5.113).

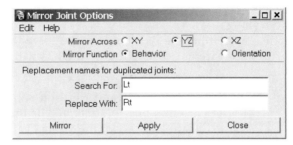

FIGURE 5.113   Mirror Joint Options window.

8. Click the Mirror button.
9. Repeat steps 1 through 8 to create the joints for the middle fin and mirror them.
10. Name these joints middleFin1, middleFin2, middleFin3, and middleFin4, left and right. At this point, you should have a skeleton as shown in Figures 5.114 and 5.115.

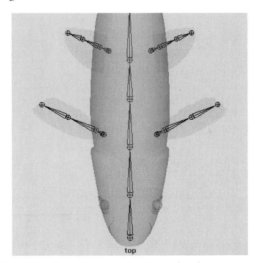

FIGURE 5.114   Fish with joints in all side fins from Top view.

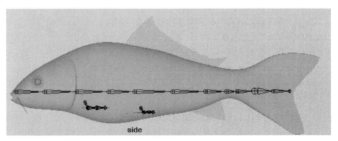

FIGURE 5.115   Fish with joints in all side fins from Side view.

Parenting the Fins' Joints

Parenting the fins' joints to the spine joints makes them move together. To parent the fin joints, do the following:

1. While holding down the Shift key, click first on LtFrontFin1, second on RtFrontFin1, and third on spine3, and then press P to parent them. Both fins' joints should be the children of spine3.
2. While holding down the Shift key, click first on LtMiddlefin1, second on RtMiddleFin1, and third on spine5. The fins should now be the children of spine5, as shown in Figure 5.116.

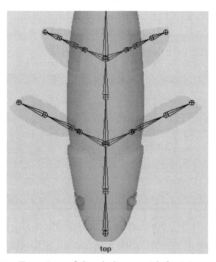

FIGURE 5.116   Top view of the skeleton with fin joints parented.

Creating the Joints for the Bottom Fin

To create the bottom fin joints:

1. Create three joints for the bottom fin.
2. Name the three joints bottomFin1, bottomFin2, and bottomFin3.
3. While holding down the Shift key, click first on bottomFin1, and second on spine7, and then press P. Now you should have a skeleton as shown in Figure 5.117.

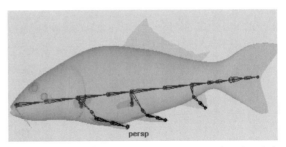

FIGURE 5.117   Bottom fin joints are now parented to the skeleton.

Binding the Skeleton to the Body

To bind the skeleton to the body:

1. Select spine1.
2. In the Hypergraph, select all the fish's body parts. Make sure you do not miss any part.
3. Select Skin > Bind Skin > Smooth Bind.
4. Select and move spine1 back and forth to test the binding. All parts of the body should move with spine1.
5. Undo the move.
6. Save your scene.

TUTORIAL 5.3: ANIMATING THE FISH ON A PATH

As described previously, our strategy is to animate the fish along a motion path. This makes it relatively easy to plan and visualize the motion. The same technique is also very useful for quickly creating rough "blocking pass" animations of humanoid characters, particularly where there is complicated character positioning to work out.

Creating the Motion Path Curve

To create the motion path curve:

1. Make sure you are in Surfaces mode.
2. Select Create > CV Curve Tool.
3. In the Top view, create a curve similar to the one shown in Figure 5.118. Start the curve in front of the fish. Make the curvature of the curve wide and smooth. Avoid elbow type curvature.

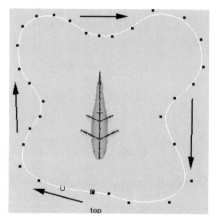

FIGURE 5.118   Motion path for the fish.

4. Select the curve's last CV. While holding the V key, move-snap the curve to the first CV.
5. Select Edit Curves > Open/Close Curves Option Box.
6. In the option window, make sure that Shape Preserve is selected and Keep Original is unchecked as shown in Figure 5.119.

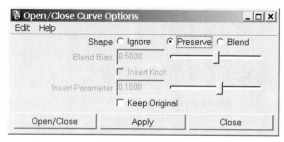

FIGURE 5.119   The Open/Close Curve Options window in its default state.

7. Click the Open/Close button.
8. Select Edit Curves > Rebuild Curve Option Box.
9. In the options window, make sure that Rebuild Type Uniform is checked and Keep CVs is also checked.
10. Click the Rebuild button. Closing and rebuilding the curve prevents the fish from flipping and allows a smooth, continuous motion.

Attaching the Fish to the Path

To attach the fish to the path:
1. Press F2 to change the mode to Animation.
2. Select Create > Locator.
3. Name the locator locator_up.

4. With the locator still selected, type 1 in the Translate Y channel of the Channel Box.
5. Click spine1, hold the Shift key, and click the curve.
6. Select Animate > Motion Paths > Attach to Motion Path Option Box.
7. In the options window, check the following:

- **Time Range:** Start/End
- **Start Time:** 1
- **End Time:** 500
- **Follow**
- **Front Axis:** Z
- **Up Axis:** Y
- **World Up Type:** Object Up
- **World Up Object:** locator_up
- **Bank**

8. Click the Attach button. Notice that the fish jumps to the beginning of the curve and stays in a vertical position as shown in Figure 5.120.

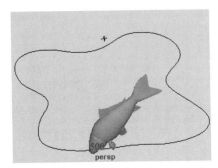

FIGURE 5.120   Fish attached to curve via spine1.

To attach the fish's body on the curve, you need to create an IK handle.

Creating the IK Spline Handle for the Spine

To create the spline handle for the spine:

1. Select Skeleton > IK Spline Handle Tool Option Box.
2. In the options window, uncheck Root on Curve, Auto Create Root Axis, Auto Parent Curve, Snap Curve to Root, and Auto Create Curve.
3. Click first on spine1, second on spine8, and third on the path curve. The fish's spine should be attached to the curve as shown in Figure 5.121.

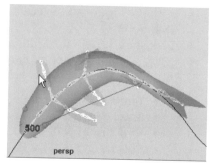

FIGURE 5.121   Fish's spine now attached to animation curve.

4. Play the animation. Oops! The fishing is swimming backward. You need to fix that.

5. Select the curve. In the Channel Box under OUTPUTS, select motion-Path1 and find the U Value setting (see Figure 5.122).

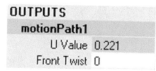

FIGURE 5.122   The U Value setting located under motionPath1 in the OUTPUTS section of the Channel Box.

6. Click the word U Value.

7. Open the Graph Editor (Panels > Panel > Graph Editor).

8. In the Graph Editor, select View > Frame All.

9. Select keyframe 1; in the Stats field, change its value to 1.

10. Select keyframe 500; in the Stats field, change its value to 0 (see Figure 5.123). This reverses the fish's motion.

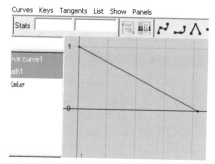

FIGURE 5.123   Graph Editor with corrected values.

11. Play the animation. The fish should be swimming forward now.
12. In the Graph Editor, select the U Value animation curve.
13. Select Curves > Pre-Infinity > Cycle and then Post-Infinity > Cycle. This will repeat the animation beyond frame 300 in a constant motion.
14. In the Graph Editor, select > View > Infinity. You should see the infinity curves as shown in Figure 5.124.

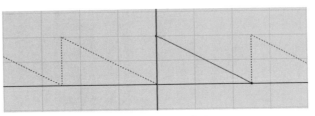

FIGURE 5.124   Animation infinity curves.

Stopping the Fish from Flipping

When you play the animation, the fish may twist on the motion path curve. To fix that, you adjust the Twist control of the spline IK handle:

1. Select the spline IK handle and open its attribute editor.
2. In the Attribute Editor click IK Solver Attribute.
3. Scroll down the window until you see an Advanced Twist Controls entry. Click it to open the section.
4. In the Advanced Twist Controls section check Enable Twist Controls. Choose World Up Type Object Up, Up Axis Positive Z, and, in the World Up Object field, type locator_up.

The fish should move on the path without flipping.

Setting Motion Path Markers

To set motion path markers:

1. Drag the time line to frame 100.
2. Select the motion path curve.
3. In the Channel Box under the OUTPUTS section, click motionPath1. You should see the U value.
4. Right-click U Value and select Key Selected. You should see the marker 100 on the curve.
5. Drag the time line to frame 200, and set another marker.
6. Drag the time line to frame 300, and set another marker.
7. Drag the time line to frame 390, and set another marker.
8. With the Move tool selected, click the markers one by one, and move them as shown in Figure 5.125.

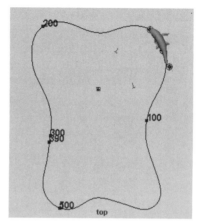

FIGURE 5.125   Motion path markers.

9. Right-click the motion path curve and select CV.
10. Select the four CVs closest to markers 300 and 390 and drag them up a bit to make a smooth hump on the curve as shown in Figure 5.126. The fish will swim up a little bit as if to eat at the water surface.

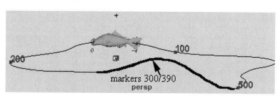

FIGURE 5.126   Hump on motion path curve.

Notice that the fish swims with different speeds now.

Adding Dynamic Secondary Motion on the Tail and Front Fin

To add dynamic secondary motion:

1. Select Create > EP Curve Tool.
2. Hold down the V (snap to point) key, click first on spine10, and click second on spine12.
3. Press Enter to finish the curve.
4. Name the curve tailCurve.
5. Press G to get the EP Curve tool again.
6. Click first on LtFrontFin2 and click second on LtFrontFin4.
7. Press Enter.
8. Name the curve LtFrontFinCurve.
9. Press G again, click first on RtFrontFin2, and click second on RtFrontFin4.

10. Press Enter.
11. Call the curve RtFrontFinCurve. You should have three EP curves (see Figure 5.127).

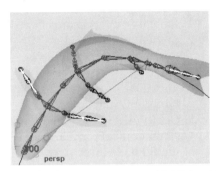

FIGURE 5.127   The three new curves are highlighted in white.

12. Select all three EP curves. Under the Surfaces menu, select Edit Curves > Rebuild Curve Option Box.
13. In the options window, make sure that Rebuild Type Uniform and Keep Ends are checked. In the Number of Spans, type 4.
14. Click the Rebuild button.
15. Press F5 to change the mode to Dynamics.
16. Select all EP curves, and select Hair > Make Selected Curves Dynamic. The curves change the color to blue.
17. Open the Hypergraph window. You should see the hair dynamic nodes as shown in Figure 5.128. Select the group hairSystem1OutputCurves. Rename its contents, curve1, curve2, and curve3, to tailDynamicCurve, LtFrontFinDynamicCurve, and RtFrontFinDynamicCurve.

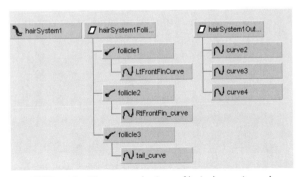

FIGURE 5.128   Hypergraph view of hair dynamic nodes.

18. Select Hair > Display > Current Position.
19. Press F2 to change the mode to Animation.
20. Select Skeleton > IK Spline Handle Tool Option Box.
21. In the options window, make sure that everything under IK Spline Handle Settings is unchecked.
22. In the Perspective view, click first on spine10, second on spine12, and third on tailDynamicCurve.
23. Press the Y key to get the IK Spline Handle tool again.
24. Click first on LtFrontFin2, second on LtFrontFin4, and third on LtFrontFinDynamicCurve.
25. Get the IK Spline Handle tool again, and click first on RtFrontFin2, second on RtFrontFin4, and third on RtFrontFinDynamicCurve. You should have three new IK spline handles.
26. Call the new IKs tailIK, LtFrontfinIK, and RtFrontFinIK.
27. In the Hypergraph, select follicle1, and open its Attribute Editor.
28. In the Attribute Editor, under Follicle Attributes, find the Point Lock parameter and change it to Base.
29. Repeat steps 27 and 28 to change the Point Lock of follicle2 and follicle3 to Base.
30. In the Hypergraph, select hairSystem1, and open its Attribute Editor.
31. Under the Dynamics section, type 0.1 in the Length Flex field, and type 1 in the Stiffness field.

Parenting the Follicles

To parent the follicles:

1. In the Hypergraph, middle-click-drag follicle1, and drag it on top of spine9. Follicle1 should be parented to spine9 as shown in Figure 5.129.

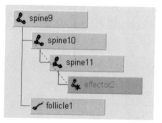

FIGURE 5.129   Follicle1 parented to spine9.

2. Middle-click-drag follicle2 on top of LtFrontFin1 as shown in Figure 5.130.

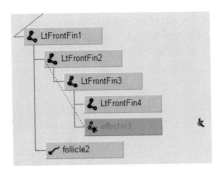

FIGURE 5.130   Follicle2 parented to LtFrontFin1.

3. Middle-click-drag follicle3 on top of RtFrontFin1 as shown in Figure 5.131.

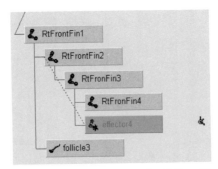

FIGURE 5.131   Follicle3 parented to RtFrontFin1.

Simulating Water

Fluid Effects is a feature that is available in Maya Unlimited. This feature allows you to create a nice fish pond.

To simulate the fish pond, follow these steps:

1. Press F5 to change Maya to Dynamics mode.
2. Select Fluid Effects > Pond > Create Pond.
3. In the Pond Attribute Editor, under Container Properties, change the size to 200, 200, and 30 as shown in Figure 5.132.

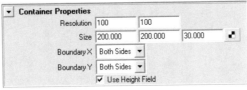

FIGURE 5.132   Pond Attribute Editor Container Properties.

4. Scroll down in the Attribute Editor until you see Shading.
5. Open the Shading tab. In the Color section, change the Selected Color setting to the color of your preference.
6. In the Shading section, move the Transparency bar approximately halfway to the right (see Figure 5.133).

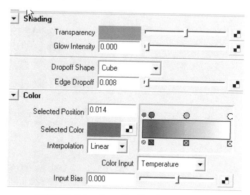

FIGURE 5.133   Pond's Shading section.

7. Adjust the position of the pond on Translate Y to make sure that the fish is under water.

Simulating Wake and Parenting It to the Fish

To simulate wake and parent it to the fish:

1. Select FluidEffects > Pond > Create Wake.
2. Name the wake WakeEmitterMouth.
3. Select spine1 then WakeEmitterMouth.
4. Press F2, and select Constrain > Parent Option Box.
5. In the options window, make sure that Maintain Offset is unchecked, and click the Add button.
6. Press F5, and select FluidEffects > Pond > Create Wake.
7. Name the wake WakeEmitterTail.
8. Repeat steps 4 and 5 to parent constrain WakeEmitterTail to spine12 (the end of the fish tail).
9. Open the wakeEmitterMouth Attribute Editor.
10. Under the Fluid Attributes tab, type 0.5 in the Density/Voxel/Sec field.
11. Open the WakeEmitterTail Attribute Editor.
12. Under the Fluid Attributes tab, type 1.0 in the Density/Voxel/Sec field. This way the tail will make a bigger splash than the mouth.
13. Make sure that the hump of the curve is in the surface of the water as if the fish food is on the water surface.

14. Play the animation. You should see the wake effect on the mouth and tail of the fish.

SUMMARY

Through the chapter's exercises, you were introduced to the basics of NURBS modeling and motion path animation. You have finished your first motion path animation with hair dynamics for secondary motion. You also have created a dynamic pond with wakes. Now you have the basic skills to model more complex NURBS characters and animate an object in a path with markers and dynamics.

CHALLENGE ASSIGNMENTS

1. Research Fish Species

Draw or find an image reference for two different fish species. Research the environment in which the fish live. For example, the fish may live on the bottom or surface of the ocean, in a fresh water pond, and so on.

2. Create Fish

Using the same techniques you used to create the koi, create two other fish. Animate them swimming along two different paths.

3. Create a Fish Environment

Using your reference materials, create an appropriate environment for your fish (water, rocks, bottom texture, etc.).

MODELING A BIPED CHARACTER

In This Chapter

- Human Anatomy for Modelers
- Tools and Methods

Biped characters are extremely common in animation, ranging from simple cartoonish forms to nearly photorealistic "hero" models. Regardless of form, a good character model's two main characteristics are that it animates well and has a visual design that graphically conveys strong personality.

Often these two requirements are somewhat at odds. For example, it is relatively easy to make a character that looks great in a static render but is too complex ("heavy") to animate smoothly. Knowing which details to keep and which to eliminate is an essential part of the character designer's and modeler's skill set. This chapter will walk you through the steps of modeling an anatomically correct biped character with a reasonable level of detail.

HUMAN ANATOMY FOR MODELERS

Human anatomy is the best starting point for modeling human and humanoid characters. A number of reference books are available on this topic. However, most are designed for traditional artists and tend to offer perspective views mixed with drawing advice. 3D modelers should look for books with reference imagery in front and side views that demonstrates a wide variety of human forms (young and old, frail and strong, etc.). One such book is *Human Anatomy for Artists* by Eliot Goldfinger (Oxford University Press, 1991).

Remember, the goal is not to try to imitate every aspect of human anatomy. That is infeasible both in terms of effort and computing power. Humans have hundreds of bones, thousands of muscles and tendons, and even very complex skin. The art of 3D character modeling is to pick up just enough basic human anatomy to make for reasonable biomechanics and enough detail to highlight what is unique about a character. For example, the human spine is composed of 33 irregularly shaped vertebrae. A typical 3D character model won't have more than a dozen simple bones used to simulate the spine, yet the curved arrangement of these bones mirrors the inflection points in the true spine. An attempt to model a straight spine with two or three bones would likely be unreasonably stiff and awkward to animate.

The main anatomic factors to consider when designing a model are the overall body proportions and the build (character-specific relationships between bones and muscle). Secondary factors include the number of fingers and facial expressions to be modeled, which in many cases is dependent on the storyboard used. Paying attention to the basics of anatomy will help you model and rig characters that deform and animate smoothly.

Body Proportions

All normal humans (and even most humanoid monsters) have their basic anatomical parts connected in the same way. The main factors that vary are the relative sizes of these parts. For example, babies' heads are a much larger proportion of their overall body length than those of adults. Although many people are not conscious of this fact, they nonetheless tend to identify characters with larger heads as cute or funny. Similarly, long legs are considered attractive in many Western cultures, so a character intended to be viewed as attractive will be modeled with proportionally longer than normal legs.

What is normal and what is ideal? The answers to such questions have, of course, changed over time and between cultures. Leonardo da Vinci's famous *Vitruvian Man* drawing was based on a model of ideal proportions established by the Roman architect Vitruvius and measured in fractions of a man's height (see Figure 6.1).

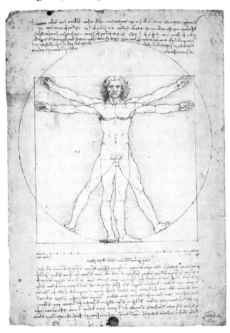

FIGURE 6.1   Leonardo da Vinci's *Vitruvian Man*.

However, artists today generally use a simpler system based on the size of a character's head.

In this system, a normal human figure is an average of 6 to 7 heads high. An idealized figure is usually 7.5 to 8 heads high, with 4 heads' height from hip to toes. The distance from shoulder to shoulder is 3 heads' width. The distance from the wrist to the fingertips is 1 head height, and that from elbow to fingertips is 2 heads (see Figure 6.2).

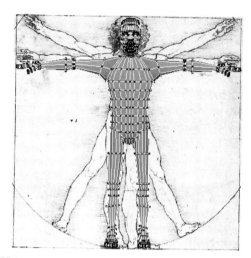

FIGURE 6.2   3D model according to da Vinci's *Vitruvian Man*.

Of course, you can use any proportions you like in your 3D models as shown in Figure 6.3. However, they will most likely be subjectively judged relative to the preceding standards and ideals. Aside from this important subjective factor, there is a practical reason to pay close attention to these proportions. All technical character rigging and animation is based on the body proportions that you initially establish. In Maya, it is sometimes possible to change these by moving joints and bones after initial rigging, but it is never easy.

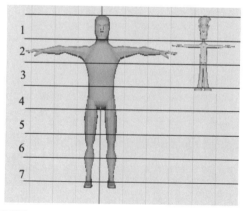

FIGURE 6.3   Two models with different proportions.

TOOLS AND METHODS

The first stage of modeling a character is to sketch a series of character images to become acquainted with its proportions and to know exactly what it should look like. The second stage is to draw the character in a "da Vinci" pose (arms outstretched with palms down) from the front view and side view. Scan the drawings and import them as image planes to use as reference. For convenience, you should size and proportion your scans equally, using a simple fixed aspect ratio. For example, you might make them both 600 pixels tall by 300 pixels wide (see Figure 6.4).

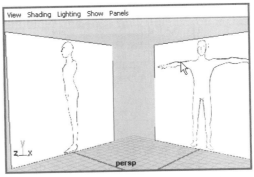

FIGURE 6.4   Character image imported into Maya as image planes.

There are many ways to model a biped using polygons. The most popular method is to start by modeling the head, then the torso, and finally the limbs. Although it is possible to create character meshes with the Create Polygon tool and extrusions, the method demonstrated in this chapter is based on the use of 3D primitive polygon forms to represent each major body mass. In this method, basic forms such as cubes and cylinders are first sculpted and then connected together. The advantages to this approach are that the position of the polygons within each massing remain relatively well aligned, and the level of detail is well balanced. The disadvantage of this approach relative to extrusion from a single mass is that a certain amount of work is required to think through and implement the connections between the various parts.

A second key concept, which can be used in any form of polygon modeling, is the use of what are called *edge loops*. These are particularly important in places like the eyes and mouth, which require fine resolution and subtle movements. The basic idea is to reflect on the polygonal surface the direction of smooth underlying muscle structures. By making these into surface loops, you help ensure that expected deformations don't apply at odd angles across your polygons (which can cause unnatural looking shearing). For example, edge loops help the skin deform correctly when the character opens, closes, or squints his eyes and when the character opens and closes his mouth. The details of this technique will be described later in the chapter when modeling the Simple Guy character.

The basic polygon editing tools were described in Chapter 3. Three additional polygon tools will be needed for the character modeling in this chapter: the Merge tool, the Append to Polygon tool, and the Bridge tool. These tools are described in the following sections.

The Merge Tool

The Merge tool merges two or more vertices into a single vertex or two adjacent border edges. When you merge vertices, the edges and UVs affiliated with those vertices are also merged (see Figure 6.5).

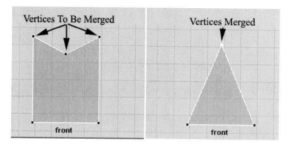

FIGURE 6.5   Merged vertices from a single polygon.

You can merge vertices from two different polygons. In this case, you first have to combine the two polygons as shown in Figure 6.6. The Combine feature combines the two polygons or meshes into one object. A *mesh* is a collection of connected polygons.

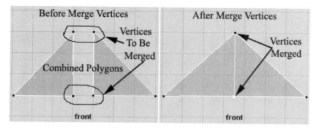

FIGURE 6.6   Merged vertices from two polygons.

Let's do a simple exercise to understand how this tool works:

1. Create a new scene.
2. Select Mesh > Create Polygon Tool.

3. In the Front view, click five times approximately in the middle of the screen to create a polygon. The polygon should be approximately four grids wide and four grids high.
4. Select the three top vertices as shown in Figure 6.7.

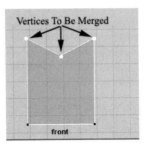

FIGURE 6.7   Three top vertices of the polygon selected.

5. Select Edit Polygons > Merge Option Box.
6. In the options window, type 6.0 in the Distance field. This increases the distance threshold to merge the vertices. The Maya default threshold is 0.01, which is too small in most cases.
7. Click the Merge Vertex button. The three vertices should become one as shown in Figure 6.8.

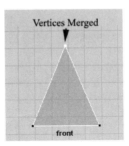

FIGURE 6.8   Three top vertices of the polygon merged.

The Append to Polygon Tool

The Append to Polygon tool creates a new polygon between two polygon edges as shown in Figure 6.9. To append two polygons from two different objects, you have to combine the polygons before you append them.

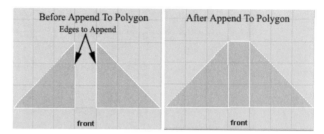

FIGURE 6.9 Two polygons appended.

For the Append to Polygon tool to work as expected, the vertex order of the polygons must be consistent—either clockwise or counterclockwise. For example, if one polygon is created clockwise and another counterclockwise, the Append to Polygon tool will create a twisted polygon, as shown in Figure 6.10.

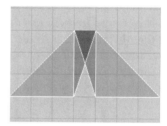

FIGURE 6.10 Two appended polygons created in different order.

You may be wondering what is going on here. When you create polygons, Maya—like most modeling packages—uses something known as the *right-hand rule* to determine which side of the polygon is the front and which is the back. If you draw vertices in clockwise order, the "front" side of the polygon will be facing you. If you draw the vertices in counterclockwise order, the "back" side of the polygon will be facing you.

Of course, you may want to append a polygon to a preexisting one and have forgotten or never known the vertex creation order of either polygon. In this case, you need to ask Maya to display the normals of the polygons to tell which are facing in which direction. This can be done by choosing Display > Polygons > Face Normals. If you want to append two polygons, make sure their normals are facing the same direction. If not, flip the normal of one of them using the Normals > Reverse command.

Let's do a simple exercise to understand how the Append to Polygon tool works:

1. Select Mesh > Create Polygon Tool.

2. In the Front view, click four times clockwise, approximately in the middle of the screen, to create a polygon quad. The polygons should be five grid units wide and four grid units high.
3. Duplicate the polygon and move it one grid unit to the right as shown in Figure 6.11.

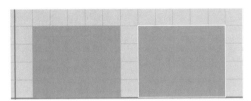

FIGURE 6.11   Duplicated polygon moved one grid unit to the right.

4. Select both polygons and select Mesh > Combine.
5. Select Edit Mesh > Append to Polygon Tool. The mouse cursor should change to a cross.
6. Click the right edge of the polygon on the left.
7. Click the left edge of the polygon on the right.
8. Press Enter to finish the tool operation. You should see a new polygon connecting the two polygons as shown in Figure 6.12.

FIGURE 6.12   Two polygons connected with the Append to Polygon tool.

The Bridge Tool

The Bridge tool is similar to the Append to Polygon Tool. It also creates a polygon between two polygon edges. The advantage of using this tool is that it allows you to select multiple polygon edges at once. As with the Append Polygon Tool, the meshes must first be combined

Let's do a simple exercise to understand how this tool works:

1. Select Create > Polygon Primitives and uncheck Interactive Creation.
2. Select Create > Polygon Primitives > Cylinder.
3. In the Perspective view, select Shading > Smooth Shade All.
4. Tumble the camera until you see the top cap of the cylinder.
5. Select and delete all faces on the top cap of the cylinder as shown in Figure 6.13.

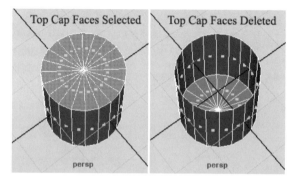

FIGURE 6.13   A cylinder with top cap faces selected and deleted.

6. In the Side view, select the cylinder and then select Edit > Duplicate or press Crtl + D.

7. With the duplicated copy of the cylinder still selected, type the following values in the Channel Box:

- Translate Y: 2.5
- Rotate Z: 180

This moves the selected cylinder up and turns it upside down.

8. Rename the cylinder pCylinder2. Now you should have pCylinder1 and pCylinder2 as two separate objects as shown in Figure 6.14.

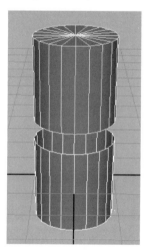

FIGURE 6.14   View of pCylinder1 and pCylinder2.

9. In the Perspective view, select pCylinder1 and pCylinder2.
10. Select Mesh > Combine.
11. Deselect both cylinders.
12. Click one of the cylinders. Notice that both are selected.

13. In the Perspective view, right-click pCylinder1 and select Edge.
14. Click several edges on the top border of pCylinder1 to select them as shown in Figure 6.15.

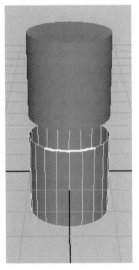

FIGURE 6.15   The top border edges of pCylinder1 are selected.

15. Right-click pCylinder2 and select the corresponding edges, as shown in Figure 6.16.

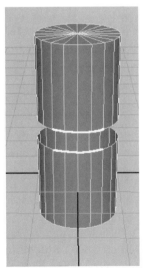

FIGURE 6.16   The edges on pCylinder2 are selected.

16. Select Edit Mesh > Bridge Option Box.
17. In the Bridge Options window type 0 in the Subdivision field. This option specifies that you will have only one polygon between the edges of the pCylinder1 and 2.
18. Click the Bridge button. You should see a polygon between each pair of edges as shown in Figure 6.17.

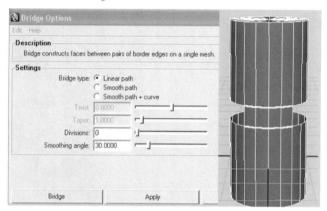

FIGURE 6.17   The Bridge Options window open and cylinders 1 and 2 with bridged edges.

    The Bridge tool accepts face selection to create the polygon bridge between the faces' border edges.

TUTORIAL 6.1: MODELING THE SIMPLE GUY CHARACTER

In this tutorial, you will model a simple human-like character in polygons (see Figure 6.18). A set of previously prepared images will serve as a blueprint to aid in modeling. Basic polygon primitives will be created and modified to create the finished polygonal model. You will modify the polygon primitives by moving vertices, splitting and extruding polygonal faces and edges, combining polygons, and appending faces. You will find that using independent primitives for different body parts allows for easier and more organized modeling.

It is important to note that polygons are initially laid out as a simple grid, with their edges running up and down and side to side as shown in Figure 6.19.

A grid is an efficient layout for a mathematically derived surface; however, character modeling, by its very nature, seeks to use 3D surfaces to create more lifelike and organic structures. Characters such as the Simple Guy model require that the grid structure be changed to accommodate the organic curvature of living surfaces. To do this, you split and append surfaces to create junctions of polygonal edges that allow for a nongrid-like curvature (see Figure 6.20).

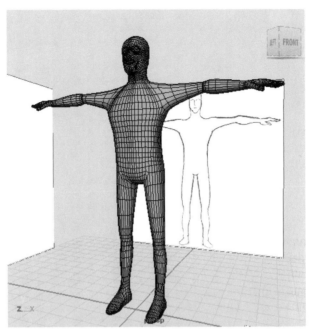

FIGURE 6.18   The Simple Guy.
(Model and step-by-step tutorial of the modeling process by Aharon Charnov.)

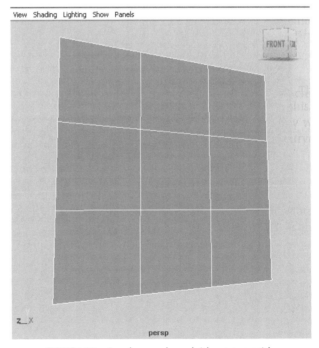

FIGURE 6.19   A polygon plane, laid out as a grid.

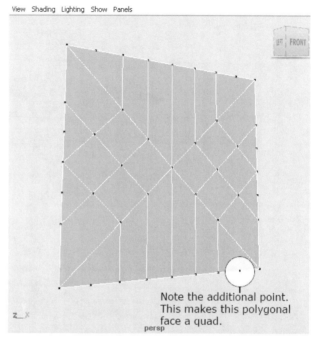

View   Shading   Lighting   Show   Panels

Note the additional point.
This makes this polygonal
face a quad.

FIGURE 6.20   A polygon plane, cut into many nongrid-like quads.

Polygons can have many sides. Although it often seems that three-sided or five-sided polygons help create curved surfaces, Maya prefers quadrangles (four-sided polygons). In this tutorial, then, you will create a polygonal character with good surface curvature in quads. An example of this more organic curvature can be seen in the Simple Guy's arms. A human-like character has arms whose surfaces can be thought of as flowing from side to side (see Figure 6.21). However, these arms also flow organically into the sides of the torso and neck as shown in Figure 6.22. In this tutorial, you will learn to model a polygonal object with good surface curvature.

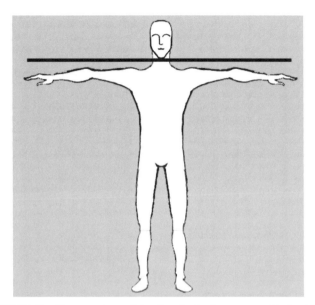

FIGURE 6.21   The curvature of the Simple Guy's arms run side to side.

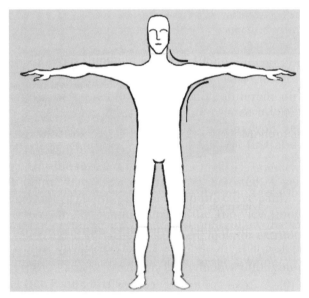

FIGURE 6.22   The curvature of the Simple Guy's arms runs into the curvature of the torso and neck.

Modeling the Simple Guy Character: Set Up

To create the Simple Guy set up, follow these steps.

1. Select File > Project > New, and name it Simple_Guy. Select Use Defaults and Accept.
2. Press F3 to go into Polygons mode.
3. Select Panels > Saved Layouts > Four View. You will find it helpful to see your model in Top, Front, Side, and Perspective views.
4. In the Front view, select View > Image Plane > Import Image.
5. Open the file called Simple_Guy_Character_front.tif from the chapter6, imagePlanes folder on the CD-ROM (see Figure 6.23).

ON THE CD

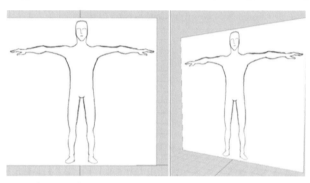

FIGURE 6.23   The Simple Guy image plane in the Front and Perspective views.

6. In the Side view, select View > Import Plane > Import Image.
7. Open the file Simple_Guy_Character_side.tif from the chapter6, imagePlanes folder on the CD-ROM.
8. In the Top view, select View > Image Plane > Import Image.
9. Open the file called Simple_Guy_Character_top.tif from the image Planes folder on the CD-ROM.
10. The image planes are centered in the origin of the axes. You are going to move and scale them. In the Perspective view, select the front image plane.
11. In the Channel Box, scroll down until you see imagePlane1 under INPUTS.
12. Enter the following values for imagePlane1 as shown in Figure 6.24.

    - Offset X, Y: 0, 0
    - Center X: –0.15
    - Center Y: 7.0
    - Center Z: –12.0
    - Width: 15
    - Height: 15

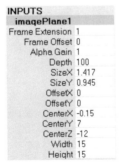

FIGURE 6.24   ImagePlane1's values.

13. In the Perspective view, select the side image plane.
14. In the Channel Box, scroll down until you see imagePlane2 under INPUTS.
15. Enter the following values as shown in Figure 6.25.

- Offset X, Y: 0, 0
- Center X: –12.0
- Center Y: 7.0
- Center Z: 0
- Width: 15
- Height: 15

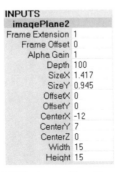

FIGURE 6.25   ImagePlane2's values.

16. Select the top image plane in the Perspective view.
17. In the Channel Box, scroll down until you see imagePlane3 under INPUTS.
18. Enter the following values as shown in Figure 6.26. Figure 6.27 shows the image planes seen from all windows.

- Offset X, Y: 0, 0
- Center X: 6.502
- Center Y: 0
- Center Z: 0.1
- Width: 2
- Height: 2

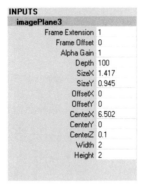

INPUTS
imagePlane3

Frame Extension	1
Frame Offset	0
Alpha Gain	1
Depth	100
SizeX	1.417
SizeY	0.945
OffsetX	0
OffsetY	0
CenterX	6.502
CenterY	0
CenterZ	0.1
Width	2
Height	2

FIGURE 6.26   ImagePlane3's values.

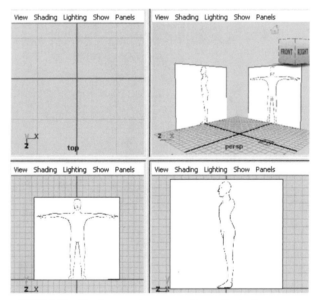

FIGURE 6.27   The image planes seen from all windows.

Modeling the Simple Guy Character: Creating the Head

You will start the head using a polygon cube, and you will sculpt it using the tools available in Maya. This is a good way to create a humanoid head for the first time. To create the head:

1. Select Create > Polygon Primitives > Cube Option Box.
2. In the Polygon Cube Options window, set the following values as shown in Figure 6.28. These specifications will give you enough edges to start sculpting the head.

- Width: 1.0
- Height: 1.0
- Depth: 1.0
- Width divisions: 4
- Height divisions: 4
- Depth divisions: 4
- Axis: Y
- Texture Mapping: Check Create UVs and Normalize

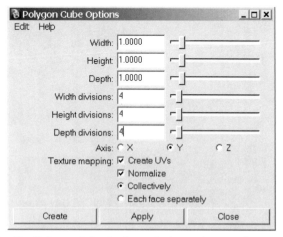

FIGURE 6.28   The Polygon Cube Options window with properly entered values.

3. Click the Create button. Maya creates the cube at the origin as shown in Figure 6.29.
4. In the Channel Box or the Hypergraph window, rename the cube head.
5. In the Channel Box, enter the following values as shown in Figure 6.30. This moves the head to the correct position and scales it to the correct dimensions.

- Translate X: 0
- Translate Y: 12.866
- Translate Z: 0.12
- Rotate X: 0
- Rotate Y: 0
- Rotate Z: 0
- Scale X: 1
- Scale Y: 1.647
- Scale Z: 1.547

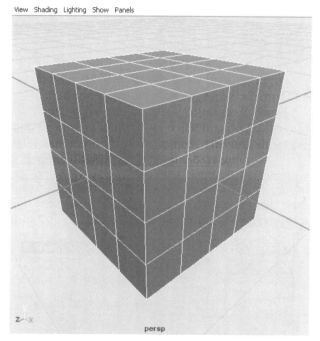

FIGURE 6.29   The new polygon cube at the origin.

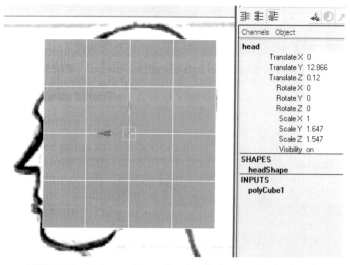

FIGURE 6.30   Cube positioned and scaled to match the head.

6. In the Top view, right-click the selected head and select Vertex from the pop-up menu.

7. Hold down the Shift key and drag-select each of the vertices in all four corners as shown in Figure 6.31.

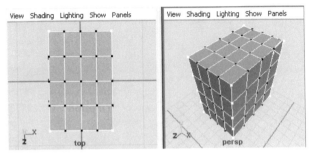

FIGURE 6.31   Top and Perspective views of the corner vertices selected.

8. With the corner vertices still selected, press the R key to change to the Scale tool.
9. Scale the vertices inward along the X axis and Z axis to make the head slightly more curved as shown in Figure 6.32.

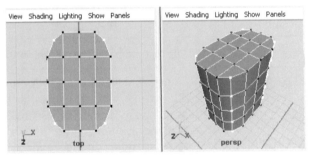

FIGURE 6.32   Top and Perspective views of the head's corner vertices scaled to correct positions.

10. In the Perspective view, with the head still selected and in Component mode, select the inner nine vertices on the top of the head as shown in Figure 6.33. Make sure that the vertices on the backside of the head aren't selected.

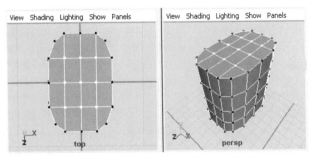

FIGURE 6.33   Top and Perspective views of the head's top middle nine vertices selected.

11. In the Side view, with the inner nine vertices still selected, press the W key to switch to the Move tool.
12. Move the middle vertices up in the Y axis to meet the top of the head on the image plane as shown in Figure 6.34.

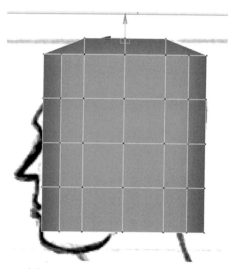

FIGURE 6.34   The top-middle nine vertices repositioned to match the top of the head.

13. In the Side view, select Shading > X-Ray to make the head transparent.
14. In the Side view, with the head still selected and in Component mode, press the W key to switch to the Move tool. Drag-select the vertices and reposition them to match the contour of the head on the image plane as shown in Figure 6.35.

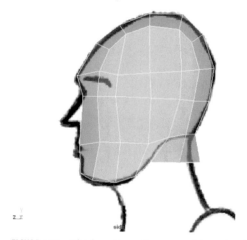

FIGURE 6.35   The head's vertices repositioned to better match the image plane in the Side view.

15. In the Side view, with the head still selected and in Component mode, right-click over the head and select Face from the pop-up menu.
16. Drag-select the faces behind the jaw and under the base of the skull. Press the Delete key. The head should now be taking shape as shown in Figure 6.36.

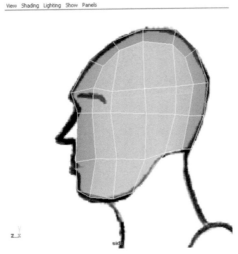

FIGURE 6.36　The faces behind the jaw and under the skull have been deleted.

17. In the Front view, drag-select the faces on the left half of the head and delete them as shown in Figure 6.37. You should now only have half of the face. You will model this half or mirror it when it is done.

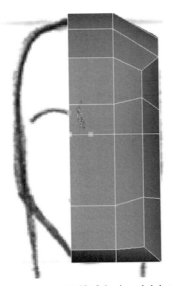

FIGURE 6.37　Half of the head deleted.

18. In the Front view, select Shading > X-Ray to make the head transparent.
19. With the head still selected and in Component mode, right-click over the head and select Vertex from the pop-up menu.
20. Press the W key to change to the Move tool. Select the vertices and reposition them to match the contour of the head on the front image plane as shown in Figure 6.38. Switch into the Perspective view as necessary to make sure the head is in form. At this point, moving vertices will no longer be sufficient to add any more of the needed detail. More polygonal faces will have to be added.

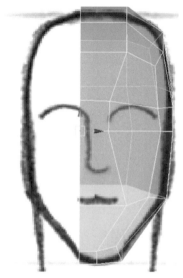

FIGURE 6.38   Vertices positioned from the front resembling the contour and details of the head.

21. Select Edit Mesh > Split Polygon Tool Options Box and set the values as shown in Figure 6.39.

- Divisions: 1
- Smoothing Angle: 0.00
- Split Only from Edges: Checked
- Use Snapping Points Along Edge: Checked
- Number of Points: 1
- Snapping Tolerance: 100

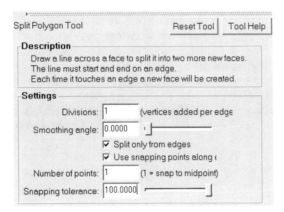

FIGURE 6.39   The Split Polygon Tool settings window.

22. With these settings, the Split Polygon tool will only create a point at an intersection of edges or at the midpoint of an edge. Use the Split Polygon tool to create more detail across the lower jaw, above and below the mouth level as shown in Figure 6.40. Reposition the vertices as needed to match the figure. Remember to continue the cuts across all the polygonal faces of the head so that the faces remain quadrangular.

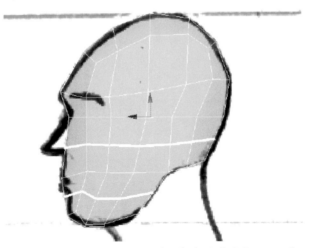

FIGURE 6.40   New edges created with the Split Polygon tool (highlighted) are placed above and below the mouth area.

23. In all the windows, deselect X-Ray shading by selecting Shading > X-Ray. This makes the head opaque.

You will now cut circular loops into the polygonal geometry to account for the accurate curvature in the skull structure. You will create good edge loops for the eye socket and mouth areas by using several tools and proceeding one step at a time.

To create more geometry for the nose area:

1. Select Edit Mesh > Split Polygon Tool Option Box.
2. Change the Number of Points to 8 as shown in Figure 6.41.

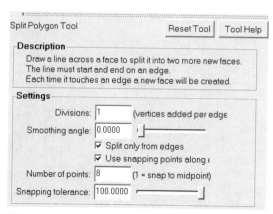

FIGURE 6.41 Updated Split Polygon Tool settings window.

3. Continue to use the Split Polygon tool to create more detail in the face area. Cut your way up the face to create a new line that will be the edge of the mouth and nose as shown in Figure 6.42. Use the Perspective view to make sure all of the cuts have created quads.

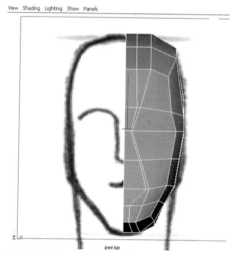

FIGURE 6.42 New edges cut for nose and mouth detail.

4. Right-click over the head and select Face from the pop-up menu.
5. Select the face over the eye area as shown in Figure 6.43.

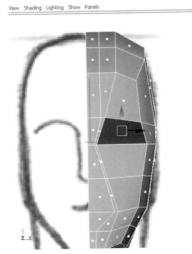

FIGURE 6.43   The eye socket face selected.

6. Select Edit Mesh > Extrude Options Box. Reset the settings and click Extrude.
7. With the face still selected, press the R key to switch to the Scale tool.
8. Scale the face inward to make the eye socket slightly more pronounced as shown in Figure 6.44.

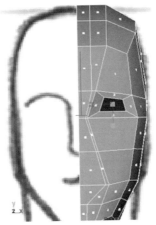

FIGURE 6.44   The eye socket's extruded, repositioned face.

9. Select Edit Mesh > Split Polygon Tool.
10. Cut new edges in the head geometry to give the eye a total of eight edges. Your resulting geometry should resemble that shown in Figure 6.45.

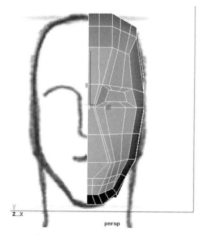

FIGURE 6.45   The eye socket's newly cut edges along the entire head.

The mouth geometry now needs to be created. You will cut irregular shapes around the mouth area and then delete edges to maintain quads.

1. Select Edit Mesh > Split Polygon Tool.
2. Cut two loops into the mouth area as shown in Figure 6.46.

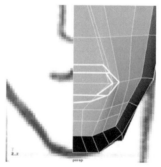

FIGURE 6.46   The mouth loop's newly cut edges.

3. This has created many triangles. You will now delete some edges to reestablish quads. Right-click over the head, and select Edge from the pop-up menu.
4. Hold down the Shift key and select the edges shown in Figure 6.47.

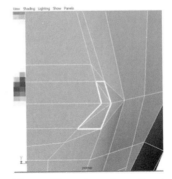

FIGURE 6.47   The selected mouth edges.

5. Select Edit Mesh > Delete Edge/Vertex. The selected edges should be deleted as shown in Figure 6.48.

FIGURE 6.48   The mouth with deleted edges.

6. There are still two nonquadrangular areas near the mouth. You will now fix these. Select Edit Mesh > Split Polygon Tool.
7. Cut two more edges into the mouth area as shown in Figure 6.49.

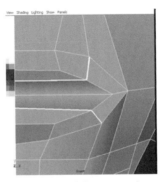

FIGURE 6.49   The mouth loop's newly cut edges.

You now need to add more detail in the eye socket by cutting around two more edge loops. After this is done, reposition the mouth and eye vertices until they resemble Figure 6.50.

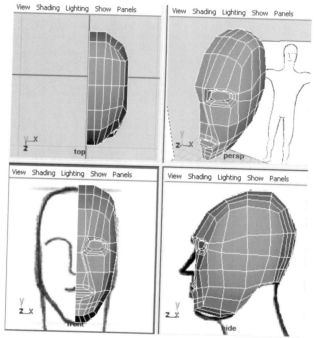

FIGURE 6.50   Updated head detail and repositioned vertices.

1. After you have finished positioning the vertices, right-click over the head and select Face from the pop-up menu.
2. Select the four faces inside the mouth (created earlier by edge loops), and press the Delete key. This creates the mouth opening.
3. Right-click over the head and select Vertex from the pop-up menu.
4. Select the vertices for the nose and upper brow area. Move them away from the face as shown in Figure 6.51.
5. At this point, you may add more details on the face if desired. When finished, save your work.

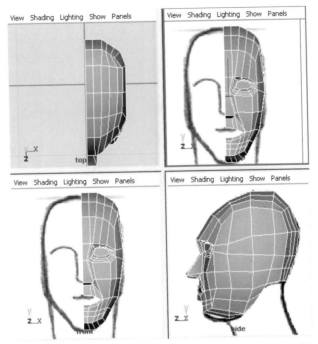

FIGURE 6.51   Finished facial detail for the Simple Guy model.

Modeling the Simple Guy Character: Creating the Body

Now with the face done, you will turn your attention to creating the body. To create the body, you will use similar techniques you used for the head. You will start the body with a cube and sculpt it to create the torso shape. First, however, you need to put the head in a new layer and template it to avoid accidental modification. Then do the following:

1. Select Create > Polygon Primitives and uncheck Interactive Creation.
2. Select Create > Polygon Primitives > Cube Options Box.
3. In the Polygon Cube Options window, set the following values as shown in Figure 6.52.

   - Width: 1.0
   - Height: 1.0
   - Depth: 1.0
   - Width divisions: 8
   - Height divisions: 8
   - Depth divisions: 4
   - Axis: Y
   - Texture: Check Create UVs and Normalize

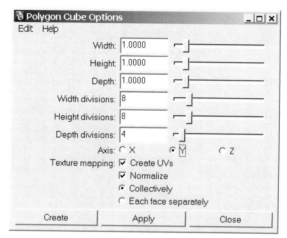

FIGURE 6.52 The Polygon Cube Options window with proper values.

4. Click the Create button. Maya creates the cube at the origin.
5. In the Channel Box or the Hypergraph window, change the name of the cube to body.
6. In the Channel Box, enter the following values as shown in Figure 6.53. This moves the body cube to the correct position and scales it to the correct dimensions.

- Translate X: 0
- Translate Y: 9.117
- Translate Z: −0.202
- Rotate X: 0
- Rotate Y: 0
- Rotate Z: 0
- Scale X: 2.271
- Scale Y: 4.145
- Scale Z: 1.844

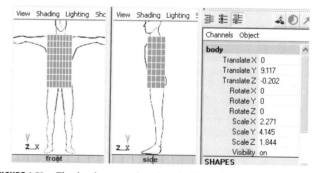

FIGURE 6.53 The body moved and scaled into the correct position.

7. In the Top view, right-click over the body and select Vertex from the pop-up menu.
8. Hold down the Shift key, and drag-select each of the vertices in all four corners as shown in Figure 6.54.

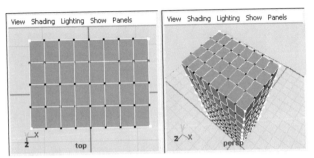

FIGURE 6.54   The body with corner vertices selected.

9. With the corner vertices still selected, press the R key to change to the Scale tool.
10. Scale the vertices inward along the X axis and Z axis to make the body slightly more curved as shown in Figure 6.55.

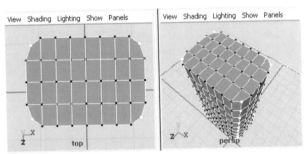

FIGURE 6.55   Body with corner vertices scaled in to round the edges.

11. Right-click over the body and select Face from the pop-up menu.
12. In the Front view, select and delete the faces on the left half of the body as shown in Figure 6.56.

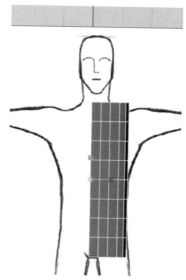

FIGURE 6.56   Half of the body remains.

13. Right-click the body and select Vertex from the pop-up menu.
14. In the Top view, drag-select the inner vertices of the body as shown in Figure 6.57.

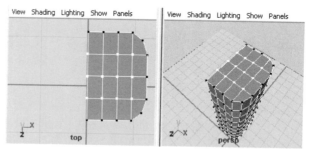

FIGURE 6.57   Top and Perspective views of the inner vertices selected.

15. In the Front view, scale the inner vertices along the Y axis. The top row should reach halfway up the neck and the bottom row distance will match the top's (see Figure 6.58).
16. In the Top view, select the three middle horizontal vertices as shown in Figure 6.59.

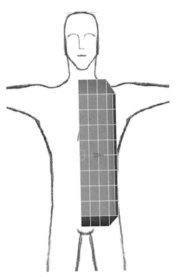

FIGURE 6.58   Inner vertices beginning to form the overall shape of the body.

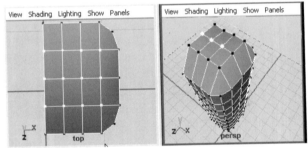

FIGURE 6.59   Top and Perspective views of the innermost selected vertices.

17. In the Front view, scale up the vertices so that they touch the jaw at the top. The bottom vertices will be scaled the same distance in the opposite direction as shown in Figure 6.60.

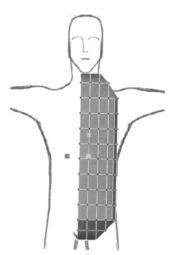

FIGURE 6.60   Vertices scaled up.

18. In the Side view, right-click over the body and select Face from the pop-up menu.

19. Select the faces that were the top of the cube (top two rows in the Front view). Press the Delete key. These faces will be filled in later with the neck's geometry. The body should now be taking shape as shown in Figure 6.61.

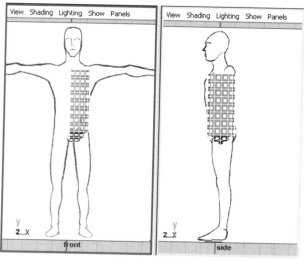

FIGURE 6.61   Front and Side views of the body.

20. In the Front view, select Shading > X-Ray.
21. In the Front view, right-click the body and select Vertex from the pop-up menu. Each horizontal line of vertices will be selected and manipulated. Select the top row and switch to the Scale tool. Press the D and X keys at the same time and snap the Scale tool to the Y axis. Scale and position each line of vertices to match the image plane. Make sure to keep the leftmost vertices aligned with the Y axis. The result should look like Figure 6.62.

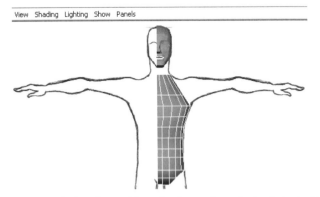

FIGURE 6.62   Edges scaled and repositioned to better form the body in the Front view.

22. The body's geometry does not extend to the shoulder area. The shoulder will be created separately. In the Side view, select Shading > X-Ray.
23. Repeat in the Side view. The result should look like Figure 6.63.

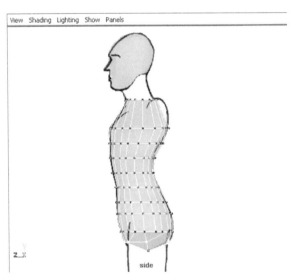

FIGURE 6.63   Edges repositioned to better form the body in the Side view.

24. Move the lower vertices of the body to round out the area where the leg will attach. Figure 6.64 shows the changes that will allow the leg to smoothly connect to the body.

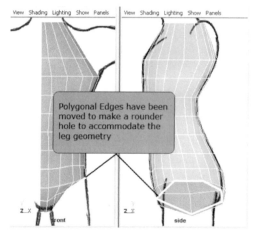

FIGURE 6.64   Vertices arranged so the leg will easily attach to the body.

25. In all windows, deselect X-ray shading by selecting Shading > X-Ray.
26. In the Side view, select faces inside the newly rounded area and press the Delete key. You have now made an open ring of edges as shown in Figure 6.65. Make sure there are 12 open edges in the body, to be connected with leg in next section.

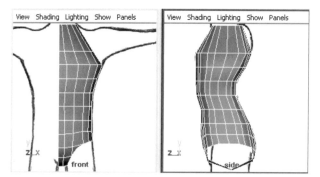

FIGURE 6.65   Front and Side views of the open ring where the leg will attach.

27. Save your work.

Modeling the Simple Guy Character: Creating the Leg

You will next create the leg geometry and connect it to the open polygonal edges on the body:

1. Select Create > Polygon Primitives > Cylinder Options Box.
2. In the Polygon Cylinder Options window, set the following values as shown in Figure 6.66. Notice that the number of axis divisions is 12 to match with the open edges of the body.

   - Radius: 0.5
   - Height: 10.00
   - Axis divisions: 12
   - Height divisions: 1
   - Caps divisions: 0
   - Axis: Y
   - Texture: Check Create UVs and Normalize

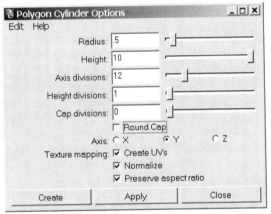

FIGURE 6.66   The Polygon Cylinder Options window with proper values entered.

3. Click the Create button.
4. In the Channel Box or the Hypergraph window, rename the cylinder leg.
5. In the Channel Box, enter the following values as shown in Figure 6.67. This moves the leg to the correct position and scales it to the correct dimensions.

   - Translate X: 1.198
   - Translate Y: 3.327
   - Translate Z: −0.647
   - Rotate X: 0
   - Rotate Y: 0
   - Rotate Z: 0

- Scale X: 1
- Scale Y: 0.586
- Scale Z: 1

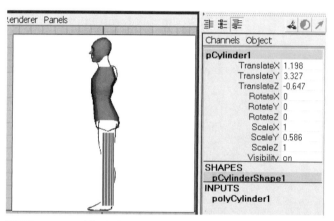

FIGURE 6.67   Modified Channel Box values for the repositioned leg.

6. Right-click over the leg and select Face from the pop-up menu.
7. In the Perspective view, select the top and bottom faces of the cylinder and press the Delete key. The cylinder should now be open at both ends. This will allow you to combine and append the leg to the body as well as to the foot after you model it.
8. Notice that the leg does not fit the shape described in either image plane. You will now move vertices to better approximate the leg's shape. In all windows, select Shading > X-Ray to make the leg transparent.
9. Right-click over the leg and select Vertex from the pop-up menu.
10. Select the leg's top row of vertices. In the Front and Side views, move and scale the vertices until they fit the upper thigh area and match the image planes.
11. Select the leg's bottom row of vertices. Press the E key to switch to the Rotate tool. In the Front and Side views, rotate and move the vertices until they fit the ankle area at the bottom of the leg.
12. When you are done moving the top and bottom row of vertices, the cylinder should look like Figure 6.68. Note the rotation of the lower vertices in the Front and Side views of the figure.

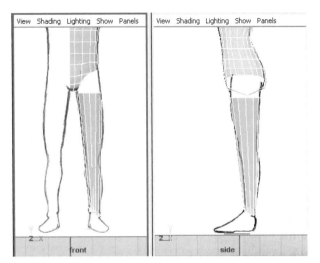

FIGURE 6.68   Front and Side views of the leg after its vertices have been repositioned.

Notice that with only a top and bottom row of vertices, it is impossible to form a curved, detailed leg. You will add more edges to help you create a leg similar to the one in the image planes. When modeling the face, you used the Split Polygon tool. For the leg, you will make cuts using the more efficient Cut Faces tool. This tool cuts many polygons in one step.

1. Select Edit Mesh > Cut Faces Tool.
2. If you click the leg with the Cut Faces tool, it will add new polygonal edges across the entire surface at once. Make sure no other object is selected because the Cut Faces tool will cut through all selected objects.
3. Make five cuts while holding down the Shift key: one just above the knee, one through the knee, one just below the knee, one just above the knee through the lower thigh, and one through the lower calf. The result should look like Figure 6.69.
4. In both the Front and Side views, select, reposition, and scale each horizontal line of vertices to more closely match the image planes. When you are done, the leg should look like Figure 6.70.

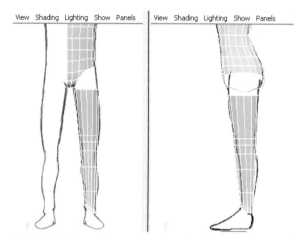

FIGURE 6.69   Leg with proper cuts using the Cut Faces tool.

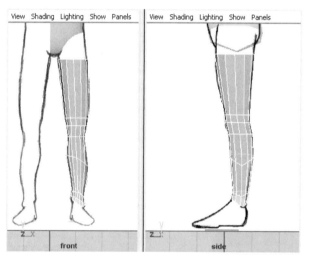

FIGURE 6.70   New vertices arranged to give the leg a more accurate shape.

5. In all windows, turn off X-ray shading.
6. Hold down the Shift key and select the body and the leg.
7. Select Mesh > Combine. The leg and body are not yet attached, but they are now one polygonal object.
8. Select Polygons > Append to Polygon Tool. The leg cylinder has 12 edges; the hole you cut in the body when you deleted the faces should also have 12 open edges.

9. Carefully select one edge on the leg and then the corresponding edge on the body. A polygonal face should be created connecting them. Repeat all the way around the leg and body. When you are done, the resulting surface should look like Figure 6.71.

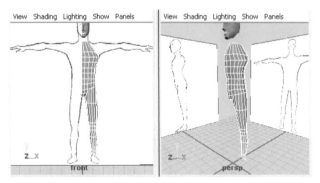

FIGURE 6.71   The body and leg now connected.

10. Save your work.

Modeling the Simple Guy Character: Creating the Foot

You will next model, combine, and append the foot:

1. In all windows, turn X-ray shading on.
2. Select Create > Polygon Primitives > Cube Options Box.
3. In the Polygon Cube Options window, set the following values as shown in Figure 6.72.

- Width: 1.0
- Height: 1.0
- Depth: 1.0
- Width divisions: 3
- Height divisions: 4
- Depth divisions: 4
- Axis: Y
- Texture: Check Create UVs and Normalize

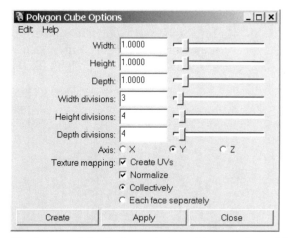

FIGURE 6.72   The Polygon Cube Options window with properly modified values.

4. Click the Create button. Maya creates the cube at the origin.
5. In the Channel Box or the Hypergraph window, rename the cube foot.
6. In the Channel Box, enter the following values as shown in Figure 6.73. This moves the foot to the correct position and scales it to the correct dimensions.

- Translate X: 1.143
- Translate Y: 0.371
- Translate Z: –0.525
- Rotate X: 0
- Rotate Y: 0
- Rotate Z: 0
- Scale X: 1
- Scale Y: 0.52
- Scale Z: 0.817

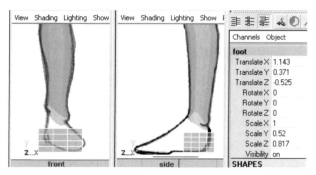

FIGURE 6.73   Foot in correct position.

7. In the Perspective view, select the back nine faces on the top and press the Delete key. This will open a hole where the foot will connect to the ankle.
8. In the Top view, round off the corners of the feet by scaling down the vertices.
9. In the Side view, move the vertices to fit the foot into the space shown in the image plane. When you are done, your foot should look like Figure 6.74. There should be 12 edges on the ankle to connect to the leg.

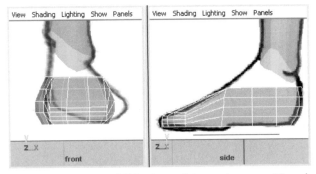

FIGURE 6.74   Front and Side views of the vertices repositioned.

10. Again, there is not enough polygonal geometry to finish modeling the foot. Cutting new faces is necessary again. To begin, select Edit Mesh > Cut Faces Tool.
11. Make two vertical cuts. One should be halfway between the front of the ankle and the toe area, and one should be halfway between the new cut and the toe area.
12. Move the points until they fit the image planes. The result should look like Figure 6.75.

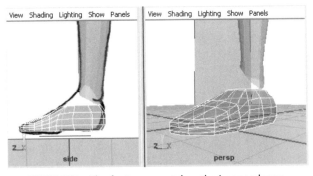

FIGURE 6.75   The foot now matches the image planes.

13. With the Shift key held down, select the body and the foot.
14. Select Mesh > Combine. The body and the foot are not yet attached, but they are now one polygonal object.
15. Select the 12 border edges on the foot and 12 corresponding border edges on the ankle.
16. Select Edit Mesh > Bridge Options Box. Set Divisions to 0. The Bridge tool creates polygons to bridge the gap between edges of equal number shown in Figure 6.76. In this case, the Bridge tool was used because it creates connecting geometry between more than one selected edge.

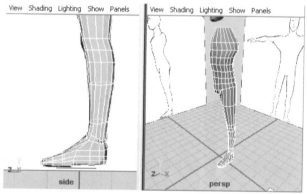

FIGURE 6.76   The body, leg, and foot are now connected.

17. Save your work.

Modeling the Simple Guy Character: Creating the Arm

The technique used to create the arm is similar to that for the leg. Here's how it's done:

1. In all views, turn off X-ray shading.
2. Select Create > Polygon Primitives > Cylinder > Options Box.
3. In the Polygon Cylinder Options window, set the following values as shown in Figure 6.77.

   - Radius: 0.5
   - Height: 5.00
   - Axis Divisions: 8
   - Height Divisions: 1
   - Subdivisions on Caps: 0
   - Axis: Y
   - Texture: Check Create UVs and Normalize

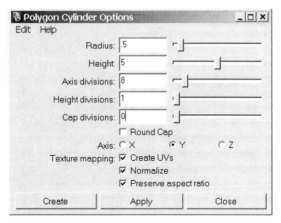

FIGURE 6.77   The Polygon Cylinder Options window with modified values.

4. Click Create.
5. In the Channel Box or the Hypergraph window, rename the cylinder arm.
6. In the Channel Box, enter the following values as shown in Figure 6.78.

  • Translate X: 4.238
  • Translate Y: 10.825
  • Translate Z: –0.519
  • Rotate X: 0
  • Rotate Y: 0
  • Rotate Z: 90
  • Scale X: 1
  • Scale Y: 1
  • Scale Z: 1

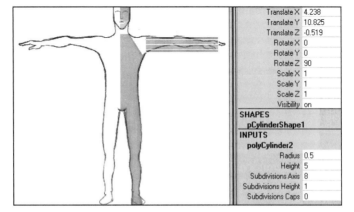

FIGURE 6.78   The arm in the correct position.

7. Select each row of the arm's vertices individually. Move and scale them in the Front view until they match the shape in the image plane.
8. Repeat in the Top view until you are satisfied with the arm's shape. When you are done, the arm should look like Figure 6.79.

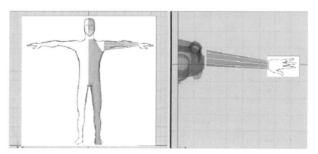

FIGURE 6.79 The arm's shape after the vertices have been repositioned.

9. Again, there is not enough polygonal geometry to finish modeling the arm. Cutting new faces will be necessary. To begin, select Edit Mesh > Cut Faces Tool.
10. Make four vertical cuts. One should be just to the left of the elbow area, one should be centered on the elbow area, and one should be just right of the elbow area. The fourth cut should be to the right of the elbow where the forearm has a slight bulge (you may want to make the last cut on a slight angle).
11. Move the vertices until they match the image planes. The result should look like Figure 6.80.

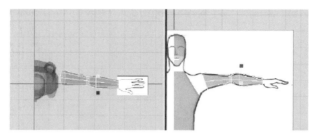

FIGURE 6.80 Newly created geometry positioned on model.

12. Select the arm's top and bottom caps (end faces) and press the Delete key. The arm should now be open near the shoulder and the wrist.
13. Select the body and the arm.
14. Select Mesh > Combine. The body and the arm are not yet attached, but they are now one polygonal object.
15. Attaching the arm is a little different from the leg because the neck area on the body does not exist. You will use a combination of techniques to connect the arm to the body. To begin, select and reposition

the vertices on the side of the body where the arm will be attached. When you are done, the side of the body should resemble Figure 6.81.

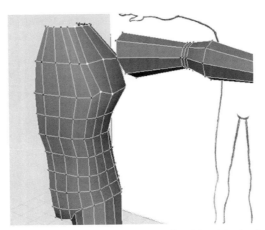

FIGURE 6.81   New vertices layout on the side of the body.

16. Select and delete the faces inside the newly positioned edges. You have now cut a hole for the arm to attach to.

17. Select Polygons > Append to Polygon Tool. The arm cylinder has eight open faces, and the body should have six open faces.

18. Carefully select one edge on the arm and then the corresponding edge on the body. A polygonal face should be created connecting them. Repeat all the way around the arm and body. When you are done, the resulting surface should look like Figure 6.82. Note that the top of the arm remains open because there was no geometry to append to.

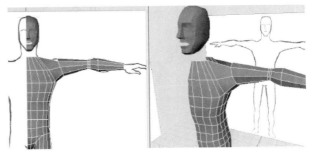

FIGURE 6.82   The body and arm are now connected except for the two faces on the top.

19. Make sure Keep Faces Together is checked by selecting Edit Mesh > Keep Faces Together.

20. Right-click the body and select Edge from the pop-up menu.
21. Hold down the Shift key and select the two open shoulder edges.
22. Select Edit Mesh > Extrude.
23. Pull the extruded edges toward the body until they are aligned with the rest of the arm. Your shoulder should now resemble Figure 6.83.

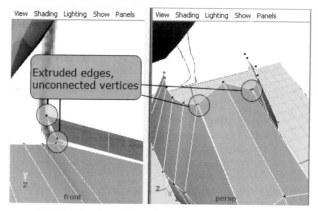

FIGURE 6.83   Extruded edges properly positioned.

24. Select the two unconnected vertices in the front of the body as shown in Figure 6.84.

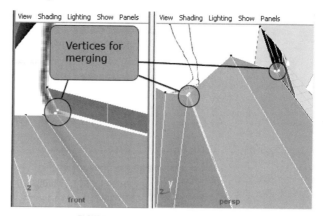

FIGURE 6.84   Vertices to be merged.

25. Select Edit Mesh > Merge Options Box.
26. Set the Distance to 1.0. Click the Apply button. The two vertices merge.
27. Repeat the process on the remaining unconnected vertices on the back of the body. Your character should now be taking shape and should resemble Figure 6.85.
28. Save your work.

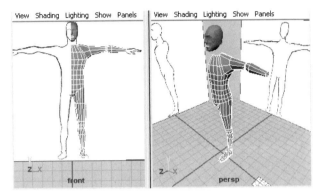

FIGURE 6.85   The body with leg and arm attached.
The head is still a separate piece of geometry.

Modeling the Simple Guy Character: Creating the Hand

You will next model, combine, and append the hand.

Hands are difficult, and fingers need a certain amount of geometry. The hands typically have more polygons than can easily attach to the arm. You will prepare the hand while taking this into account. You will create a hand that has most of its polygonal faces at the fingers. You will create looping polygonal edges to trap that geometry at the fingers so that the body of the hand can be light enough to easily attach to the arm geometry.

1. Select Create > Polygon Primitives > Cube > Options Box.
2. In the Polygon Cube Options window, set the following values as shown in Figure 6.86.

  - Width: 1.0
  - Height: 1.0
  - Depth: 1.0
  - Width divisions: 2
  - Height divisions: 2
  - Depth divisions: 2
  - Axis: Y
  - Texture: Check Create UVs and Normalize

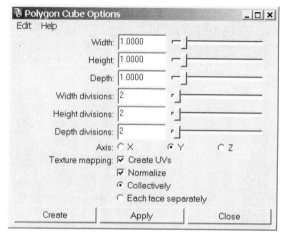

FIGURE 6.86   The Polygon Cube Options window with modified values.

3. Click the Create button. Maya creates the cube at the origin.
4. In the Channel Box or the Hypergraph window, rename the cube finger.
5. In the Channel Box, enter the following values as shown in Figure 6.87. This moves the finger to the correct position and scales it to the correct dimensions.

- Translate X: 6.687
- Translate Y: 10.872
- Translate Z: 0.146
- Rotate X: 0
- Rotate Y: 0
- Rotate Z: 0
- Scale X: 0.49
- Scale Y: 0.09
- Scale Z: 0.168

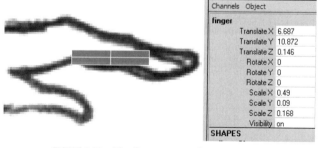

FIGURE 6.87   The finger properly positioned.

6. In the Side view, with the Shift key held down, select and slightly scale the four corners inward. This will help round the finger.

7. In the Front view, select and move the vertices until you have approximated the shape of the finger on the image plane.

8. Repeat this last step in the Top view until you have approximated the shape of the finger on the image plane. Your finger should now look like Figure 6.88.

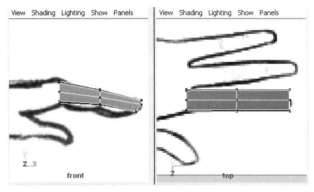

FIGURE 6.88   Finger positioned with adjusted vertices.

9. In all views, select Shading > X-Ray.

10. The finger does not completely match the image plane. Because there is not enough geometry to make the shape, you must cut faces to add geometry to the finger. To begin, make five vertical cuts at the finger joints. Your finger should look like Figure 6.89. The vertical cuts will create more geometric detail where the finger bends. This helps the finger geometry to deform properly when the finger is animated.

FIGURE 6.89   Finger geometry cut at joints.

11. In the Front view, move the vertices until the finger's shape matches the image plane. When you are done, the finger should look like Figure 6.90.

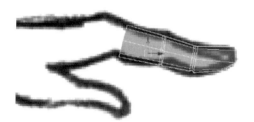

FIGURE 6.90   Finger vertices properly arranged.

12. Press the F8 key to go into Object mode.
13. Press the Insert key to see to the finger's pivot point.
14. Move the pivot point to the base of the finger, as shown in Figure 6.91.

FIGURE 6.91   The finger's pivot point repositioned to the bottom of the finger.

15. Press the Insert key to lock the finger's pivot point in its new position.
16. Select the faces on the bottom end of the finger and press the Delete key. This will open the bottom of the finger and allow you to append the finger to other fingers after you create them.
17. In the Top view, select Edit > Duplicate.
18. Move the duplicated finger into the correct position for the next finger.
19. Rotate and scale the finger to make its shape match the image plane.
20. Repeat these steps for the third finger. When you are finished, the three fingers should look like Figure 6.92.

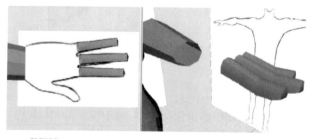

FIGURE 6.92   Fingers properly positioned and scaled.

21. Hold down the Shift key and select all three fingers.
22. Select Mesh > Combine. The fingers are not yet attached, but they are now one polygonal object. Name this object hand.
23. Select Edit Mesh > Append to Polygon Tool.
24. Carefully select one edge of the open finger and then the corresponding edge on the next finger. A polygonal face should be created that connects them. Repeat for all three fingers. When you are done, the resulting surface should look like Figure 6.93.

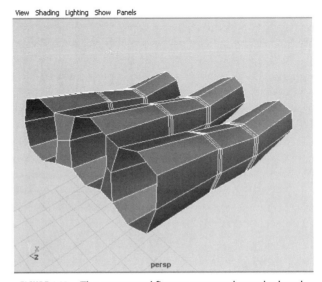

FIGURE 6.93   The connected fingers start to shape the hand.

You are now ready to create the rest of the hand. There are 20 open edges that will need to ultimately connect to the eight open edges on the arm.

1. Right-click the hand and select Edge from the pop-up menu.
2. Hold down the Shift key and select the open edges along the rim of the hand as shown in Figure 6.94.
3. Select Edit Mesh > Extrude.
4. In the Top view, pull the new geometry away from the fingers so that your hand now resembles Figure 6.95.

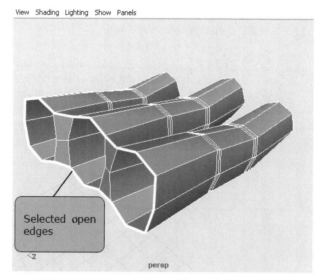

FIGURE 6.94 Selected edges of fingers to be extruded.

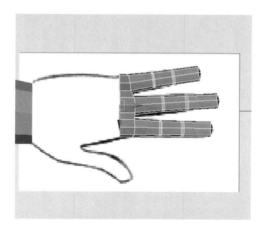

FIGURE 6.95 Properly extruded finger edges.

5. The problem here is that you just created a new layer that is also 20 edges around. You will now reduce this number. To begin, select Edit Mesh > Split Polygon Tool.
6. In the Top view, start with the area just left of the middle finger and cut two triangles (ignore the spaces between the fingers).
7. Make the same two cuts behind the other two fingers so that they resemble Figure 6.96.

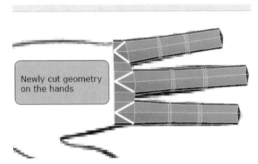

FIGURE 6.96   Triangle cuts on top of hand.

8. Repeat these cuts on the bottom of the hand as well.
9. In the Front view, cut two more triangles on the side of the hand so that the hand resembles Figure 6.97. These triangles will help to deform the knuckles when the hand is animated. They also can combine the edge loops on the hand.

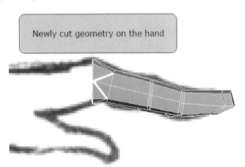

FIGURE 6.97   Triangle cuts on side of hand.

10. Make the same cuts on the other side of the hand.
11. Earlier in this tutorial, it was stated that quads are preferred in Maya. You will now delete edges to once again change triangles into quads.
12. Right-click the hand and select Edge from the pop-up menu.
13. Hold down the Shift key and select all of the straight edges in this newly extruded row of faces. Do not select the diagonal edges.
14. Holding the Shift key, right-click and select Delete Edge. The selected edges should be deleted, and you should be left with eight open edges that resemble Figure 6.98.
15. In the Front view, there are still two triangles as shown in Figure 6.99. You will overcome this by splitting edges. To begin, select Edit Mesh > Split Polygon Tool.

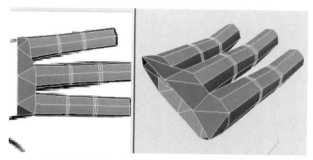

FIGURE 6.98   Hand with most triangles removed.

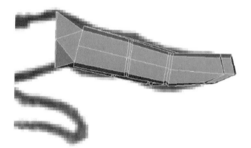

FIGURE 6.99   Location of remaining triangles on hand.

16. Split horizontally between the triangles.
17. Right-click over the hand and select Edge from the pop-up menu.
18. Hold down the Shift key and select the triangular edges.
19. Holding the Shift key, right-click and select Delete Edge. The selected edges should be deleted. You should be left with two quads that resemble Figure 6.100.

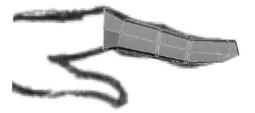

FIGURE 6.100   Hand geometry with no triangles.

20. Repeat these steps on the other side of the hand. You now have eight open edges ready to attach to the arm.
21. Hold down the Shift key and select the hand and the body.

22. Select Mesh > Combine. The hand and body are not yet attached, but they are now one polygonal object.
23. Select Edit Mesh > Append to Polygon Tool.
24. Carefully select one edge on the hand and then the corresponding edge on the arm. A polygonal face should be created connecting them. Repeat all the way around the hand and arm. When you are done, the resulting surface should look like Figure 6.101.

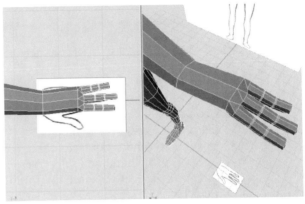

FIGURE 6.101   The body and hand are now connected.

25. In the Top view, select and move the vertices on the wrist to better match the image plane in the top and/or front. The hand does not perfectly match, and there is no thumb. You will fix this with the Cut Faces tool.
26. Select Edit Mesh > Cut Faces Tool.
27. In the Top view, make three straight cuts so that the hand resembles Figure 6.102.

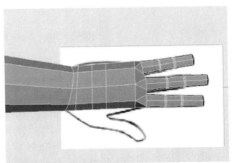

FIGURE 6.102   New cuts in the hand.

28. Select and reposition the vertices so that the hand now resembles Figure 6.103.

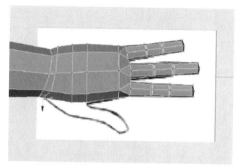

FIGURE 6.103   Newly cut edges positioned in the hand.

29. Select the faces on the side of the hand where the thumb should be.
30. Select Edit Mesh > Extrude.
31. Move the new faces out to cover about half of the thumb's base.
32. Select Edit Mesh > Extrude.
33. Move the second set of faces out to cover the rest of the thumb's base.
34. Right-click the hand and select Vertex from the pop-up menu.
35. Move the vertices to refine the thumb's shape until it resembles Figure 6.104.

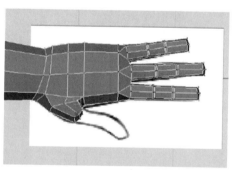

FIGURE 6.104   Newly extruded thumb base.

36. Right-click the hand and select Face from the pop-up menu. Select the faces in front of the thumb base.
37. Select Edit Mesh > Extrude.
38. Move the new geometry out. Rotate and scale it until it matches the next section of the thumb on the image plane.
39. Repeat these steps until you have finished the thumb shape.
40. Right-click the hand and select Vertex from the pop-up menu.
41. Select and continue to move the vertices until you are satisfied with the thumb shape. You will need to add three cut lines for the thumb joint using the Cut Faces command like before. At that point, the thumb should resemble Figure 6.105.
42. Save your work.

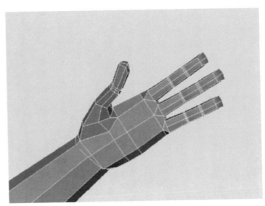

FIGURE 6.105   Finished hand with thumb.

Modeling the Simple Guy Character: Combining the Head with the Body

Now that you have the body and the head sculptured, you have to attach them. My decision to attach the head and body at the end of the modeling process relates to modeling strategy and preference.

1. The body should have 12 open edges in the shoulder and neck area. If the cuts you've made have resulted in a head that has fewer than 12 open edges, you should cut more faces into the head until it has 12 open edges.
2. Select Edit Mesh > Cut Faces Tool.
3. Split faces from the top of the head down to the opening beneath the jaw as shown in Figure 6.106. The head's open edges now match the body's open edges.
4. Hold down the Shift key and select the body and the head.
5. Select Mesh > Combine. The head and body are not yet attached, but they are now one polygonal object.
6. Select Edit mesh > Append to Polygon Tool.
7. Carefully select one edge on the head and then the corresponding edge on the body. A polygonal face should be created connecting them. Repeat all the way around the head and body. When you are done, the resulting surface should look like Figure 6.107.

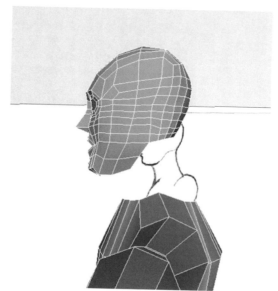

FIGURE 6.106 Head with the same number of faces as the open body.

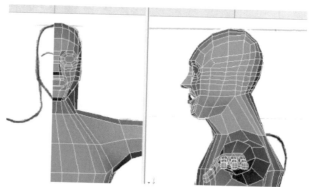

FIGURE 6.107 The head is now connected to the body, but the neck needs refinement.

8. Select Edit Mesh > Cut Faces Tool.
9. Make two horizontal cuts through the neck.
10. Select the vertices on the neck. Move and scale them to better match the neck shape in the image planes. The neck should now look like Figure 6.108.
11. Save your work.

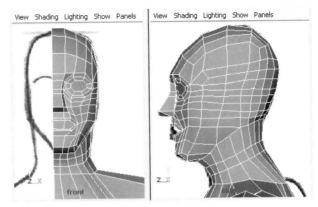

FIGURE 6.108   The refined neck.

You will next duplicate the model and combine it into a whole character.

1. Select the polygon character.
2. Press the F8 key to go into Component mode. Make sure the leftmost line of vertices is on the Y axis.
3. Press the F8 key to go into Object mode.
4. Select Edit > Duplicate Special Options Box.
5. In the Duplicate Special Options window, set the scale X value to –1 as shown in Figure 6.109.

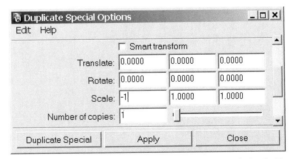

FIGURE 6.109   The Duplicate Special Options window with Scale X set to –1.

6. Click the Duplicate Special button. The duplicate of the model should now be on the other side of the Y axis as shown in Figure 6.110.

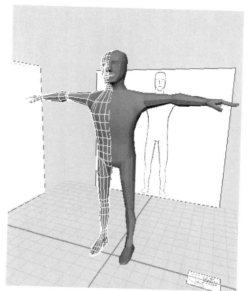

FIGURE 6.110   The body successfully mirrored.

7. Hold down the Shift key and select both sides.
8. Select Mesh > Combine. The bodies are not yet attached, but they are now one polygonal object.
9. Press the F8 key to go into Component mode. Drag-select the vertices along the Y axis.
10. Select Edit Mesh > Merge Options Box.
11. Select Edit > Reset Settings. Click the Apply button. The vertices should merge. The Simple Guy character is now a complete model as shown in Figure 6.111.
12. Select the model.
13. Select Edit > Delete by Type > History. This clears the model of all of the history created in the tutorial.
14. Select Mesh > Smooth. The completed model will now become smooth as shown in Figure 6.112. It should be noted that the eye socket was never actually quadrangular. Once you smooth the polygonal mesh, its faces will convert to quads.
15. Save your work.

View Shading Lighting Show Panels

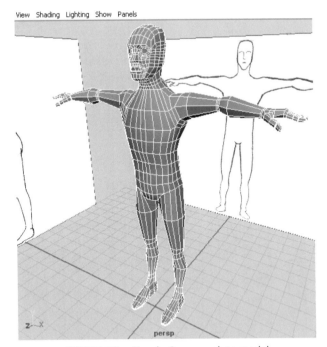

FIGURE 6.111   Simple Guy complete model.

View Shading Lighting Show Panels

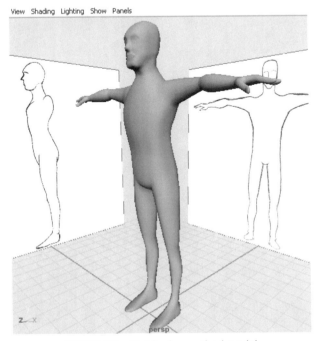

FIGURE 6.112   Finished smoothed model.

SUMMARY

In this chapter, you learned the importance of anatomy for models and body proportions. You also learned how to model a biped by sculpting and connecting polygonal primitives. In the next chapter, you will rig a biped.

CHALLENGE ASSIGNMENT

Create and Model a Character

Create and model your own character based on the Simple Guy. Base the character on either yourself or someone you know.

RIGGING A BIPED CHARACTER

In This Chapter

- The Skeleton
- Creating and Rigging an Advanced Spine

THE SKELETON

ON THE CD

There are many different ways to rig a biped, ranging from relatively simple to very complex. This chapter describes some basic anatomical principles important to biped rigging and then introduces a few key technical topics. The bulk of the chapter is a very detailed tutorial.

For clarity, the rigging described in this lesson is relatively basic. However, this kind of rigging is sufficient for many animations. On the accompanying CD-ROM, a more advanced rig is provided with the Henry character. This is described near the end of this chapter in a section on advanced rigging.

Maya Full Body IK

ON THE CD

Recent versions of Maya include a built-in rigging system known as *full body IK* (FBIK). The advantage to this system is that it provides a pretty solid rig very quickly and interoperates efficiently with an external product called MotionBuilder (which can be particularly useful for real-time game engine animation). For instructional purposes, however, this text describes the full conventional rigging process and provides several rigs on the attached CD-ROM.

There are several reasons for this approach. First, no automated rigging system can cover the full range of characters and situations you are likely to encounter. Second, understanding the basic principles involved in rigging is essential for fixing problems that inevitably occur. Finally, rigging style is often a matter of personal preference, and what feels right to one animator may not work for another. By learning the full range of options, you will be able to use existing rigs and alter them to suit your needs.

Joint Placement

Although the flour sack rigged in Chapter 4 was relatively forgiving about joint placement, more naturalistic human models are not. Correct placement is not only critical to anatomically expected behavior but can help you avoid a tremendous amount of drudgery in painting skin weights (as described in Chapter 4 under "Smooth Bind Challenges")

In the real world, bodies are built on top of skeletons and not vice versa. Most sculptors also work in this order, first creating an armature and then shaping clay, stone, or metal around it. However, modelers and riggers normally create geometry first and then fit a skeleton within it. This is particularly hard in simple geometric models where muscle masses are not apparent or with clothed models. In theory, it would be helpful to obtain a 3D model of an actual human skeleton, scale and place that

within the 3D skin, and then position Maya joints at the appropriate locations. However, in practice, a series of joint-specific rules of thumb provides a good starting point with significantly less effort. The following list
explains the rule of thumb for each listed body part.

- **Pelvis.** The pelvis or root joint should be placed at hip level, a little bit
  toward the back of the body, as shown in Figure 7.1 The two top
  joints of the legs should be placed approximately one-third of the distance between the bottom and top of the pelvis. The pelvis joint and
  the two top legs joints should create a triangle seen in the Front view
  as shown in Figure 7.2. However, these joints should not be "copla-
  nar"—the pelvis joint sits behind the legs.

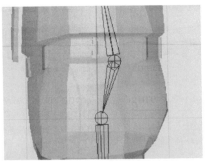

FIGURE 7.1   Pelvis joint seen from the Side view, positioned toward the back of the body.

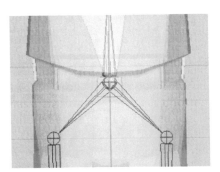

FIGURE 7.2   Pelvis joint and the two top leg joints
seen from the Front view, creating a triangle.

- **Spine.** The spine is shaped like a gently inverted letter Y, which follows the curvature of the back. The bones of the spine should be oriented up toward the head. The spine starts at the pelvis, aiming
  slightly toward the belly, and then changes orientation, pointing toward the back base of the neck. At the base of the neck, it reverses
  orientation again, curving slightly forward (see Figure 7.3).

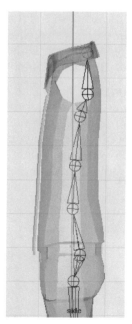

FIGURE 7.3   Curvature of the spine seen in Side view.

- **Shoulder joints.** The shoulder joints should not be vertically cen-tered within the arms. They should be placed closer to the top of the shoulder to get appropriate skin deformation behavior as shown in Figure 7.4. From front to back, the shoulder joints are centered as shown in the Top view in Figure 7.5.

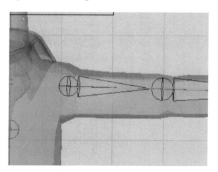

FIGURE 7.4   Front view of shoulder and elbow joint placement.

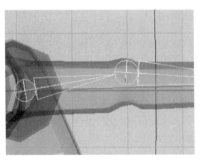

FIGURE 7.5   Top view of shoulder and elbow joint placement.

- **Elbows.** This asymmetrical joint positioning also holds true for the elbow. The elbow joint should be placed close to the back of the elbow geometry, as shown in Figure 7.6.

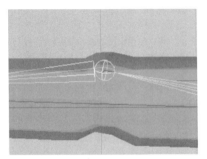

FIGURE 7.6   Top view of elbow joint placement.

- **Knees.** The knee joint is positioned in the front portion of the leg geometry as shown in Figure 7.7. In anatomically correct models, note that the center of rotation should be slightly above the kneecap.

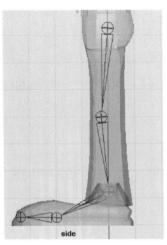

FIGURE 7.7   Knee joint seen from the Side view.

Driven Keys

The use of driven keys allows you to establish relationships between parts of your rig beyond those possible with hierarchies, constraints, or IK systems. For instance, using normal Maya keyframes will let you change an object's attribute values over time. You might keyframe the translation of a foot controller over two different points in time. Driven keys, however, are special keys that establish a relationship among several different objects' attribute values at that same point in time. For example, you might establish a set driven key relationship between a master controller object and your foot control. In this setup, one object's attributes will affect another's simultaneously. For a small translation in X of your controller object, you might want a larger translation in Y of the foot. To do this, you would set controller object X's translation channel as a driver and set the Y translation of the foot as the driven object. You would then set a series of keys to define the relationship between them.

In general, set driven keys are useful when you want the transformation of one object to drive that of another but where the distance or direction traveled by the two objects varies. (If the distance or direction were the same, you might just use a constraint.) For example, when the arm of a biped moves forward, the shoulder often rotates forward slightly around the clavicle. To establish such a relationship in your rig, you would create a set driven key between the arm and the shoulder rotations.

It is also often useful to create new attributes on existing objects and to create set driven key relationships based on them. You might add a toe curl attribute to your foot controller with values ranging from 0 to 10. You could then use this new custom attribute to drive toe joint rotations.

To understand how to add an attribute to an object and set driven keys, you will do a simple exercise. You will add an attribute to a locator object and then establish a driven key relationship between that attribute and the rotation of a simple joint.

Add an Attribute to an Object

To add an attribute to an object, follow these steps:

1. Create a new scene.
2. Create a locator and translate it 3 units in Y and −1 in Z.
3. Select the Joint tool.
4. In the Side view, create four joints to the right of the locator and approximately at the middle of the grid as shown in Figure 7.8.

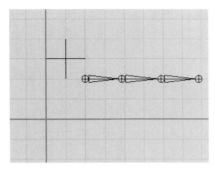

FIGURE 7.8   A locator and four joints.

5. Select the locator.
6. Select Modify > Add Attribute.
7. In the Add Attribute options window check Override Nice Name and choose the following attributes (see Figure 7.9):

- Attribute Long Name: Attribute to Move locator Up and Down.
- Nice Name: Move
- Data Type: Float
- Numeric Attribute Properties: Minimum: 1
- Maximum: 10
- Default: 1

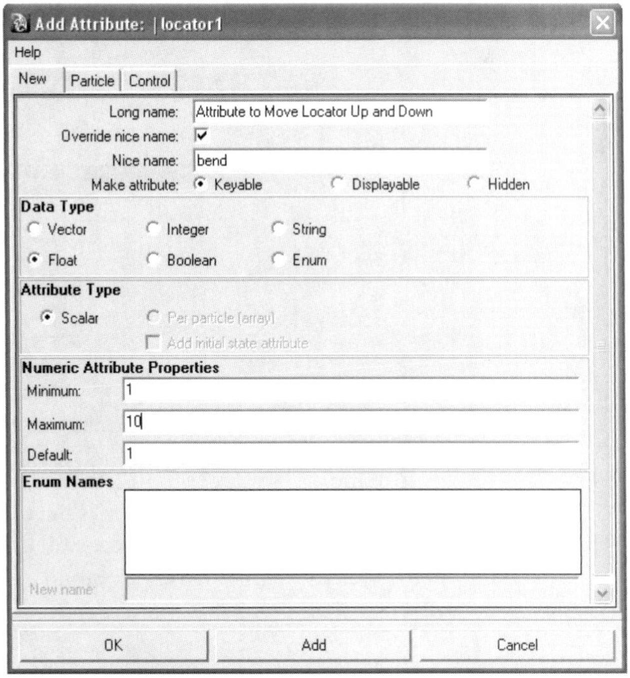

FIGURE 7.9   The Add Attribute window.

8. Click the OK button. You should see the new attribute in the Channel Box. Notice that only the Nice Name appears in locator channels.

Setting Driven Keys

To set driven keys:

1. Make sure you are in Animation mode.
2. Select Animate > Set Driven Key > Set Option Box as shown in Figure 7.10.

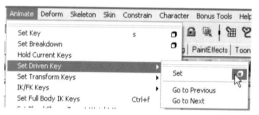

FIGURE 7.10   Set Driven Key menu.

3. Select the locator and, in the Set Driven Key window, select Load > Selected as Driver. You should see the locator1 transform channels in the right side of the window.
4. Click the bend parameter. A blue selection marker highlights it, indicating that it is selected as driver (see Figure 7.11).

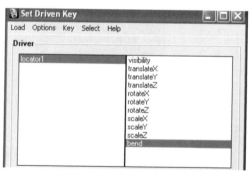

FIGURE 7.11   The bend attribute selected in the Set Driven Key window.

5. In the Side view, select joint2 and joint3.
6. In the Set Driven Key window, select Load > Selected as Driven.
7. In the Set Driven Key window, click joint2 and joint3. You should see the joints' transform and visibility channels in the right side of the window.

8. Click rotateZ. A blue selection marker appears on rotateZ, indicating that it is selected as driven (see Figure 7.12).

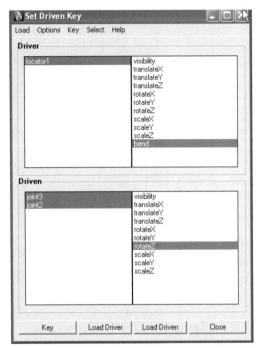

FIGURE 7.12   The joint2 and joint3 rotateZ channel selected in the Set Driven Key window.

9. At this point, the locator1 bend attribute should have a value of 1 and joint2 and joint3 should have a Rotate Z value of 0. Click the Key button in the Set Driven Key window to set the first driven key. Note that to set a driven key, the locator and the joints do not have to be selected in the Maya views. They can be selected in the Set Driven Key window only.

10. Select locator1 and change the bend value to 10 in the Channel Box. This is the maximum value of the bend attribute.

11. Select joint2 and rotate it –90 in Z.

12. Select joint3 and rotate it –90 in Z. You should have the two joints rotated as shown in Figure 7.13.

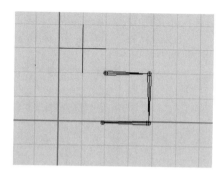

FIGURE 7.13   Joint2 and joint3 rotated –90 in Z.

13. Click the Key button in the Set Driven Key window to set the second driven key.
14. In the Channel Box, change the bend value to 5.5. The joints should be rotated –45 degrees on Z.

Alternatively, with the bend attribute selected, you can position the mouse cursor on the Side view. With the middle mouse button pressed, drag the mouse to the left and right to see the value changing and the joints rotating.

The Connection Editor

The *Connection Editor* is another feature available in Maya to create a relationship between two objects' attributes. You can connect the output of an object's attribute to the inputs of another object's attribute, and they will have a one-to-one transformation relationship. Character rigging has many node connections, which makes the Connection Editor a powerful tool.

Working with the Connection Editor

The best way to understand the Connection Editor is with a simple, if unrealistic, illustration. For example, let's connect the X translation attribute of a cone to that of a sphere:

1. Press Ctrl+N to create a new scene.
2. Select Create > NURBS Primitives > Sphere. Make sure Interactive Creation is not checked.
3. In the Channel Box, enter the value 5 in the Translate X channel.
4. Select Create > NURBS Primitives > Cone. Leave it at the origin.
5. Select Window > General Editors > Connection Editor, as shown in Figure 7.14. The Connection Attribute Editor opens as shown in Figure 7.15.

FIGURE 7.14   The Connection Editor command under the Window menu.

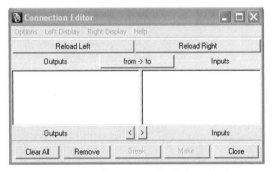

FIGURE 7.15   The Connection Editor window.

6. Select the sphere, and click the Reload Left button in the Connection Editor.
7. Select Translate Z in the Outputs window as shown in Figure 7.16.

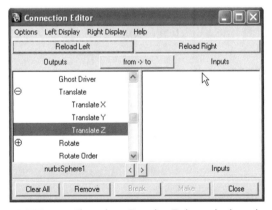

FIGURE 7.16   The sphere TranslateZ channel selected.

8. Select the cone and click the Reload Right button in the Connection Editor.
9. Select TranslateZ in the Inputs window as shown in Figure 7.17.

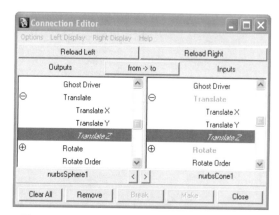

FIGURE 7.17   The cone TranslateZ channel selected in the Connection Editor.

10. Select the sphere and enter the value 10 for the Translate Z channel in the Channel Box. Notice that the cone also translated 10 units in Z.

Although connecting translations is something that could be done several other ways in Maya, keep in mind that pretty much any channel in Maya can be connected to any other. The only restriction is that the channels be of the same type (a color to a color, an integer to an integer, and so on).

TUTORIAL 7.1: CREATING A BIPED SKELETON

Chapter 4 introduced a few rigging concepts and tools. Although the sack is a much simpler character, the same rigging concepts apply to rigging a biped (see Figure 7.18). In this tutorial, you will learn some additional complementary methods, such as using set driven keys, isolating the hips and head from the upper body, and making a reverse foot. Isolating the hips and the head helps you pose the character properly because the hips and the head can rotate independently from the rest of the body. The reverse foot helps eliminate inadvertent slipping or sliding of the feet on the ground.

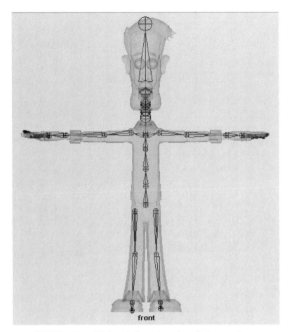

FIGURE 7.18   A biped showing the skeleton rig.

Lower Body

In the rigging of the lower body of the sack in Chapter 4, a very simple and straightforward approach was used: a single IK chain. However, in a biped character that will be shown walking or running, the animator has to do many foot plants (making sure the foot hits the ground solidly). To make this process as easy as possible for the animator, a bit more upfront rigging work is required. As noted previously, you will be implementing a reverse foot. Also, in this rig, a rotation plane (RP) IK solver is used to allow better control of the position of the knees.

Creating the Legs

To create the legs of a biped skeleton:

ON THE CD

1. Open a file called Henry.mb in the MayaWorkingFiles subfolder from the chapter7 folder on the CD-ROM.
2. Template all the layers so you don't accidentally select the geometry components when creating the skeleton.
3. In the Side view, create a joint hierarchy for the left leg. First, place a joint on top of the leg, and then on the knee, ankle, foot ball, and toe as shown in Figure 7.19.

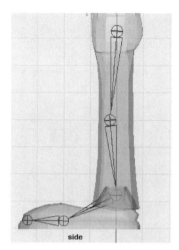

FIGURE 7.19 Leg skeleton.

4. Name the joints LtTop, LtKnee, LtAnkle, LtBall, and LtToe.
5. In the Front view, move the joint hierarchy to the middle of the left leg geometry. Make sure the bones are inside the geometry in all views.
6. Select the first joint of the hierarchy and mirror it to create the right leg (see Figure 7.20).

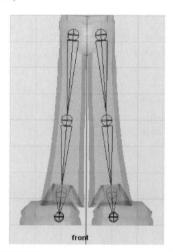

FIGURE 7.20 The leg skeleton mirrored.

7. Name the joints of the right leg RtTop, RtKnee, RtAnkle, RtBall, and RtToe.

Creating the IK Handle for the Legs

To create the RP IK handle for the legs:

1. Select the IK Handle tool and make sure the Current Solver is set to ikRPsolver.
2. First, click the top joint of the left leg to place the IK handle root and then click the ankle joint to place the end effector (see Figure 7.21).

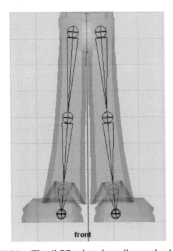

FIGURE 7.21   The ikRPsolver handle on the left leg.

3. Move the IK handle up and down to make sure the knee is bending correctly.
4. Undo the action and make sure the IK handle is back to the original position.
5. Repeat the steps to create the right leg IK handle.
6. Name the IK handles LtLegIK and RtLegIK.

Adding a Pole Vector Constraint for the Knees

The pole vector constraint will help you to control the knee joint position. To add a pole vector constraint for the knees:

ON THE CD

1. Import a file called PVCcontrol.mb from the chapter7, Rigging_Controls folder on the CD-ROM.
2. In the Front view, move and snap PVCcontrol to the LtKnee joint.
3. In the Channel Box, enter the value 0.3 for the Scale X, Y, and Z settings.
4. In the Side view, move PVCcontrol 4 grid units in front of the left knee joint, as shown in Figure 7.22.

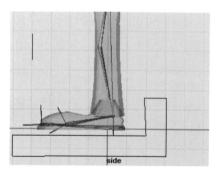

FIGURE 7.22 PVCcontrol in front of the left knee.

5. Freeze the PVCcontrol transformations.
6. Name the PVCcontrol PVCleftKnee.
7. Duplicate the PVC once.
8. Call the duplicate PVCrightKnee.
9. In the Front view, move and snap PVCrightKnee to the right knee joint.
10. In the Side view, move PVCrightKnee 4 units in front of the right knee joint.
11. Freeze the PVCrightKnee transformations.
12. Click PVCleftKnee to select it and then click LtLegIK.
13. Select Constrain > Pole Vector.
14. Click PVCrightKnee to select it first and then click RtLegIK.
15. Select Constrain > Pole Vector.
16. Select LtLegIK. You should see a line constraining the IK handle RP vector root to PVCleftKnee.
17. Repeat the step to see the PVCrightKnee constrain as shown in Figure 7.23.

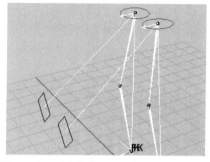

FIGURE 7.23 Left and right knees pole vector constrain lines.

Creating the IK Handles for the Foot

Foot IK handles will be used to connect the foot joints to the reverse foot joints. To create an ikSCsolver IK handle for the ball of the left foot:

1. Select the IK Handle tool and click first on the left ankle joint and second on the left foot ball.
2. Name the IK handle LtBallIK.
3. Now create an ikSCsolver IK handle for the left toe. Select the IK Handle tool and click first on the left foot ball and second on the left toe.
4. Name the IK handle LtToeIK.

Creating the Reverse Foot

The reverse foot helps to stop the foot sliding on the ground when animated. To create a four-joint hierarchy for the left reverse foot:

1. Create the first joint of the reverse foot in the lower back of the foot, the second joint close to the toe joint, the third joint close to the ball joint, and the fourth close to the ankle joint (see Figure 7.24).

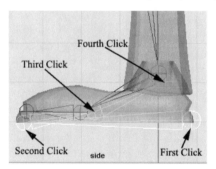

FIGURE 7.24   Four clicks to create four joints of the reverse foot.

2. Call the first joint of the hierarchy LtRfoot, the second joint LtRtoe, the third joint LtRball, and the fourth joint LtRankle.
3. Snap the LtRtoe joint to LtToe, LtRball to LtBall, and LtRankle to the LtAnkle (see Figure 7.25). To snap the joints, hold down the V key while moving them.

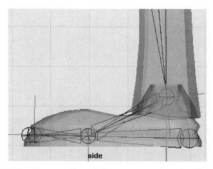

FIGURE 7.25   Reverse foot joints snapped to the foot joints.

4. Next, parent the left foot IK handles to the left reverse foot joints. To begin, click LtlegIK and then click LtRankle and press P.
5. Click LtBallIK and then click LtRball and press P.
6. Click LtToeIK and then click LtRtoe and press P.
7. Select LtRfoot and move it up and down to test the connections. All of the leg joints should move with it.
8. Repeat the same steps to create the right reverse foot.

Creating the Foot Control

To create the foot control:

1. Select the CV Curve Tool Option Box and select Curve Degree 1 Linear in the options window.
2. Draw a figure as shown in Figure 7.26.

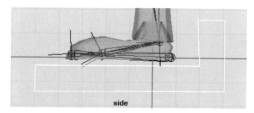

FIGURE 7.26   Foot control created with the CV Curve tool.

3. In the Front view, place the control under the left foot and freeze its transformations.
4. Name the control LtFootControl.
5. Snap the pivot of LtFootControl to LtRfoot.
6. Now, select LtFootControl first and then select LtRfoot.
7. Select Constrain > Point Option Box. Make sure Maintain Offset is off and click the Add button.
8. Move LtFootControl. The entire leg should move with it as shown in Figure 7.27.

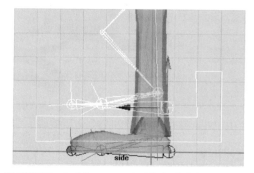

FIGURE 7.27   Left leg moved with the left foot control.

9. Repeat the steps to create the right foot control.

Adding an Orient Constraint

You are going to constrain LtRfoot to the LtRFoot control so that when you rotate LtFootControl, the foot will rotate as well.

1. Select LtFootControl first and then select LtRFoot.
2. Select Constrain > Orient. In the options window, make sure Maintain Offset is unchecked.
3. Click the Add button.
4. LtRFoot rotates 90 degrees on Y, which is incorrect. You have to fix it. In the Hypergraph, select the Orient Constrain node that is parented to LtRFoot.
5. In the Channel Box, you will see the orient constraint channels. Enter the value –90 in the OffsetY channel as shown in Figure 7.28. LtRfoot should point forward now.

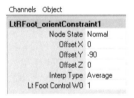

FIGURE 7.28   Left foot orient constrain OffsetY showing the value –90 in the Channel Box.

6. Repeat steps 1 through 5 to constrain RtRfoot to the RtFootControl.

Adding an Attribute to the Foot Control

To add an attribute to the foot control:

1. Select LtFootControl.
2. Add an attribute to LtFootControl.
3. In the Add Attribute options window, name the attribute ball Rotation and make sure the Data Type is set to Float. Leave the Minimum, Maximum, and Default boxes blank. You should see the new ballRotation in the Channel Box.
4. Repeat the steps to add a ballRotation attribute to the right foot control.

Using the Connection Editor

To use the Connection Editor:

1. Select Window > General Editors > Connection Editor. The Connection Editor window opens.
2. Select LtFootControl and click the Reload Left button.
3. Select the BallRotation attribute in the Outputs window as shown in Figure 7.29.

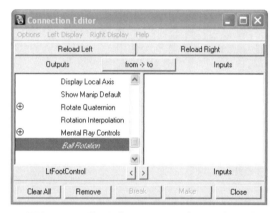

FIGURE 7.29   The BallRotation attribute selected in the Outputs window of the Connection Editor.

4. Select LtRball and click the Reload Right button.
5. Select the RotateZ attribute in the Inputs window as shown in Figure 7.30.

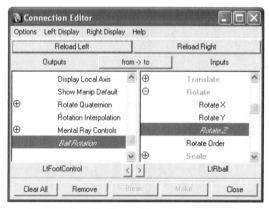

FIGURE 7.30   The RotateZ attribute selected in the Inputs window of the Connection Editor.

6. Select LtFootControl and change the value of the Ball Rotation to 20 in the Channel Box. Notice that LtRball rotates 20 degrees.

7. Repeat the steps to create a connection of the RtFootControl ball rotation to RtRBall RotateZ.

Creating and Rigging the Spine

For our Henry character, we will use a relatively simple spine. Our rig will use Maya's spline IK, controlled by four clusters. These clusters will be parented to the shoulder and hip controllers. Because of the parenting, rotation of the shoulders and hips will be inherited by the clusters, which will twist the spine.

Creating the Spine

To create the spine:

1. In the Side view, start the spine joint hierarchy at the hips and create five joints toward the head. The last joint should be just below shoulder level as shown in Figure 7.31.

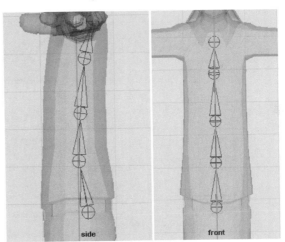

FIGURE 7.31   Side and Front views of the spine.

2. Name the joints hips, spine1, spine2, spine3, and spine4.

Creating the Spine Clusters

To create the spine clusters:

1. Select the IK Spline Handle tool and click the Reset Tool button in the options window.
2. Click the hips joint to place the root of the IK spline and then click spine4 to place the end effector. You should see the IK and the IK NURBS curve in the Hypergraph.
3. Name the IK handle spineIK and name the curve spineCurve.
4. Right-click spineCurve and select Control Vertex. You should see four CVs.
5. Select the bottom CV on the curve and create a cluster with the default setting.
6. Repeat the steps for the other three CVs. Create the clusters in order from bottom to top. You should see cluster1Handle, cluster2Handle, cluster3Handle, and cluster4Handle (see Figure 7.32).

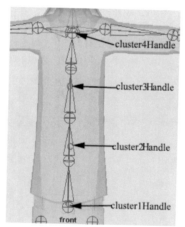

FIGURE 7.32   The four spine cluster handles.

Isolating the Hips

To isolate the hips:

1. Create a NURBS circle. Scale it 5 units in XYZ, and snap it to spine1, as shown in Figure 7.33.

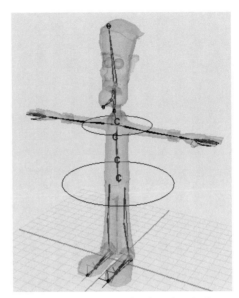

FIGURE 7.33   NURBS circle placed at the hips.

2. Freeze the circle transformations.
3. Name the circle hipsControl.
4. Select each of the leg top joints and parent them under hipsControl.
5. Select cluster1Handle and cluster2handle and parent them under hipsControl.
6. Select hips and parent it under hipsControl.
7. In the Side view, move hipsControl on Z to see the effect. The spine should move as shown in Figure 7.34. In the Hypergraph, you should have a hipsControl hierarchy as shown in Figure 7.35.

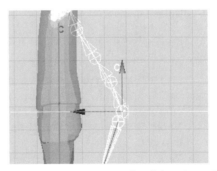

FIGURE 7.34   Spine moved with hipsControl.

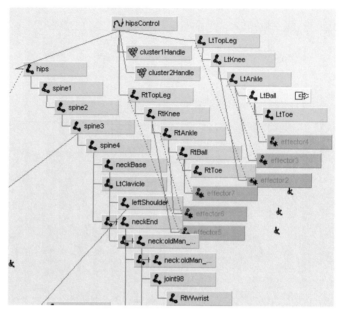

FIGURE 7.35   HipsControl nodes hierarchy.

The Upper Body

The upper body rig demonstrates a number of features beyond those in the basic sack rig. First, our humanoid has a head, which is isolated for ease of animation. Second, our character has fingers, which are controlled using custom attributes and a set driven key. Third, an important addition for realistic deformation of the shoulder region is the clavicle control.

Creating the Arm Joints

To create the arm joints:

1. In the Front view, place a joint on the collarbone, shoulder, elbow, forearm, and wrist as shown in Figure 7.36.
2. In the Top view, move the elbow joint a bit toward the back of the elbow geometry as also shown in Figure 7.36.
3. Name the joints LtCollarBone, LtShoulder, LtElbow, LtForearm, and LtWrist.
4. Repeat the steps to create the right arm joints. Name the joints RtCollarBone, RtShoulder, RtElbow, RtForearm, and RtWrist. Alternatively you can mirror the left arm joints and rename them.

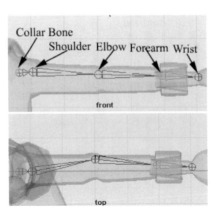

FIGURE 7.36   Collarbone, shoulder, elbow, forearm, and wrist joints.

Creating the Hand

To create the hand:

1. In the Top view, first place a joint in the middle of the palm.
2. Create a four-joint hierarchy for the index finger.
3. In the Side and Front views, move the joints to the center of the hand geometry.
4. Duplicate the index finger joint hierarchy three times. Move and adjust the duplicated hierarchy for the other fingers.
5. Parent each finger joint's hierarchy to the palm joint.
6. Parent the palm joint to the wrist joint.
7. Create a three-joint hierarchy for the thumb. Parent the thumb joint hierarchy to the wrist (see Figure 7.37).

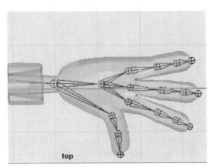

FIGURE 7.37   Hand skeleton.

8. Name all of the hand's joints properly.

Creating the Head

For the purpose of this tutorial, the head joints are created to move the head structure only and not for facial expressions or speaking. For facial expressions you would use technique called blend shapes, which are discussed in Chapter 9, "Facial Animation." To create the head:

1. In the Side view, start the skeleton from the neck toward the top of the head. First, place a joint in the middle of the neck, one just below chin level, one just to the left of the lower hairline, and the last one on the very top of the head.
2. Name the joints neckBase, neckMiddle, headBase, and headTop.
3. If character is going to open its mouth, you also need to create the lower jaw joints. Create a joint very close to the one by the hairline, another one further down approximately in the middle of the chin, and the last joint at the end of the chin.
4. Name the joints jaw1, jaw2, and jaw3.
5. Parent jaw1 to headBase (see Figure 7.38).

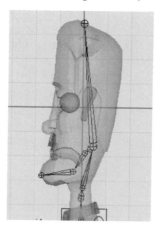

FIGURE 7.38   Head and lower jaw joints.

Parenting the Arms and Head to the Skeleton

At this point, you should have all of the skeleton parts. It would be difficult to animate the character this way because each part would move independently. Parenting the arms, legs, and head to the spine will solve this problem.

Parenting the Arms

To parent the arms:

1. Select the collarbone joints and parent them to spine4, as shown in Figure 7.39.

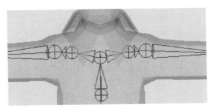

FIGURE 7.39   Arms parented to the spine.

Parenting the Head

To parent the head:

1. Select the base joint of the neck.
2. Parent it to spine4, as shown in Figure 7.40.

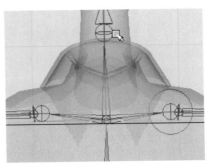

FIGURE 7.40   Head parented to the spine.

Creating the IK Handle for the Arms

To create an ikRP handle for the arms:

1. Select the IK Handle tool and make sure Current Solver is set to ikRPsolver. In the Front or Top view, first click the left shoulder joint to place the IK handle root and then click the left forearm joint to place the end effector (see Figure 7.41).

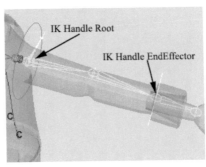

FIGURE 7.41   The ikRPsolver handle on the left arm.

2. Now you will have to move the end effector of the IK handle to the wrist joint. However, the end effector node is hidden. You have to open the IK handle node to see the end effector.

3. In the Hypergraph, select the IK handle and click the Input and Output Connections button. You should see three nodes connected to the IK handle node. The middle one is the end effector node, as shown in Figure 7.42.

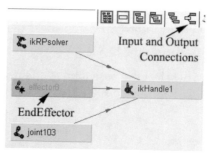

FIGURE 7.42 IK handle node input connections.

4. Make sure you have the Move tool selected.

5. Select the end effector node and press the Insert key on the keyboard to see the node pivot.

6. Move and snap the pivot to the wrist joint as shown in Figure 7.43. To snap the pivot on the wrist joint, hold the V key while moving it.

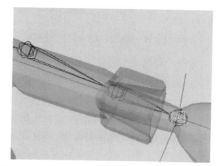

FIGURE 7.43 The end effector pivot moved to the wrist joint.

7. Move the IK handle to the left and right to make sure the elbow is bending correctly.

8. Repeat the same steps to create an ikRP handle for the right arm.

9. Name the IK handles LtArmIK and RtArmIK.

Adding a Pole Vector Constraint for the Elbows

To add a pole vector constraint for the elbows, do the following:

1. Import the file PVCcontrol.mb from the chapter7, Rigging_Controls folder on the CD-ROM.
2. In the Top view, move and snap the PVCcontrol to the LtElbow joint.
3. In the Channel Box, enter the value 0.3 for the Scale X, Y, and Z settings.
4. In the Top view, move the PVCcontrol 3 grid units behind of the left elbow joint, as shown in Figure 7.44

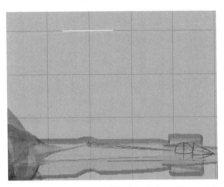

FIGURE 7.44   PVCcontrol behind the elbow joint.

5. Freeze the PVCcontrol transformations.
6. Name the PVCcontrol PVCleftElbow.
7. Duplicate the PVC once.
8. Call the duplicate PVCrightElbow.
9. In the Top view, move and snap the PVCrightElbow to the right elbow joint.
10. In the Top view, move the PVCrightElbow 3 units behind of the right elbow joint.
11. Freeze the PVCrightElbow transformations.
12. Click the PVCleftElbow to select it, and then click LtArmIK.
13. Select Constrain > Pole Vector.
14. Click the PVCrightElbow to select it and then click RtArmIK.
15. Select Constrain > Pole Vector.
16. Select LtArmIK. You should see a line constraining the IK handle rotation plane RP vector root to PVCleftElbow.
17. Repeat the step to see the PCVrightElbow constraint as shown in Figure 7.45.

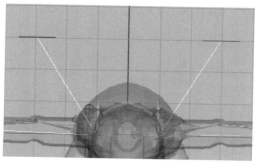

FIGURE 7.45   PVCcontrol behind the left and right elbow joints.

Creating the Upper Body Control

To create the upper body control:

1. Create a NURBS circle and scale it 3 units on XYZ. Snap the circle to spine4.
2. Freeze the circle's transformations.
3. Name the circle upperBodyControl.
4. Parent cluster3Handle and cluster4Handle under upperBodyControl.
5. Select Rotate Y in the Channel Box and lock and hide it. UpperBody-Control should rotate the shoulders on X and Z, and the IKSpline-Handle Twist attribute should rotate the shoulders on Y. In the Perspective view, you should have a skeleton like the one shown in Figure 7.46, and in the Hypergraph, you should have an upperBody-Control hierarchy as shown in Figure 7.47.

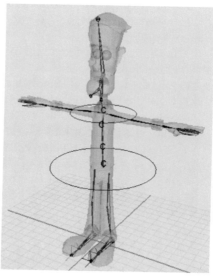

FIGURE 7.46   Full body skeleton with hips and upper body controls.

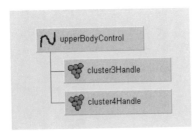

FIGURE 7.47   The UpperBodyControl nodes hierarchy.

Creating the Arm Controls

To create the arm controls:

ON THE CD

1. Import the cube.mb file from the chapter4, Rigging_Controls folder on the CD-ROM.
2. Snap the cube to the LtWrist joint.
3. Scale the cube 2 units on XYZ as shown in Figure 7.48.

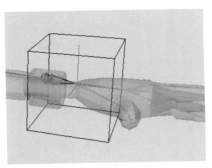

FIGURE 7.48   Cube snapped to the wrist joint.

4. Freeze the cube's transformations.
5. Point-constrain LtArmIK to the cube.
6. Move the cube. The arm should move with it as shown in Figure 7.49.

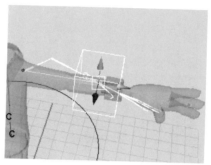

FIGURE 7.49 Cube moving entire arm.

Creating Clavicle Controls

To create the clavicle controls:

1. Create a NURBS circle.
2. In the Channel Box, enter the value 90 in the Rotate Z channel.
3. Move and snap the circle to the LtClavicle joint.
4. In the Channel Box, type 0.3 in the Scale X, Y, and Z channels.
5. Move the circle approximately 1 grid unit behind the clavicle joint.
6. Freeze the circle's transformations.
7. With the circle still selected, press the Insert key on the keyboard.
8. Move and snap the circle's pivot on top of LtClavicle joint.
9. Select the circle first and then select LtClavicle joint.
10. Select Constrain > Point Constrain. Make sure Maintain Offset is unchecked in the options window.
11. Name the circle LtClavicleControl.
12. Move LtClavicleControl. The LtClavicle joint should move with it.
13. In the Channel Box, select the Rotate X, Y, and Z channels and the Scale X, Y, and Z channels.
14. Right-click the selected channels and click Lock and Hide Selected. Only the clavicle control should translate.
15. Repeat the steps to create a clavicle control for the right clavicle joint.

Isolating the Head

Isolating the head means that the head will not move or rotate with the shoulders. This is useful when you want to have separate rotations for the shoulders and the head.

To isolate the head:

ON THE CD

1. Import the cube from the chapter4, Rigging_Controls folder on the CD-ROM.

2. Move it on the head and scale it to the size of the head as shown in Figure 7.50.

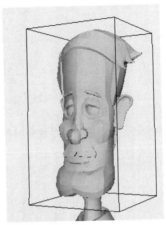

FIGURE 7.50   The cube moved and scaled to the size of the head.

3. Snap the cube's pivot to the neckBase joint.
4. Freeze its transformations.
5. Name the cube headControl.
6. To point-constrain headControl to neckBase, select neckBase first and then select headControl.
7. Select Constrain > Point. Make sure Maintain Offset is unchecked and click the Add button.

Orient Constrain the neckBase Joint to headControl

Orient constraining the neckBase joint to headControl creates a rotation relationship between them, so that when headControl rotates, neckBase follows its orientation.

1. Select headControl first and then select neckBase.
2. Select Constrain > Orient. Make sure Maintain Offset is unchecked and click the Add button. The joint incorrectly rotates 90 degrees in X and Z to follow the box orientation, so you need to fix it.
3. In the Channel Box, open the neckBase orient constraint channels.
4. Type 90 in the OffsetX and OffsetZ fields. neckBase should straighten up again (see Figure 7.51). Now the box will follow the position of the neck joints when you animate the body. The head will only rotate when the box is rotated.

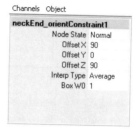

FIGURE 7.51   Orient constraint channels.

Adding Custom Attributes to the Arm Controls

To add custom attributes to the arms controls:

1. Make sure the finger joints are named as follows:

   - Index finger: LtIndex1, LtIndex2, LtIndex3, and LtIndex4
   - Middle finger: LtMi1, LtMi2, LtMi3, and LtMi4
   - Pinky finger: LtPinky1, LtPinky2, LtPinly3, and LtPinky4
   - Thumb: LtThumb1, LtThumb2, and LtThumb3

2. Make sure the palm and all finger joints have 0 rotation on the XYZ channels.
3. Select LtArmControl and select Modify > Add Attribute.
4. In the Attribute Long Name field, type index and click the Add button. The Add Attribute window should stay open.
5. Create three more attributes: middle, pinky, and thumb.
6. In the Channel Box, you should see the index, middle, pinky, and thumb attributes as shown in Figure 7.52.

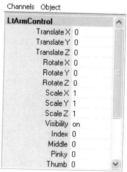

FIGURE 7.52   The index, middle, pinky, and thumb attributes in the Channel Box.

Using Set Driven Keys to Animate the Fingers

To animate the fingers with set driven keys:

1. Open the Set Driven Key window.
2. Load LtArmControl as the driver and click the index attribute to select it.
3. Select LtIndex1, LtIndex2, and LtIndex3 and load them as driven.
4. Click LtIndex1, LtIndex2, and LtIndex3 to select them and select rotateZ as shown in Figure 7.53.

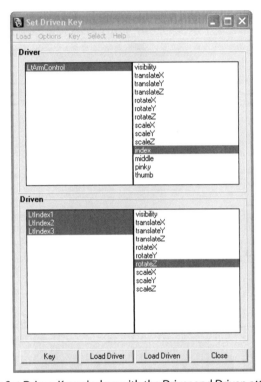

FIGURE 7.53　The Set Driven Key window with the Driver and Driven attributes selected.

5. Click the Key button to set the first set driven key for the index attribute and index finger joints at zero rotation.
6. Select LtArmControl and change the value of the index attribute to 10 in the Channel Box.
7. In the Top or Perspective view, select LtIndex1, LtIndex2, and LtIndex3. Rotate them each at –45 degrees on Z as shown in Figure 7.54.

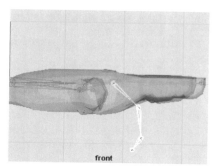

FIGURE 7.54 Index finger joints rotated –45 degrees.

8. Click the Key button to set a driven key for the finger's rotation.
9. In the Channel Box, select the index attribute and move the mouse cursor over the Side view. With the middle mouse button, click-drag to the left and right to see the index finger curling.
10. Repeat the steps to create the attributes on the right arm control and set driven keys for the middle finger, pinky, and thumb.

The thumb is a bit trickier to get an accurate movement using only one directional rotation. Try using these steps on the X, Y, and Z values for each thumb.

CREATING AND RIGGING AN ADVANCED SPINE

ON THE CD

Providing rigidity, but nevertheless remaining twistable and flexible, the spine is one of the most complex parts of the body to rig well. Maya's default IK treats the spine as a single joint chain of fixed length, with a single rotation at its base (the pelvis). The Simple Guy rig we've worked on so far takes a slightly more sophisticated approach, using clusters parented to controllers to twist the spine from each end. This approach is generally sufficient for simple walk cycles and for characters that don't require much torso movement. However, for more expressive characters, some more advanced techniques are required to simulate natural spine movements. Examples of these can be found on the Henry rig on the attached CD-ROM and are briefly described here.

Some general characteristics of an effective spine rig include the ability to visualize the line of action, stretchiness, and twist interpolation.

Visualizing the Line of Action

In planning both biped animation and cinematography, one important concept is that of *line(s) of action*. In 3D terms, this can be thought of as the projection of the spine and dominant limb positions onto the camera plane (as shown in Figure 7.55). A strong pose has a clear line of action, and a good camera position often emphasizes changes in the line of action. In hand sketching, artists often start by literally drawing these lines. In 3D, however, this can be harder to visualize because the spine joint hierarchy may look busy and is often obscured by geometry. By linking a graphical proxy object such as a plane to the spine, it can be easier to read the line of action at a glance when posing.

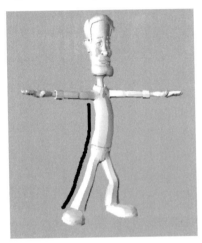

FIGURE 7.55 Line of action.

Stretchiness

A real human spine can both stretch and compress. However, default IK chains in Maya can do neither. A fair bit of extra work is involved in adding this feature to rigging; however, the reward is much better character performance. This feature is very helpful for exaggeration, especially in cartoony rigs (see Figure 7.56).

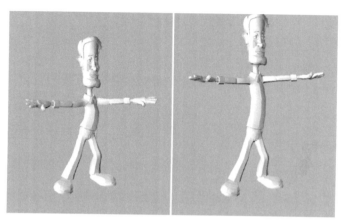

FIGURE 7.56   The character's spine is stretched up.

There are two main methods for achieving stretchiness in the spine. The first approach is to scale the joints of the spine according to the distance between the base and the end effector. This distance can be dynamically calculated using a special Maya length node.

The second technique, demonstrated in the Henry rig, is a broken hierarchy spine. Rather than forming a continuous chain, the joints are kept independent from each other. A controller is point-constrained to the top and bottom of the spine so that it always stays halfway between them. This allows simple and consistent control of the stretch. However, this technique can make it a bit more difficult to get a smooth spine arc than with a standard IK system.

Twist Interpolation

When a real human spine twists, it does not simply rotate from the pelvis. Instead, it is fixed at the pelvis and actually rotates a bit between each vertebra. The angle of rotation falls off progressively going along the spine. Several controllers can be added to the spine to achieve this effect (see Figure 7.57). If you can picture a warping ladder or twisting ladder, then you have the concept of twist interpolation. In the Henry rig, three locators are positioned along the spine (oldMan_spine01Bttm_pos, oldMan_spine01Mid_pos, oldMan_spine01Top_pos). In Maya, locators are visual representations of transformation nodes, also known as "nulls." They maintain a position and a rotation but contain no geometry. In addition to the nulls along the spine itself, three other nulls are off to the side of the spine, arranged like rungs on a ladder (oldMan_spine01Bttm_up, oldMan_spine01Mid_up, oldMan_spine01Top_up). Finally, there are two controllers with circular geometry designed to be directly manipulated. The m_hip_CON controller allows rotation and positioning of the hips, and m_Chest_CON controls the chest.

FIGURE 7.57   Spine twist interpolation.

The top null on the spine (oldMan_spine01Top_pos) is a child of the chest controller (m_Chest_CON). The bottom null on the spine (old-Man_spine01Bttm_pos) is a child of the hip controller (m_hip_CON). Each of the three nulls along the spine is constrained to its corresponding locator along the side. This allows twisting in the horizontal plane. The middle controller corresponding side null is position constrained to both the top and bottom spinal nulls, so it tries to stay in between them and distributes any twisting motion.

SUMMARY

Congratulations! You should now have a reasonably well-rigged biped character, which is perhaps the most technically complex part of character animation. You have learned that for a character to move properly, it needs to be modeled and rigged correctly according to its anatomy. Along the way, you learned some techniques of general utility in animation, such as the use of a set driven key. Now that you have a rigged character, it is time to move on to the actual process of character animation, the subject of the next few chapters.

CHALLENGE ASSIGNMENT

Biped Model

Part A: Creating a Lower Body Rig

Create a lower body rig for the biped you modeled in Chapter 6, "Modeling a Biped Character." Test your rig by binding it to the character and creating poses for a walk cycle.

Part B: Creating a Spine Rig

Create a spine rig for your biped using any of the techniques shown. Test your rig by binding it and creating poses that show the character crouched or fully extended as if stretching to dunk a basketball.

Part C: Creating an Upper Body Rig

Create an upper body rig for your Chapter 6 character. Test your rig by binding it and creating poses as if your character were drawing a bow and arrow. Pay particular attention to the shoulder deformations.

THE ART AND SCIENCE OF ANIMATION

In This Chapter

- Muybridge's Observations of Motion
- The Process of Walking
- Adding Emotion and Character to Your Walk Cycles

MUYBRIDGE'S OBSERVATIONS OF MOTION

More than 100 years ago, the photographer Eadweard Muybridge was posed a challenging question: Does a running horse ever have all four feet in the air simultaneously? At the time, high speed photography was hardly known. A typical portrait required the subjects to sit very still for several minutes. Could Muybridge take a picture that would capture a horse mid-air and answer this question? The challenge led Muybridge to experiment and invent several technologies in the process, helping create both a new science (*kinesiology*, the study of motion) and a new industry (the motion picture).

What Muybridge came up with first was the idea of exposing a dozen or more cameras in rapid succession. As it turned out, this not only allowed him to understand how a horse gallops and trots but also to record a wide variety of human and animal movements, which for all of prior history, had been too rapid to study systematically. Muybridge shot the photos from known fixed perspectives, including orthogonal to the direction of motion and perpendicular to it, and he shot against a large background grid that gave a scale reference.

Eventually, Muybridge also came up with a means of displaying these images in rapid succession. The succession was rapid enough to produce a flickery approximation of continuous motion and earn him credit as one of the fathers of not only the movie industry, but also animation.

Appropriately enough, animators turn to Muybridge's images, even a century later, because they are still a useful reference to basic human (and animal) kinematics. Consider, for example, Figure 8.1, showing a man walking.

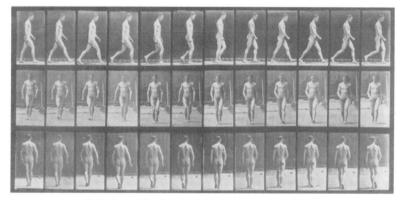

FIGURE 8.1   Muybridge's study of a man walking.
(Collections of the University of Pennsylvania Archives.)

The Process of Walking

Walking is such a common process for us that it is usually an unconscious act. However, after you begin to break down the steps, it becomes clear that several things are going on at the same time. Start by considering the feet and then work your way up the body. As Muybridge's photos first clearly showed, a normal walk is a symmetrical activity—our steps to the left are nearly exact mirrors of our steps to the right. (Even the slightest variation in this symmetry is immediately perceived as a limp.) There are five basic positions (see Figure 8.2).

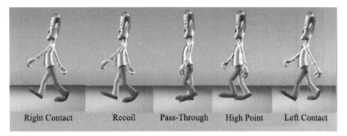

FIGURE 8.2   Five basic walk positions.

- **Right contact.** The starting point of the walk cycle is usually taken to be the moment when the right heel strikes the ground. This is the extreme pose of the walk, where arms and legs are extended. Note, however, that both arms and legs are not fully extended; they retain a slight bend.
- **Recoil.** The second point of the walk cycle is when the right leg catches the full weight of the body, still with the knee slightly bent.
- **Pass-through.** Also known as the "passing position," this is the mid-point of the walk cycle. The upper body lifts up, and the trailing leg passes underneath the body.
- **High point.** The back leg propels the body to its maximum height.
- **Left contact.** The step is completed as a nearly exact inverse of the starting right contact position.

Timing in classic animations done for cinema are at a rate of 24 frames per second (fps); a normal walk is timed so that each step takes 12 frames, and the intermediate positions are evenly distributed on the sixth, third, and ninth frames (usually drawn in that order). Each step is $^1/_2$ second, and a full cycle takes 1 second. When working at video frame rates of 29.97 fps, the frame timings don't work out so evenly, so animators often use a 32-frame cycle for convenience. The positions are distributed in frames 1, 8, 16, 24, and 32.

Hip and Shoulder Rotation

Getting the foot and leg positions correct is only the first part of creating a convincing walk cycle. What animators term "secondary motion" is just as important. For a walk cycle, the basic secondary motions are actions that we take to keep in balance while performing the major leg movements.

The first of these are horizontal hip swings, which are best seen from the Top view. In the right contact position, the right hip swings forward, and the left swings back as shown in Figure 8.3.

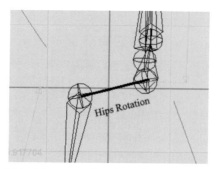

FIGURE 8.3   Hips rotated at the right contact position.

In the left contact position, the reverse situation is true, with the hip swung to the left. Only in the passing position are the hips not rotated horizontally.

A second, compensating motion is that of the shoulders and arms. Basically, the arms swing in the opposite direction as the legs, providing better balance. The shoulders pivot about the clavicle, supporting this movement and running exactly counter to the horizontal hip swing. Even when the arms are consciously held still during the walk, the shoulders will still swing a bit to maintain balance with the hips (see Figure 8.4).

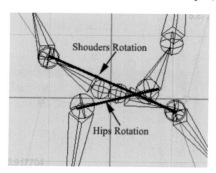

FIGURE 8.4   Shoulder rotation at the right contact position.

After the horizontal secondary motion is considered, we can turn our attention to vertical secondary motions. The hips and shoulders also cycle in this plane. In the right contact position, the hip is level. However, it rotates down toward the left foot and reaches its lowest point in the passing position. From the passing position to the left contact, it rotates back up to level.

While the hips are moving vertically, the shoulders are again compensating by moving in the opposite direction. At the right contact position, they are level. As the left leg lifts into the passing position, the left shoulder rises. It levels out again at the left contact position.

Arm Movement

During a normal walk, the right arm is almost straight down during the right contact position. The left arm is positioned a little bit forward. The elbow is rotated approximately 10 degrees as shown in Figure 8.5.

FIGURE 8.5   The arms' positions during the right contact position.
(Collections of the University of Pennsylvania Archives.)

The arms gradually straighten up during the recoil and pass-through positions, as shown in Figure 8.6. In a normal walk, each arm swings in the direction opposite the corresponding leg. At the left contact position, the left arm is fully back, and at the right contact position, the right arm is back, as shown in Figure 8.7. The arms swing from back to front and create an arc-like movement as shown in Figure 8.8.

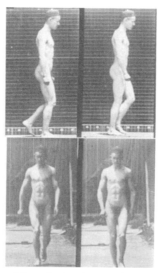

FIGURE 8.6   The arms' positions during the recoil and pass-through positions. (Collections of the University of Pennsylvania Archives.)

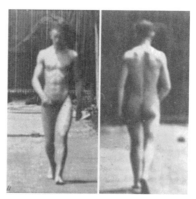

FIGURE 8.7   The arms swinging in the opposite direction of the legs during the high point position. (Collections of the University of Pennsylvania Archives.)

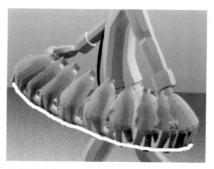

FIGURE 8.8   Arm swing arc movement.

The Spine and Head

In a normal walk, the spine contracts and expands a bit with each step, bending to absorb the impact of the hips moving up and down. The overall form of the spine is an important part of the posture of the character. As we will discuss soon, posture varies greatly depending on both the physical characteristics of the character and the character's emotional state and personality.

The head tilts slightly from right to left and bobs at the same time to create a curve movement from left to right and vice versa (see Figure 8.9).

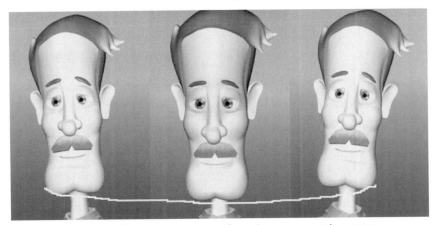

FIGURE 8.9   Three heads showing the swing movement in a curve.

TUTORIAL 8.1: A NORMAL WALK CYCLE

To animate a character walking involves positioning the character in several main poses and setting keyframes for these poses. The computer will do the in-between poses. Think of yourself as the main animator and the computer as the tweener.

This tutorial will walk you through the technical steps to create a basic walk cycle. However, a walk can and should show the character's personality and emotion, which we will discuss later in the chapter.

As mentioned earlier, a normal film walk cycle is 24 frames. For increased clarity, this tutorial will animate a slow (half speed) walk over 48 frames.

Animating the Legs at the Right Contact Position

To animate the legs at the right contact position:

ON THE CD

1. Open the file HenryRiggedIsolatedHead.mb from the AdvancedRig subfolder in the chapter8, MayaWorkingFiles folder on the CD-ROM.

2. Open the Maya preferences window (Window > Settings/Preferences/Preferences), make sure Default In Tangent and Default Out Tangent are set to Clamped, and make sure Weighted Tangents is checked, as shown in Figure 8.10. Under Settings, set your working units to Film (24 fps). Also, under Settings > Timeline, make sure your Playbook speed is set to Real-time (24 fps). This will ensure that what you see is what you get in terms of timing. The clamped tangent is used because this tangent setting combines spline and linear tangents. When the value of two adjacent keys are very close, the tangent will be linear; when the values of adjacent keys are farther apart, the tangent will be a spline. This will help to prevent foot and pelvis joints from sliding.

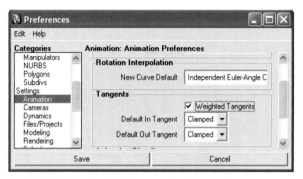

FIGURE 8.10   Setting Maya animation preferences.

3. Select the left reverse foot control.
4. In the Channel Box, enter –4 in the TranslateZ channel.
5. Select the right reverse foot control.
6. In the Channel Box, enter –3 in the TranslateZ channel (see Figure 8.11).

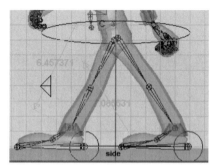

FIGURE 8.11   Right leg extended forward and left leg extended backward.

7. The left and right legs are over-extended, but this is okay for now.
8. Make sure the right and left reverse foot controls are selected.
9. Select Animate > Set Key Option Box.
10. In the Set Key Options window, check Set Keys at Prompt.
11. Click the Set Key button to open a Set Key window.
12. In the Enter List of Times field, type 1,48. This means you are setting a keyframe for the foot control at frame 1 and frame 48, which are the first and last keyframes (see Figure 8.12).

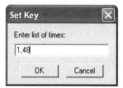

FIGURE 8.12   Set Key window showing the keyframe numbers.

13. Click the OK button.
14. Advance the time line to frame 24.
15. Select the left reverse foot control and enter 3 in the TranslateZ channel in the Channel Box.
16. Select the right reverse foot control and enter –4 in the TranslateZ channel in the Channel Box.
17. Make sure the left and left reverse foot controls are selected.
18. Select Animate > Set Key Option Box.
19. In the Set Key Options window, check Set Keys at Current Time.
20. Click the Set Key button.
21. Play the animation. The feet should drag on the ground.

Animating the Legs at the Passing Position

To animate the legs at the passing position:

1. Move the time line to frame 12.
2. Select the left reverse foot control and, in the Channel Box, enter the following:

    - Translate X = 0
    - Translate Y = 1.5
    - Translate Z = 0

3. Select the right reverse foot control and, in the Channel Box, enter 0 for the Translation X, Y, and Z settings (see Figure 8.13).

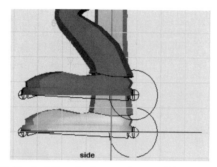

FIGURE 8.13   Left foot in the passing position on frame 12.

4. Make sure the right and left reverse foot controls are selected.
5. Select Animate > Set Breakdown Keys Option Box.
6. In the Set Breakdown Keys window, make sure Set Breakdown at Current Time is checked.
7. Click the Set Breakdown key.
8. Move the Time Slider to frame 36.
9. Select the right reverse foot control.
10. In the Channel Box, enter the following values:

   - Translate X = 0
   - Translate Y = 1.5
   - Translate Z = 0

11. Select the left reverse foot control and, in the Channel Box, enter 0 for the Translation X, Y, and Z settings (see Figure 8.14).

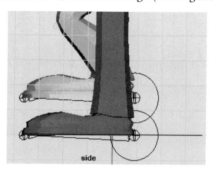

FIGURE 8.14   The right foot in the passing position on frame 36.

12. Make sure the right and left reverse foot controls are selected and select Animate > Set Breakdown Key.
13. Play the animation. You should see both feet animated on the passing position.

Setting Driven Keys for the Ball Rotation

To set driven keys for the ball rotation:

1. Select Animate > Set Driven Key > Set Option Box. The Set Driven Key window opens.
2. In the Set Driven Key window, select Load > Select as Driver.
3. Select ballRotation on the right side of the window, as shown in Figure 8.15.

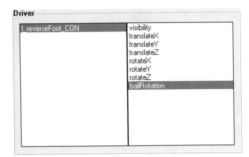

FIGURE 8.15   The left reverse foot control ballRotation attribute selected in the Set Driven Key window.

4. Select the left ball joint.
5. In the Set Driven Key window, select Load > Select as Driven.
6. Select rotateZ in the right side of the window as shown in Figure 8.16.

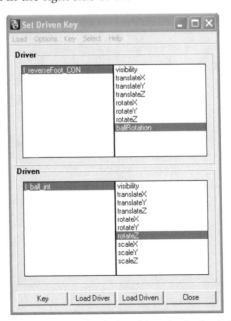

FIGURE 8.16   Left ball joint rotateZ loaded as driven in the Set Driven Key window.

7. Make sure the left reverse foot ballRotation value is set to 0 in the Channel Box.
8. Make sure the left foot ball joint Rotation X, Y, and Z values are 0 in the Channel Box.
9. Click the Key button in the Set Driven Key window.
10. Select the left reverse foot control.
11. Change the left reverse foot ballRotation value to 10.
12. Select the left ball joint.
13. In the Channel Box Rotate Z channel, enter 65.
14. Click the Key button in the Set Driven Key window.
15. Test the set driven key by changing the ballRotation values. The left foot ball should rotate.
16. Repeat steps 1 through 15 to create the set driven keys for the right reverse foot ballRotation.

Animating the Left and Right Ball Rotation

To animate the left and right ball rotation:

1. Move the time line to frame 1.
2. Select the left reverse foot control.
3. In the Channel Box, enter the value 10 in the Ball Rotation channel. The left ball should rotate 65 degrees as shown in Figure 8.17.

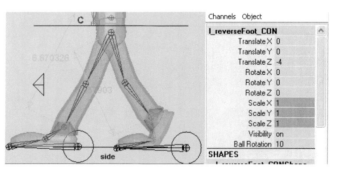

FIGURE 8.17   The left reverse foot Ball Rotation value set to 10 in the Channel Box.

4. Still in frame 1, select the right reverse foot control.
5. In the Channel Box Rotate X channel, enter –33. The foot should be rotated pointing up as shown in Figure 8.18.

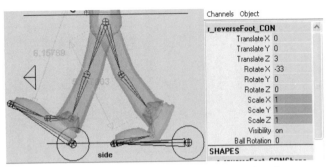

FIGURE 8.18   The right reverse foot control rotated on frame 1.

6. Select the right reverse foot control and the left reverse foot control.
7. Select Animate > Set Key Option Box.
8. In the options window, change Set Key At to Prompt and click the Set Key button.
9. In the Set Key window, enter 1,48 in Enter List of Times field.
10. Click the OK button.
11. In the Set Key Options window, change Set Key At to Current Time.
12. Move the time line to frame 24.
13. Select the right reverse foot control and, in the Channel Box, enter Rotate X = 0 and Ball Rotation = 10.
14. Select the left reverse foot control and in the Channel Box, enter Rotate X = –33 and Ball Rotation = 0 (see Figure 8.19).
15. Select Animate > Set Key Option Box.
16. In the Set Key Options window, change Set Keys At to Current Time.
17. Click the Set Key button.
18. Play the animation to test the keys. Notice that the right foot and left foot balls have rotation on the pass position, which needs to be fixed.
19. Move the Time Slider to frame 12.
20. Select the right reverse foot control and, in the Channel Box, enter Rotate X = 0 and Ball Rotation = 0. The right foot should be flat on the ground.
21. Select the left reverse foot control and, in the Channel Box, enter Rotate X = 20 and Ball Rotation = 0. On frame 12, both feet should be as shown in Figure 8.20.

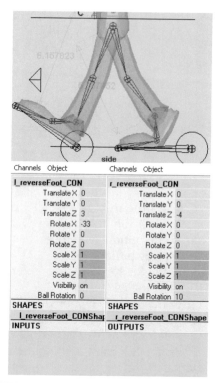

FIGURE 8.19   The left reverse foot rotated and right reverse foot ball rotation also rotated on frame 24.

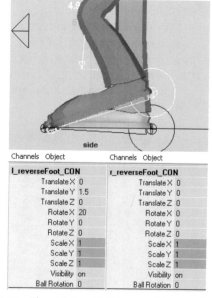

FIGURE 8.20   The right and left foot positions on frame 12.

22. Select the right reverse foot control and the left reverse foot control.
23. Press S to set another key for the controls on frame 12.
24. Move the Time Slider to frame 36.
25. Select the right reverse foot control and, in the Channel Box, enter Rotate X = 20 and Ball Rotation = 0.
26. Select the left reverse foot control and, in the Channel Box, enter Rotate X = 0 and Ball Rotation = 0 (see Figure 8.21).

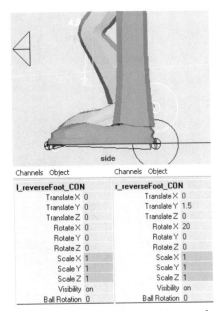

FIGURE 8.21   Right and left foot positions on frame 36.

27. Select the right reverse foot control and the left reverse foot control and press S to set another key for both foot controls on frame 36.
28. The motion curves for the left and right reverse foot controls and left and right ball rotations should look like the curves shown in Figure 8.22.
29. Select the left reverse foot control and the right reverse foot control.
30. Open the Graph Editor.
31. In the Graph Editor, select View > Frame All. You should see all the motion curves.
32. Select Curves > Post Infinity > Cycle, as shown in Figure 8.23. This extends the length of the animation curve by repeating the sequence of existing keyframes on that curve forever. In this case, this will continue the walking motion indefinitely, which makes it much easier to judge visually than by looking at a single isolated cycle.

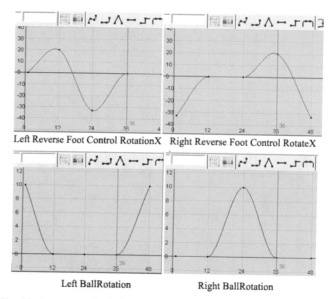

Left Reverse Foot Control RotationX   Right Reverse Foot Control RotateX

Left BallRotation   Right BallRotation

FIGURE 8.22   Motion curves for left and right reverse foot controls and ball rotations.

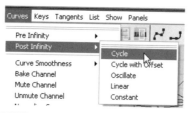

FIGURE 8.23   The Post Infinity Cycle menu.

33. In the Graph Editor window, select View > Infinity. The infinity curves will appear as broken lines as shown in Figure 8.24.

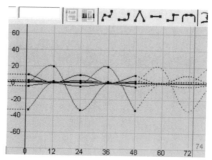

FIGURE 8.24   Post Infinity curves in the Graph Editor.

Animating the Hips and Shoulders

The hips are the center of gravity of the body and the center of the body's balance. During a walk cycle, the hips and the shoulders move in opposite directions to keep the body in balance. When the right hip is forward, the right shoulder is back and vice versa. When the right hip tilts up, the right shoulder tilts down and vice versa.

To animate the hips and shoulders:

1. Set the timeline to frame 1.
2. Select the hips control (m_hip_CON node) and, in the Channel Box, enter Rotate Y = 13 and Rotate Z = 9. This rotates the hips forward and backward and tilts the hips up and down. The left hip should be higher than the right hip.
3. Select the chest control (m_Chest_CON node) and, in the Channel Box, enter Rotate Y = –13 and Rotate Z = **–9**. Notice that the shoulders rotate and tilt in the opposite direction, as shown in Figure 8.25.

FIGURE 8.25   Hips and shoulders rotating and tilting in the opposite direction in frame 1.

4. Advance the time line to frame 24.
5. Select the hips control and, in the Channel Box, enter Rotate Y = –13 and Rotate Z = –9.
6. Select the chest control and, in the Channel Box, enter Rotate Y = 13 and Rotate Z = 9 (see Figure 8.26).

FIGURE 8.26   Hips and shoulders rotating and tilting in the opposite direction in frame 24.

7. Select Animate > Set Key Option Box and change Set Key At to Current Time.
8. Click the Set Key button.
9. Select the hip and chest controls.
10. In the Graph Editor, select View > Frame All.
11. In the Graph Editor, select Curve > Post Infinity > Cycle.
12. Play the animation.

Animating the Hips Up and Down

To animate the spine compression in this rigging, you need to animate the hips and the chest up and down.

1. Select the hips control.
2. In the Channel Box, enter the value –0.2 for the Translate Y channel.
3. With the hips control still selected, press the W key to change to the Move tool. You should see the Move tool in the middle of the hips.
4. Click the green arrow (Y axis) of the Move tool to select it. The green arrow becomes yellow when selected (see Figure 8.27).

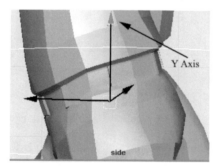

FIGURE 8.27   The green arrow (Y axis) of the Move tool selected.

5. Select Animate > Set Key Option Box.
6. In the options window, check Current Manipulator handle in the Set Keys On section and, in the Set Keys At section, select Prompt.
7. Click the Set Key button. The Set Key window appears.
8. In the List of Times field, enter 1,24,48 as shown in Figure 8.28.

FIGURE 8.28   List of times.

9. Click the OK button.
10. With the hips control still selected, change the value of Translate Y to 0.1 in the Channel Box.
11. Press S. The Set Key window appears.
12. In the Enter List of Times field, enter 12,36 as shown in Figure 8.29.

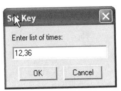

FIGURE 8.29   List of times in the Set Key window showing 12 and 36.

13. Click the OK button. In the Graph Editor, the motion curve should be like the one shown in Figure 8.30.

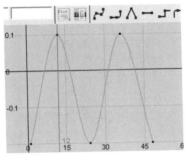

FIGURE 8.30   Motion curves of the hips moving up and down.

Animating the Spine Up and Down

To animate the spine up and down:

1. Select the chest control and, in Channel Box, enter the value −0.4 for the Translate Y channel.
2. Using the Set Key prompt, set a keyframe for frames 1, 24, and 48.
3. With the chest control still selected, change the value of the Translate Y channel to 0.2.
4. Set a keyframe for the frames 12 and 36.

Animating the Arms

You will animate the arms using forward kinematics (FK) to properly create the arm arc movement. The arms' inverse kinematics (IK) are disabled. To enable the arms' IK handles, select them and, in the Channel Box, change the Blend value to 1.

Animating the Shoulder

To animate the shoulder:

1. In the Channel Box, make sure the Arms IK Blend value is set to 0.
2. Select the left shoulder joint (OldMan_lArm01_jnt).
3. In the Channel Box, enter Rotate X = 35, Rotate Y = –15, and Rotate Z = –62.
4. Select the right shoulder joint (OldMan_rArm01_jnt) and, in the Channel Box, enter Rotate X = 0, Rotate Y = 30, and Rotate Z = –72.
5. Select the left and right shoulders joints.
6. Select Animate > Set Key and make sure the Prompt option is checked in the options window.
7. Set a keyframe for both shoulder joints on frames 1 and 48, as shown in Figure 8.31.

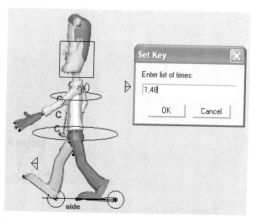

FIGURE 8.31   Set Key window showing a list of keys.

8. Select the left shoulder joint and, in the Channel Box, enter Rotate X = 0, Rotate Y = 20, and Rotate Z = –72.
9. Select the right shoulder joint and, in the Channel Box, enter Rotate X = 35, Rotate Y = –38, and Rotate Z = –62.
10. Select the left and right shoulder joints and press S. The Set Key prompt appears.
11. In the List of Times field, enter 24 as shown in Figure 8.32 and click the OK button.

The motion curves for the shoulder joints should look like the ones shown in Figure 8.33.

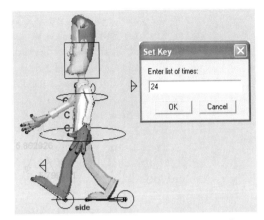

FIGURE 8.32 Set Key window showing the number 24.

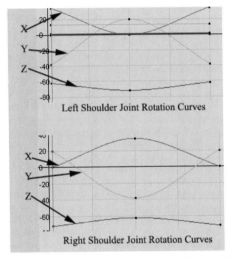

FIGURE 8.33 Rotation curves for the left and right shoulder joints.

Animating the Elbows

To animate the elbows:

1. Select the left elbow joint (OldMan_LArm02_jnt) and, in the Channel Box, enter Rotate X = 0, Rotate Y = –20, and Rotate Z = 0.
2. Select the right elbow joint (OldMan_rArm02_jnt) and, in the Channel Box, enter Rotate X = 0, Rotate Y = –20, and Rotate Z = 0.
3. Select the left and right elbow joints and, using the Set Key prompt, set a keyframe in frames 1 and 48.
4. Select the left elbow joint (OldMan_lArm02_jnt) and, in the Channel Box, enter Rotate X = 0, Rotate Y = 0, and Rotate Z = 0.

5. Select the right elbow joint (OldMan_rArm02_jnt) and, in the Channel Box, enter Rotate X = 0, Rotate Y = 0, and Rotate Z = 0.
6. Select the left and right elbow joints and, using the Set Key prompt, set a keyframe in frames 12 and 36.
7. Select the left elbow joint and, in the Channel Box, enter Rotate X = 0, Rotate Y = –20, and Rotate Z = 0.
8. Select the right elbow joint and, in the Channel Box, enter Rotate X = 0, Rotate Y = –20, and Rotate Z = 0.
9. Select the left and right elbow joints and press S. In the List of Times, enter 24 and click the OK button. The rotation Y curves for the elbow should look like the ones shown in Figure 8.34.

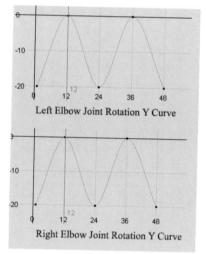

FIGURE 8.34   Elbow joints' rotation Y curves.

Animating the Clavicles

To animate the clavicles:

1. Select the left clavicle control (l_clavicle_CON).
2. In the Channel Box enter 0.07 in the Translate Z channel.
3. Set a key for this value at frames 1 and 48.
4. Change the Translate Z channel value to –0.28.
5. Set a key for this value at frame 24.
6. Select the right clavicle control (r_clavicle_CON).
7. In the Channel Box, enter –0.28 in the Translate Z channel.
8. Set a key for this value at frames 1 and 48.
9. Change the Translate Z value to 0.07.
10. Set a key for this value at frame 24. The rotation Z curve for the clavicles should look like the one shown in Figure 8.35.

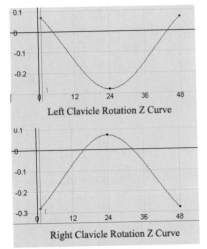

FIGURE 8.35   Left and right clavicles' rotation Z curve.

If the shoulder joints do not move with the clavicle joints, select the left shoulder joint and select the BlendPoint2 attribute in the Channel Box. Right-click BlendPoint2 and select Break Connections. Change the attribute value to 1. You'll see that the shoulder socket pops back into place.

Animating the Head

The head tilts and bobs at the contact position. To animate the head bob:

1. Select the head control (m_headBox_CON).
2. In the Channel Box, enter 10 in the Rotate X channel.
3. Set a key for this value at frames 1 and 48.
4. Change the Rotate X value to –5.
5. Set a key for this value at frame 24.
6. To animate the head tilt, select the head control (m_headBox_CON).
7. In the Channel Box, enter –5 in the Rotate Z channel.
8. Set a key for this value at frames 1 and 48.
9. Change the Rotate Z value to 5 and set a key for this value at frame 24. The motion curves for the head control should look like the ones shown in Figure 8.36.

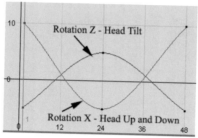

FIGURE 8.36   Rotation X and Z of the head up and down and head tilt.

Congratulations! You have finished your first walk cycle animation. A walk cycle is one of the hardest types of animation because it involves many principles of animation such as overlap action, follow through, weight, and timing. Because we are so used to looking at people walking, even non-animators can be tough critics.

ADDING EMOTION AND CHARACTER TO YOUR WALK CYCLES

One of the interesting things about watching people walking is just how much we can tell about a character from the way he walks. First, you can rapidly judge the gender, the physical health, and general age of the character. Beyond that, you can also tell much about the state of mind and personality of the character just by observing timing and body language. For example, when a character is happy, he walks faster than normal; when sad, the character walks slower than normal. Normally, when we walk, we minimize the expenditure of energy by lifting our feet only very slightly—less than a centimeter—during the passing position. An energetic or brash character, however, will briskly lift his feet and raise them to a noticeably higher passing position.

Figure 8.37 shows the character walking without any emotion, and Figure 8.38 shows the character walking happily.

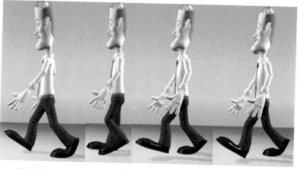

FIGURE 8.37   The character walking without emotion.

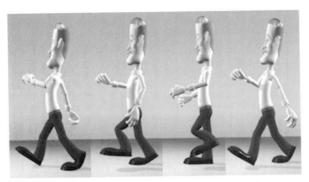

FIGURE 8.38   The character walking happily.

Notice that in Figure 8.38, the character's chest is forward, the arms are widely forward and backward, and the feet move higher than the character in Figure 8.37.

When the character is sad, the pacing of the walk and the body language is the opposite. Figure 8.39 shows the character walking sadly.

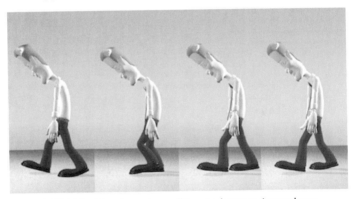

FIGURE 8.39   The character walking and expressing sadness.

Notice in Figure 8.39 that the head is leading the walk. The character's body is curved forward. The head is looking down. The shoulders are scrunched and hanging down. The arms are almost straight down, and the feet are moving close to the ground.

The Jump

Like walk cycles, jumps involve several principles of animation—in this case, anticipation, squash and stretch, weight, overlapping action, and follow through.

In Figures 8.40 and 8.41 you can see a character jumping on and off a box. Figure 8.40 shows the first part of the jump. First, you see the character standing looking at the box. Then he prepares himself to jump by retracting his body in the opposite direction, anticipating his action. After the anticipation, he pushes his body up a bit above the box and puts his arms in front of the body to keep a balance until his feet reach the box. When he lands on the box, he recoils again to absorb the shock of his feet hitting the box. Following the recoil, he stands on the box in balance.

FIGURE 8.40   The character jumping on a box. (Courtesy of Aaron Walsman.)

FIGURE 8.41   The character is jumping off a box. (Courtesy of Aaron Walsman.)

Figure 8.41 shows the second part of the jump. The character moves to the edge of the box and pushes his body off the box. He extends his left leg, anticipating the landing. When he lands on the ground, he moves his right foot forward ahead of the left foot to balance the landing. He recoils again to absorb the shock of the feet on the ground. Following the impulse of his body, he moves his left foot close to the right and stands up in balance. Notice the recoil of the head at the shock of the landing. Also notice that in this jump, the character's body was always in balance.

Character Exerting Mostly Horizontal Force

When the character is exerting a force, such as pushing a heavy object, the character must overcome the resistance of the object's weight and the friction between the object and the ground.

In computer animation, the object's weight is conveyed by the character's anticipation and action. For example, in Figure 8.42, the character is standing with her right hand on her chin and her left hand on her hips looking at a big box. Based on her pose, you can tell that she is thinking. Then she goes closer to the box to examine it. Based on the character's anticipation, she is obviously going to try to move the box.

FIGURE 8.42   The character thinking. (Pushing a Heavy Object character animation and images are courtesy of Marcos Romero.)

In Figure 8.43, you see the character lifting her arms anticipating that she will apply a strong force against the box. You also see that there is a big force resisting the push. The resistance is conveyed by the character's body language. She places both hands on the box, her head between the hands, her right knee bent, and her left leg straight backwards. She is putting her body out of balance and using her weight to push.

FIGURE 8.43   The character anticipating the action. (Pushing a Heavy Object character animation and images are courtesy of Marcos Romero.)

Character Exerting Vertical Force: Lifting a Heavy Object

When a character exerts a vertical force, such as lifting a heavy object, the whole body participates in the action. There are two basic ways to lift an object from the ground: using the back and using the legs. The back is much weaker than the legs, so normally the back is used mostly for light lifting. Some lifts combine the two approaches. For example, in Figure 8.44, the character starts by bending over a barbell and then changes the spine position completely to attempt again by lifting from the legs. This shift in method emphasizes the weight being lifted.

FIGURE 8.44   The character lifting a heavy object. (Courtesy of David Suroviec.)

After the weight gets to chest height, the character changes approaches once again. The grip and the spinal position both invert. From a pulling action with tensed abdominal muscles, the figure pivots to a new line of motion, pushing the weight up. Again, the division of a single lift into multiple shifting positions emphasizes the heaviness of the weight. We "feel" the weight because of the relative slowness of the start of each shift and because we see the anticipation and opposing action.

SUMMARY

This chapter introduced you to the process of biped locomotion. You learned the most important body positions of a walking cycle and a jump. You also learned the body language to convey a sad walk and a happy walk. Finally, you learned how to create animations involving physical forces and how to express these forces through your characters.

CHALLENGE ASSIGNMENT

Walk Cycles

Part A: Creating a Normal Walk Cycle

Using the character you rigged for Chapter 7, create a normal walk cycle.

Part B: Showing Emotions

Adapt the normal walk cycle to show two emotions: happiness and sadness.

2. Jumping

Animate Henry jumping onto a box and then back off again. Make the box at least knee height and have him catch his balance after he lands.

3. Lifting

Animate Henry lifting a 100-pound barbell above his head. Make sure he has to work for it.

4. Pushing and Pulling

Animate Henry pushing an almost impossibly heavy object or dragging a heavy object up stairs. False starts and having to start over again are encouraged.

FACIAL EXPRESSION

In This Chapter

- The Anatomy of the Face (Physiognomy)
- Universal Human Emotions and Their Physical Expression
- Other Aspects of Head and Facial Animation
- Overall Workflows for Facial Animation

Facial expression is one of the most difficult—and the most reward-ing—aspects of character modeling and animation. Modeling facial expression is difficult because human beings are extraordinarily sensitive to the most minute nuances of facial expression and because most of us are unaware of exactly what signals we are constructing or re-sponding to. As with other aspects of modeling and animation, observa-tion and reference can be strong allies, particularly when studied closely in slow motion. The reward is that facial modeling and animation done well can be a joy to watch and a source of great professional satisfaction.

Because this topic is complex and advanced enough to be a book in itself, this chapter will only introduce the main concepts and technical mechanisms. In particular, we will not address lip sync in detail. For those interested in learning more, we highly recommend Jason Osipa's book *Stop Staring: Facial Modeling and Animation Done Right* (Sybex, 2007). The good news is that a few basic techniques are sufficient for accom-plishing most of what is needed. Lip sync and additional expressions are performed mainly by layering on additional detail using the same techni-cal mechanisms described here.

THE ANATOMY OF THE FACE (PHYSIOGNOMY)

The study of the human face has a long and colorful history in art, sci-ence, and even pseudoscience. (In the late nineteenth and early twenti-eth centuries, a group of practitioners claimed to be able to recognize the characteristics of criminals solely based on their physiognomy.)

In creating animatable models of the face, artists have wide latitude. Facial features can be highly abstracted. They can be implemented as painted textures, as geometry, as bump map displacements, or even as separate floating geometry. However, even simple representations in-clude certain features, often exaggerated for emphasis. These include large and obvious features such as the nose, but also more subtle aspects, such as the disproportionate importance of eyebrows.

Most emotional expression is carried by the top portion of the face: the eyes, eyelids, and eyebrows. The forehead and upper cheeks also come into play. As in all things in animation, anticipation and overlap-ping action are important. In the context of expressive speech, for exam-ple, this means the emotional shifts should precede the spoken line.

The eyebrows are controlled by two sets of muscles. One set extends across the forehead and can lift any portion of the brow. A second set runs from the eyebrows diagonally to the bridge of the nose. Contracting these muscles leads to a noticeable furrow in the skin between the brows—a "brow squeeze." The overall vertical position of the brows is usually an indicator of alertness or overall vocal volume. Anxious or aggressive expressions usually have the brow lifted, as do characters that are yelling. Meanwhile, some degree of brow squeeze is involved in almost all expressions, usually indicating the degree of thought or concentration (see Figure 9.1).

FIGURE 9.1   Upper face with three expressions: disgust, neutral, surprise.

Eyelids can, of course, be opened or closed to varying degrees. The important emotionally expressive aspect of the eyelids is that their position tends to be judged not in absolute terms but rather relative to the pupil and iris. An alert expression will have the eyes wide open, made visible and obvious by showing the white of the eye above and below the iris. By contrast, a sleepy expression will have the lids partially covering the iris.

Overall eye squeeze (or "squint") intensifies any expression (see Figure 9.2), for example, the visual difference between a little bit angry and very angry.

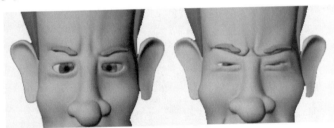

FIGURE 9.2   Eye squeeze.

UNIVERSAL HUMAN EMOTIONS AND THEIR PHYSICAL EXPRESSION

One of the interesting things about human faces is that we can express at least six emotions that are universally recognized. Researchers in psychology have empirically measured this and found that this recognition starts at a very young age and transcends a huge variety of human cultures and customs. If you find yourself lost and scared anywhere on earth, locals will easily discern your facial expression, even with no shared basis in language and despite very different social and cultural conventions. Facial expressions are routinely gathered and processed even when seen very briefly, at a distance, or under difficult lighting conditions.

The six basic expressions are as follows (see Figure 9.3):

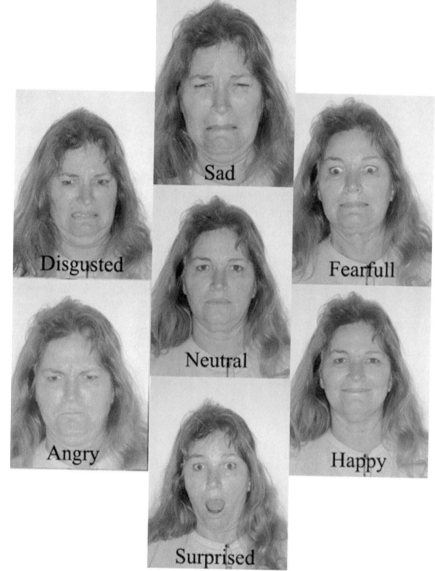

FIGURE 9.3 Composite photographic view of neutral and the six basic human emotions.

- **Happiness.** The mouth is typically at least partially open, with mouth corners pulled back toward the ears (not simply lifted vertically). Eyebrows are relaxed.
- **Sadness.** The mouth is relaxed with corners either level or pulled down. The eyes are partly closed with inner eyebrows bent upward.
- **Surprise.** The upper eyelids are wide open with lower lids relaxed. The jaw is open, and the eyebrows are raised.
- **Anger.** The eyes are wide open with inner eyebrows pulled downward and together, causing a distinct furrow above the nose. The mouth is open with teeth exposed or closed with the lips pressed together.
- **Fear.** Eyes are open—tense and alert. Brows are raised and pulled together with inner brows bent upward.
- **Disgust.** Eyebrows and lids are relaxed. The upper lip is lifted and curled (often asymmetrically).

Happiness

A happy facial expression is something that most people think they understand—even non-artists usually grow up drawing "smiley" faces. However, some important differences exist between real smiles in 3D and 2D line drawings (see Figure 9.4). The first and most important is that in a smile, the corners of the mouth pull *back* as well as lifting up. This can most easily be seen in a side view of the face. In a photorealistic character, a rule of thumb is that the smile is about a third deeper than the neutral expression, as well as a third wider.

 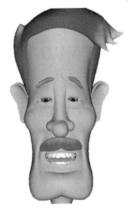

FIGURE 9.4   Happy faces.

In the Henry character, the base pose starts with a bit of a smirk because the character is happy-go-lucky at the core. Henry's chin protrudes much farther forward than that of a realistic character, actually extending forward of his rather bulbous nose. Because of this, it wasn't possible to pull the mouth corners very far back. In a more realistically proportioned face, the distance back would be approximately equal to the vertical displacement.

In 3D, you must also consider how far the lips part. A good rule of thumb here is that both move about one lip height. In Henry's case, the upper lip moves to remain just visible under the moustache.

Smiles expose a character's teeth. However, the most important part of a legible smile is not the mouth itself but the large crease in the cheeks that it typically causes. This is most subtle in a young girl and most obvious in an old man. In our Henry character, the cheek line is strong enough that it would read as a crease even with a toon shader. The fold is a tension line that starts from just below the fold in the middle of the chin, is redirected by the flesh of the cheek, and ends near the sides of the nose.

The displacement of the cheeks is a third issue to consider. The main concern here is to maintain the cheek volume and then move the cheeks outward as well as up and back. Rather than just lifting up, think of them as migrating slightly around the skull toward the ears.

Working our way up the face, we note that because of the cheek movement, a smile causes the eyes to squint. Depending on the age and design of the character, this squint can be accentuated with crow's feet radiating from the corner of the eye and small extensions of the normal lower eyebrow crease toward the ears. In general, eyebrows are relaxed in a smile.

Sadness

Is a frown just a smile upside down? Well, not exactly, but close (see Figure 9.5). A frown does pull the corners of the mouth down and back, and it does read strongly in the cheek folds. A realistic frown can be closed mouthed, with the center of the mouth staying still. In the case of Henry, a slightly open mouth was used to exaggerate the expression. Here, the center of the top lip was actually lifted a bit, and the bottom lip was pulled down to expose the lower teeth in the corners. This is not realistic in anything except perhaps a Rottweiler, but it is dramatic. Just in case anyone missed it, in this character, we mirrored the mouth downturn with the mustache.

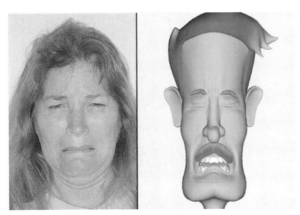

FIGURE 9.5   Sad faces.

In the lower face, the secondary effects of the frown are more subtle than those of the smile. The cheek folds are much smaller vertically and tend to bunch up a bit, often causing multiple folds. The cheeks aren't so much pulled down as they are flattened out.

In the upper portion of the face, however, the secondary effects of the frown are much stronger than those of a smile. The eyes squint down, in Henry's case to the point of being closed and even compressed. The eyebrows are in the lowest possible position, pulling down a major portion of the forehead. Sometimes the brow is raised a bit in the middle. With intense sadness there is also a full brow squeeze.

Anger

In anger, we show as much of our canine teeth as possible, leading to a very distinctive upper lip position (see Figure 9.6). We also tend to lean forward or back and show the whites of our eyes. We sometimes flare our nostrils, as well.

Because anger is an intense expression, it is perhaps not surprising that we get some squinting and a lot of brow action. The combination of brows down with eyes relatively open is unique to anger. Even in realistic characters, the brows can tilt inward rather distinctly—a trait often exaggerated for effect. Unlike in the sad expression, the eyes do not close. They stay open while the squinting muscles around the eyes are in a state of high tension.

FIGURE 9.6   Angry faces.

Disgust

Disgust is interesting in that it is the most asymmetrical of expressions as shown in Figure 9.7. The mouth twists one way or another, with the upper lip pulled into a sneer. The brows and the eyes move much less than in the stronger emotions discussed so far, but the center brow usually lowers slightly. There is a lot of individual variation in disgust, but in general, the tendency is to tighten up the whole face. This squinching effect exaggerates any inherent asymmetries in the face.

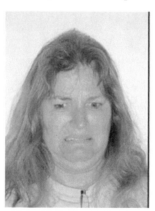

FIGURE 9.7   Disgusted faces.

Surprise

Surprise is characterized by the eyes being as wide open as possible, with the brows lifting to their maximum (see Figure 9.8). There is no brow furrow whatsoever.

FIGURE 9.8   Surprised faces.

Subtle forms of surprise can be indicated entirely with the upper face, but the expression is deepened and emphasized in the lower face with "slack jaw" and a narrow open mouth.

Fear

Fear is very similar to surprise and is often combined with it (see Figure 9.9). In both cases, the eyes and brows are similar—wide open. However, the wideness of the mouth is the key difference. In a fearful expression, the corners of the mouth pull back, and the mouth is often partly or fully open.

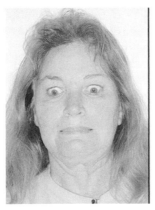

FIGURE 9.9   Fearful faces.

Mixed Emotions

Not surprisingly, these expressions can be mixed with each other, and simple combinations are also well recognized. For example, a mixture of surprise and anger is easily interpreted (see Figure 9.10). However, combinations of opposites, such as happiness and sadness, can lead to ambiguous results.

FIGURE 9.10   Mixture of surprise and anger.

A second issue to be noted is that there are emotional expressions beyond these simple six that may be well recognized within a particular culture but misinterpreted within another context. This situation is analogous to that of aspects of body language previously discussed. Disdain, for example, can be reflected in facial expressions but is not as well recognized as the basic six.

One non-obvious issue is that various emotional expressions have characteristic head tilts. For example, in anger, we sometime lift our chin and throw our head back, whereas in sadness, we tilt our head down. These tilts are often relative to a preexisting head position but can be accentuated with appropriate cinematography.

OTHER ASPECTS OF HEAD AND FACIAL ANIMATION

The human head is constantly active, and animators must pay attention to these basic motions just to make a character look alive. There are three major types of motion to consider: the head itself, the eyes and eyelids, and breathing.

If you look at head motion in reference footage from a scene in which two characters are talking, you will notice that both characters' heads are constantly shifting to slightly different positions. For a character that is speaking, this motion will be coordinated with the speech pattern, particularly tone. For a character that is actively listening, the motion will often include nodding to indicate agreement or disagreement.

Eye contact between the characters will also be clearly apparent. There may be some cases where a character being spoken to is not looking at the speaking character, but only if they are bored or not paying attention. In typical conversation, characters spend most of their time looking into each other's eyes, with brief glances around. The obvious way of doing this would be to have your two characters facing each other dead on and to center the gaze of one character's eyes on the other's. Unfortunately, this is too obvious and quickly becomes boring to watch. Therefore, try to stage your characters at an angle to one another, even putting a prop between them such as a table. Then have them look at each other a bit off-center. This leads to an interesting "gaze line" across your shots. (It also helps to give your characters something plausible to look at or fiddle with while another character is talking.)

Blinking is another important indicator of liveliness, and the frequency and timing of blinking is related to speech pattern, head location, and emotional state. An average blink interval is on the order of six seconds, all other things being equal. When agitated, a character might blink every two seconds; when very sedate, a character only blinks every eight seconds. The length of a blink must also be considered. Typically, the blink of an alert character might take two frames for closing the eye and three frames for reopening. A drowsy character blink might be four frames for closing and five for reopening. We often blink at the end of a statement in a conversation, which can be a signal to the person being addressed that they are being given an opportunity to respond.

Most of the time, we shift our heads slightly and quickly, maintaining our eye focus. However, when something of interest is more than about 20 degrees from the center of our current gaze, we shift our gaze in a characteristic manner. First, we refocus our eyes in the new direction; then we quickly shift our head position, re-centering our gaze. If this shift is over a small range of neck motion, it might occur in a straight line. However, longer head turns are accompanied by a distinctive head bob downward, which is accompanied by a blink.

Finally, our basic head (and body) position often shifts in synchronization with our speech and breath patterns. Inhaling causes us to lift our heads slightly, and exhaling causes us to lower our heads. However, unless we are breathing very heavily, this motion is more subtle than that driven by speech and is masked by it.

Speech and Sync

Visual representation of speech is an important and highly specialized component of facial animation. The basic process is as follows. First, the character voice track is recorded both in audio and visual form. Unlike other parts of animation, which are preplanned using storyboards, actual reference footage is absolutely critical here. This footage forms the essential timing reference, and the visuals are also highly useful for the rest of the process.

Next, the script is analyzed in detail. Each word in any language is actually pronounced using a set of "phonemes" that represent the fundamental audio building blocks of language. Usually, these are the combination of a consonant and a vowel (i.e., "ta") or two vowels ("oo"). There are more phonemes in a language than there are letters, but fortunately for the animator, not all of these are visually distinct. For example, try pronouncing the following phonemes out loud: "da" and "ta." Notice that your mouth position does not vary significantly. Based on this important simplification, lip syncers translate immediately from a written script into "visemes." A *viseme* is a component of human speech that is visually distinct.

In lip sync animation, the animator first models a set of visemes and then animates them. Although it is highly detailed work because of the amount of keys required, overall this is exactly the same technical process used for simulating facial expressions.

Technical Approaches to Facial Animation

There are two basic technical approaches to facial animation: the use of joints bound to the skin and the application of blend shapes. Because of the limitations of current implementations of joints, blend shapes are generally the preferred approach. This may change over time, particularly as systems begin to incorporate the ability to simulate muscle mass and skin folding and sliding. At the moment, however, the best way to get highly expressive faces is to individually model a base geometry and then a series of deformations of this geometry. *Blend shapes* are linear interpolations between these geometries, at a vertex-by-vertex level. Maya's implementation of blend shapes allows multiple "targets" that each can represent a different expression or mouth shape. Each blend shape pair is controlled by a slider bar and may be keyframed over time.

TUTORIAL 9.1: BLEND SHAPES

This tutorial will introduce you to the Maya blend shape system. You will use blend shapes to create a facial rig simulating the major facial expressions. You will use set driven keys to establish the relationship between major facial expressions and secondary blend shape actions. For the Henry character, these include the eyebrows and mustache. Secondary blend shapes are necessary in this case because the character's eyebrows and mustache were modeled as objects separate from the head.

The use of set driven keys allows great flexibility in the behavior of secondary objects. The secondary objects need not have a linear relationship to the primary facial expression. This allows overlapping action, where one part of the face begins to move before another part. However, you can also establish simpler relationships using the Connection Editor. The best technique to use depends on how the face was modeled. In the case of the Henry character, the expression faces and the eyebrows were modeled based on a one-to-one relationship, so the Connection Editor would work as well.

The basic process of blend shaping requires two or more objects with an exactly equivalent number and arrangement of vertices. One object becomes the base, and the others are called *targets*. In this process, any transforms on the objects are ignored, so the location of the geometries does not matter. However, the operation is sensitive to the picking order.

To create a blend shape, you select the targets first and the base (neutral) face last. A blend shape bar is created in the Blend Shape window in the order the targets were selected. For each target object, Maya creates a slider bar with a name based on the target geometry's original name. The values on the slider bar range from 0 to 1, where 0 represents the base geometry and 1 represents a 100 percent morph to the target. A value of 0.5 gives you geometry in which each vertex is exactly halfway between its position in the base and the target geometries. By mixing targets together, you can get an array of results.

Creating Blend Shapes

The hard work in creating blend shapes is actually in the modeling (which, in this example, we have done for you). After you have your models organized, the process of generating the blend is surprisingly simple for a technique with such powerful results.

Head Blend Shape

To create the head blend shape:

1. Press F2 to change the mode to Animation.
2. Open a file called facial_exercise.mb from the chapter9, blend_shape folder on the CD-ROM.
3. In the Hypergraph, hold down the Shift key and select, in order, HappyFace, SadFace, ScaredFace, AngryFace, SurprisedFace, DisgustedFace, and baseFace (neutral).
4. Select Deform > Create Blend Shape Option Box.
5. In the BlendShape node field, type headShape.
6. Click the Create button. The blend shape is created but is not visible yet.
7. Select Window > Animation Editor > Blend Shape, as shown in Figure 9.11. The Blend Shape window opens with six sliders.

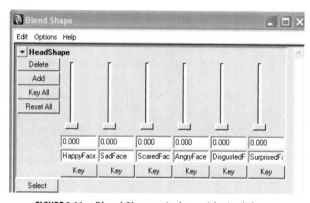

FIGURE 9.11   Blend Shape window with six sliders.

Left Eyebrow Blend Shape

To create the left eyebrow blend shape:

1. In the Hypergraph, hold down the Shift key and select, in order, HappyEyebrow_L, SadEyebrow_L, ScaredEyebrow_L, AngryEyebrow_L, SurprisedEyebrow_L, DisgustedEyebrow_L, and Eyebrow_L.
2. Select Deform > Create Blend Shape Option Box.
3. In the BlendShape node field, type LeftEyebrow.
4. Look in the Blend Shape Editor (from the Window menu). You should see six sliders, as shown in Figure 9.12.

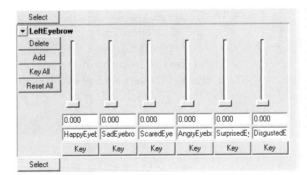

FIGURE 9.12   The Blend Shape window with the six new eyebrows sliders.

5. In the Hypergraph, select HappyEyebrow_R, SadEyeBrow_R, Scared-Eyebrow_R, AngryEyebrow_R, SurprisedEyeBrow_R, and Disgusted-Eyebrow_R.
6. Select Deform > Create Blend Shape Option Box.
7. In the options window BlendShape node field, type RightEyebrow.
8. Click the Create button. Look in the Blend Shape Editor, and you should see nine sliders.

Setting Driven Keys for the Eyebrows

To create set driven keys for the eyebrows:

1. Select Animate > Set Driven Key > Set. The Set Driven Key window opens.
2. In the Hypergraph, open the HappyFace dependency graph and select the headShape node.
3. In the Set Driven Key window, load headShape as the driver and select HappyFace on the right side, as shown in Figure 9.13

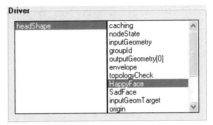

FIGURE 9.13   HeadShape selected as the driver with the HappyFace attribute selected on the right side.

4. In the Hypergraph, click the Scene Hierarchy button to close the HappyFace dependency graph.
5. Select HappyEyeBrow_L and open its dependency graph.
6. Select the LeftEyebrow node.
7. In the Set Driven Key window, load LeftEyebrow as driven, and select HappyEyeBrow_L in the right side (see Figure 9.14).

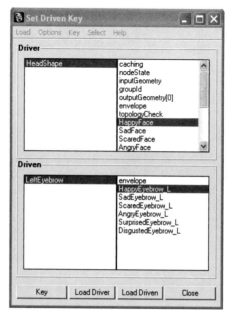

FIGURE 9.14   HeadShape and LeftEyebrow loaded in the Set Driven Key window.

8. In the Hypergraph, click the Scene Hierarchy button to close the HappyEyebrow_L dependency graph.
9. In the Blend Shape window, make sure the HappyFace and the HappyEyebrow_L sliders have the value 0.
10. In the Set Driven Key window, click the Key button.
11. In the Blend Shape window, enter the value 1 for the HappyFace slider and enter the value 1.0 for the HappyEyebrow_L slider, as shown in Figure 9.15.

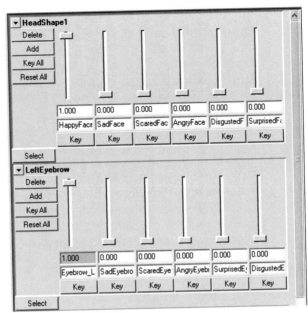

FIGURE 9.15   The Set Driven Key window showing the HappyFace and HappyEyebrow_L values.

12. In the Set Driven Key window, click the Key button.
13. Move the HappyFace bar up and down and notice that the HappyEyebrow_L slider moves with it.
14. Repeat steps 5 through 12 to set a driven key for SadEyebrow_L, ScaredEyebrow_L, AngryEyebrow_L, SurprisedEyebrow_L, and DisgustedEyebrow_L.
15. Repeat the preceding steps to create a blend shape for the right eyebrows. Name the new blend shape RightEyebrow and create set driven keys.

The most important thing to remember about blend shapes is that your base level model and your target models must have identical topology at the vertex level. That means you can't add or delete vertices to your expression targets. This in turn means the workflow for creating blend shapes must be a bit iterative.

Your starting expression will essentially be a blank neutral staring pose—the most boring possible face. A good strategy is to make your second expression a dramatic one such as an open-mouthed happy expression. At this point, make sure you have enough vertices in the right places to make a strong expression. If you find that you need more, you will have to go back and add them to your base geometry.

As you learned in considering physiognomy, a few areas are worthy of special attention. In the lower face, be sure to consider the crease lines for your character's cheeks. These are very important visual clues that help us recognize a smile. In the upper face, consider the articulation of the eyelids and skin creases around the eyes (for example, crow's feet).

You will also need to develop a strategy for representing eyebrows and brow furrows. For this task, there are multiple and very different technical strategies. Eyebrows can be modeled as geometry, and in the case of cartoonish characters, can even be entirely separate from the face and floating out a little bit in space. They can also be done as texture and bump maps or even be created using Maya's fur or PaintFX. In more cartoony characters such as Henry, the brow furrow can be modeled using geometry. For more photorealistic characters, however, this requires a lot of CVs and a great deal of detailed modeling. In such cases, the best strategy when brow furrow detail is required is to use texture and bump maps.

OVERALL WORKFLOWS FOR FACIAL ANIMATION

You can approach facial animation in many ways, which can result in very different workflows. However, a recommended starting workflow might be the following.

- **Blocking and camera.** Review reference footage, if available. Block out the scene in terms of the camera angles and note the emotional segments and gaze angles. If the character is speaking, plan the relationship between its speech pattern and corresponding actions.
- **Sync.** For speaking characters, translate the script into phonemes and visemes. With reference (or final) sound, do preliminary lip sync.
- **General emotion.** Use blend shapes to key major emotional expressions and their transitions.
- **Head tilt.** For each major segment or spoken phrase, break out a series of head positions. The timing of these will roughly correspond to any sync and also to emotional shifts that you want to emphasize.
- **Eyes.** Animate the eyes, including direction and blink. Use head turns and emotional shifts as starting points and fill in between.
- **Eyelids.** Using the pupil and iris as a central reference point, adjust the eyelids as appropriate for the expressions needed. Use squint to emphasize more intense moments.
- **Brows.** Adjust the brow positions from the overall expression, if needed for emphasis. Use brow furrow to highlight concentrated versus relaxed moments.
- **Finesse.** Do final passes through your sequence and look for opportunities to add anticipation and overlapping action.

Summary

Although facial animation is a complex and challenging topic, this chapter has introduced you to the key issues to consider and to tools and workflows for conducting facial animation using blend shapes in Maya.

Challenge Assignment

Expressions

Part A: Showing Expressions

ON THE CD

Open the file called facial_exercise.mb from the chapter9, Blendshape folder on the CD-ROM. Modify the face to show three expressions: happiness, sadness, and fear.

Part B: Morphing Expressions

Create blend shapes showing a sad face morphing into a happy face and then to a fearful face.

A

MAYA BOOT CAMP: CREATING YOUR FIRST MAYA SCENE

In This Appendix

- An Overview of the Maya Interface
- Creating a Project
- Creating a Scene
- Previewing a Scene
- Saving a Scene
- Framing a Scene
- Texturing an Object
- Lighting a Scene
- Rendering a Test Frame
- Layers
- Snapping Tool

An Overview of the Maya Interface

When you open Maya, it shows the default window configuration, which is a perspective camera window on the left, and the Channel Box on the right as shown in Figure A.1.

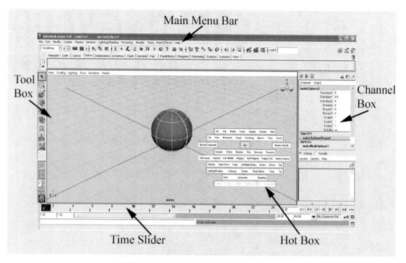

FIGURE A.1 Maya interface overview.

The camera window provides a view into a 3D scene and contains only a small placement grid at the beginning. The Channel Box describes properties of objects when selected.

After the window is open, you can select the Perspective view by clicking anywhere inside the window. Note that the window frame becomes highlighted to indicate its selection. In addition to the Perspective view, Maya also creates three orthographic views: Top, Side, and Front (see Figure A.2).

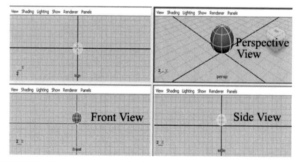

FIGURE A.2 Maya orthogonal views and Perspective camera view.

You can see these by selecting Panels > Layouts > Four Panes or by selecting the Perspective view and pressing and releasing the spacebar. To make one of the orthographic views fill the screen, click in it and press and release the spacebar quickly. Pressing the spacebar quickly again will return you to your previous layout. Pressing and holding down the spacebar will bring up the hotbox. The *hotbox* is an alternative way to access the menus at the cursor level as well as switch rapidly between windows and layouts.

Manipulating the Views

Maya allows you to manipulate the four views (Perspective, Top, Front, and Side). With the Perspective view highlighted, you can rotate, zoom, and pan the camera. With the orthogonal views highlighted, you can zoom in and out and pan the camera.

Rotating a View

To rotate the camera, click the Perspective view window, hold down the Alt key (Windows and Linux) or Option key (Mac OS X), click, and then drag the mouse around. The grid should spin around while you drag.

Tracking a Scene

To track the scene, hold the Alt key (Windows and Linux) or Option key (Mac OS X), middle-click, and drag around. Translation works in all windows.

Zooming into an Object

To zoom the camera in and out, press the Alt key (Windows and Linux) or Option key (Mac OS X), right-click, and drag. As you drag right, the scene gets larger; as you drag left, the scene gets smaller. Alternatively you can zoom by scrubbing the mouse scroll wheel. The zoom works in all windows.

Working Modes

The basic Maya interface is divided into five major sections or modes: Animation (F2), Polygons (F3), Surfaces (F4), Dynamics (F5), and Rendering (F6) (see Figure A.3).

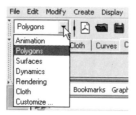

FIGURE A.3   Maya modes.

Each mode displays a very different set of menus and tools. For example, most of the tools and menus you will need for the creation and editing of geometry are grouped under the Polygons and Surfaces modes. To switch between modes, either use the pop-up menu on the left of the toolbar or press the keyboard shortcut indicated. Note that File, Edit. Modify. Create, Display, and Window menus are available in all modes.

Working Units

By default, the working units in Maya are centimeters. If you want to change the units, go to the main menu and select Window > Settings/ Preferences > Preferences. Click the Settings tab and choose the appropriate one (meter, inch, foot, or yard) as shown in Figure A.4.

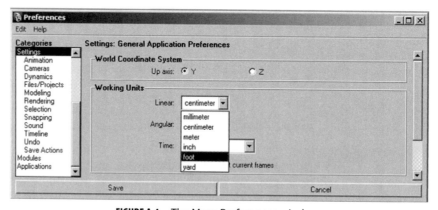

FIGURE A.4   The Maya Preferences window.

You can change your working units at any time. Changes will not affect existing objects, but new objects will be created in the newly selected units.

   For the purpose of this book's exercises, we will use the centimeter setting.

CREATING A PROJECT

When working with Maya, the first thing you have to do is create a project. This allows you to organize your files in specific folders created by Maya. It is very important that you create your project before saving the scene in Maya. Otherwise, everything goes to the default folder, which rapidly becomes very cluttered and confusing.

1. Select File > Project > New.
2. In the name field, type my_first_project.
3. Specify the location where the project is going to be saved.
4. Click Use Default. Maya will create all the directories you need for your workflow.
5. Click Accept.

File names cannot have spaces (Maya was originally a UNIX-based program and retains this restriction in both Windows and Mac versions).

CREATING A SCENE

Now that you have a project, you can create a scene. A *scene* is a 3D space where you create objects, textures, and lights. You can have as many objects as you want in a scene. There are two major types of predefined objects in Maya: NURBS and polygon primitives. You will learn about the differences between them in the tutorials in this book. For the moment, just think of them as a set of convenient starting points for constructing more complicated objects.

Creating a NURBS Primitive

Maya offers two ways to create a primitive: Interactive Creation and Non-interactive Creation. The Maya default is Interactive Creation, which allows you to create primitives by clicking and dragging on the grid. Non-interactive Creation allows you to create primitives by selecting the option in the main menus.

For the purpose of this book, you will use Non-interactive Creation.

1. Set the Surfaces mode by pressing F4.
2. From the main menu, select File > New Scene and click the option box (see Figure A.5). Notice that a window opens, allowing you to modify the preference of the scene. For the purpose of this book, we will leave the default preferences.

FIGURE A.5   New Scene Option Box.

3. Many Maya menu items have both a name and a drop-shadowed option box. Selecting the name executes the command directly; selecting the option box allows you to specify custom options first. It also lets you apply the command multiple times by clicking the Apply button. Click New. Maya will ask if you want to save the scene. Click the Save button. Call it my_first_scene and click the Save button. Notice that Maya saves the file in the Scenes folder of my_first_project, which you've created.
4. Select Create > NURBS Primitives and uncheck Interactive Creation.
5. Select Create > NURBS Primitives > Cylinder Option Box (see Figure A.6).

FIGURE A.6   NURBS Primitives Cylinder option box.

Customizing a Primitive

Let's create a cylinder with radius 2 and height 6.
1. In the NURBS Cylinder Options window, enter the value 2 for the radius and 6 for the height. Click Create (see Figure A.7).

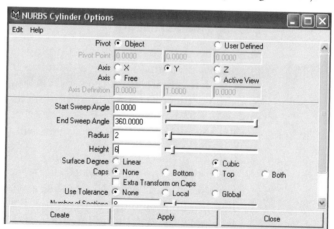

FIGURE A.7   NURBS Cylinder Options window.

Moving, Rotating, and Scaling Objects

Besides specifying object sizes on creation, Maya also lets you manipulate objects directly so that you can move, rotate, and scale them in any camera view. These operations are so common that you should take the time to learn the keyboard shortcuts.

Manipulator Keyboard Shortcut Keys

These shortcut keys allow you to work quickly.

- The Q key puts Maya in Select mode (you can select but not modify an object in the scene).
- The W key sets Maya in Move mode.
- The E key sets Maya in Rotate mode.
- The R key sets Maya in Scale mode.
- The G key sets Maya back to execute the last command.

Moving an Object

To move an object:

1. Press Q on the keyboard to get the Selection tool.
2. Click the object to select it.
3. Press the W key on the keyboard to get the Move tool.
4. In the Perspective view, pull the blue and green handles and move the object out of the center of the window (see Figure A.8).

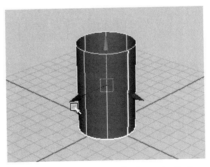

FIGURE A.8   NURBS cylinder selected.

When you select an object with the Move tool, notice that three manipulator handles appear. Pulling on the red handle moves in X, green in Y, and blue in Z. The yellow manipulator handle in the middle of the object(s) allows you to drag the object in any direction.

Scaling an Object

To scale an object:

1. With the object selected, press the R key to get the Scale tool. The Scale tool works the same way as the Move tool. Pulling on the red handle scales in X, green in Y, and blue in Z.
2. To scale uniformly in all directions, click and drag in the center of the object (see Figure A.9).

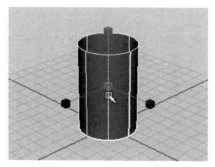

FIGURE A.9   NURBS cylinder with the Scale tool.

Rotating an Object

To rotate an object:

1. With the object selected, press the E key to get the Rotation tool. The Rotation tool works the same as the Move and Scale tools.
2. You also can click View Compass to see the object from the Perspective, Top, Bottom, Front, Back, Left, and Right views (see Figure A.10). The View Compass doesn't rotate an object, just the view.

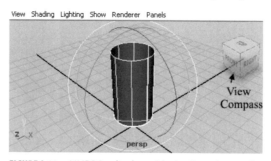

FIGURE A.10   NURBS cylinder with the Rotation tool.

Manipulating an Object Using the Universal Manipulator Tool

The Universal Manipulator tool combines the Translation, Rotation, and Scale tools. To see the Universal Manipulator tool, select the object and then select the Manipulator icon in the toolbox (See Figure A.11) or select Modify > Transformation Tools > Universal Manipulator Tool. The keyboard shortcut is Ctrl+T.

FIGURE A.11   Universal Manipulator icon.

To translate, rotate, or scale the object, click and drag the manipulator handles (see Figure A.12). To move the object freely, click the center point of the manipulator and drag it.

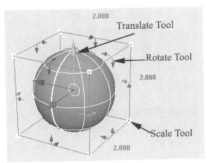

FIGURE A.12   A sphere showing the Universal Manipulator tool.

Creating a Polygon Primitive

To create a polygon primitive:

1. Select Create > Polygon Primitives and uncheck Interactive Creation.
2. Select Create > Polygon Primitives > Sphere (see Figure A.13).

FIGURE A.13   Create a polygon primitives sphere.

3. Press the R key to get the Scale tool.
4. Click and drag on the center of the sphere to scale it to approximately double the original size.

PREVIEWING A SCENE

To preview a scene, select Smooth Shade under the Shading menu of the Perspective window.

There are two shortcuts to preview a scene:

- Pressing the number 4 previews the scene in Wireframe mode.
- Pressing the number 5 previews the scene in Smooth Shade All mode (see Figure A.14).

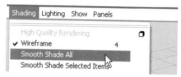

FIGURE A.14   Smooth Shade All option.

Note that Maya gives you a default ambient light that is sufficient for previewing the scene.

SAVING A SCENE

To save a scene, select File > Save As.

FRAMING A SCENE

Maya has important features to avoid getting lost in 3D. Try out the following:

- Look at Selection
- Frame All (see Figure A.15)
- Frame Selection (f)

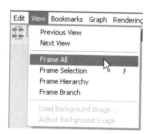

FIGURE A.15   The Frame All option.

TEXTURING AN OBJECT

By default, the objects created in Maya are gray. However, you can change their color at any time. Maya organizes sets of surface attributes called a shader group into an object. *Shader groups* are composed of sub-objects such as textures and procedural materials. All of these can be manipulated in a special kind of panel called the *Hypershade*. The details of working with the Hypershade panel are discussed in Chapter 3, but here are the basics.

1. Select any of the orthogonal windows.
2. Select Panels > Panel > Hypershade to open the Hypershade panel (see Figure A.16).

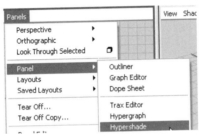

FIGURE A.16   Opening the Hypershade panel.

Creating Materials and Choosing Color

A shading model is a mathematical method for calculating how a surface should appear within a given lighting environment. In Maya, these are also known as *materials*. Maya's built-in renderers support several different standard shading models. The most common of these are as follows:

- **Lambert.** This is Maya's default. Lambert materials have flat lighting with no highlights. This is ideal for surfaces such as pottery, where a chalky appearance is appropriate.
- **Phong.** This shader type allows for glossy materials with specular highlights, such as plastic or porcelain. The highlights can be a little harsh, however.
- **Phong E.** This shader is a faster-rendering version of Phong with softer highlights.
- **Blinn.** This shader is similar to Phong, but has more accurate calculations of highlights. Blinn shaders are often used for metallic objects where highlights are very important.

To create materials and choose color:

1. Select Create > Materials > Phong from the Hypershade menu (see Figure A.17).

FIGURE A.17   Creating a Phong material.

2. Double-click the Phong icon to open the Attribute Editor on the right side of the screen (see Figure A.18).

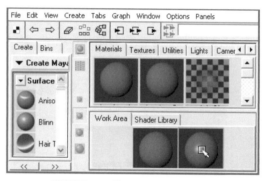

FIGURE A.18   Phong material icon.

3. In the Attribute Editor, type in a new name for your surface—for example, blue_sky.
4. Under Common Material Attributes, double-click the gray color swatch (see Figure A.19). The Color Chooser appears.

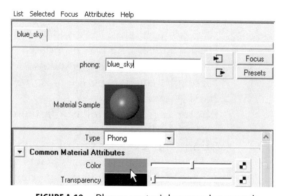

FIGURE A.19   Phong material gray color swatch.

5. Pick a color by clicking on it and click Accept.
6. Click the Hide/Show Channel Box button in the upper-left corner of the screen to close the Attribute Editor and go back to the Channel Box (see Figure A.20).

FIGURE A.20   Hide/Show Channel Box button.

Assigning Materials

To assign the new material, click the Phong ball in the Hypershade, middle-click, and drag it onto the sphere (see Figure A.21), or right-click and choose Assign to Selection.

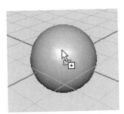

FIGURE A.21   Assigning a material to the sphere.

Notice that the mouse cursor has a + attached to it. Repeat this process to assign a material to the cylinder.

LIGHTING A SCENE

Lighting a scene properly is very important. You have several choices of light types in Maya.

1. Go to the main menu and select Create > Lights > Spot Light (see Figure A.22). By default, Maya creates a spot light at the origin, pointing to the right.

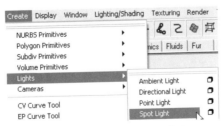

FIGURE A.22   Creating a spot light.

2. For the real-time preview of the lighting in the Perspective window, select Lighting > Use All Lights (see Figure A.23). You also can use the shortcut for this function by pressing the number 7 on the keyboard.

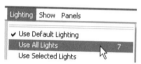

FIGURE A.23   The Use All Lights menu option.

Moving and Rotating a Light

To move and rotate a light:

1. Press Ctrl+T to get the Universal Manipulator tool.
2. Click the light and move it up above the sphere.
3. Click the rotation handles and rotate the light –90 degrees. Rotate the light in all axes until you get the effect you want. You may need to use all the windows to make a good light adjustment. Maya also allows you to see the object through the light. For better lighting adjustment, click the light and select Panel > Look Through Selected.
4. Double-click the Lights icon on the Hypershade to open the light Attribute Editor.
5. Type Intensity = 1.5 and Cone Angle = 90 (see Figures A.24 and A.25).

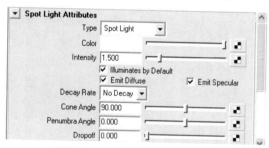

FIGURE A.24   Light Attribute Editor.

FIGURE A.25   Light above the sphere.

RENDERING A TEST FRAME

Now that you have created and lit a scene, you are ready to render a test. By rendering a test frame you can preview what your scene looks like. Based on this rendering, you adjust the objects, colors, and light as desired.

You can render a test of any view. However, to see your scene in 3D, you must render in the Perspective window.

1. Change Maya to the Rendering mode.
2. Click the Perspective window to select it.
3. Select Render > Render Current Frame (see Figure A.26). You should see your scene rendered.

FIGURE A.26   The Render Current Frame option.

Saving the Test Rendered Frame

To save the rendered frame:

1. Go to File on the rendered image and select Save Image. The computer will ask you where you want to save it.
2. Select an appropriate place and click the Save button.

LAYERS

Layers can be extremely useful when you work with more than one object in a scene or you are modeling a complex object. Placing objects or parts of an object on layers allows you to manage your work easily and efficiently. For example, you can easily select an object behind another.

To create a new layer, click the Create a New Layer button on the lower right as shown in Figure A.27.

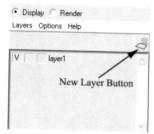

FIGURE A.27   Create a New Layer button.

To add an object or a group of objects to a layer, select them, position the cursor on top of the new layer, right-click, and choose Add Selected Objects.

SNAPPING TOOL

The Snapping tool allows you to transform an object or a component by snapping on the grid, curves, or points.

To use the Snapping tool, you can click the icons below the main menu bar (see Figure A.28) or use Maya's default hotkeys.

FIGURE A.28   Snapping icons.

The hotkeys are listed here:

- Press X and click and drag to snap to grid.
- Press C and middle-click-drag to snap to curve.
- Press V and click and drag to snap to a point.

Let's try this out.

1. Select Create > CV Curve Tool.
2. Hold down the X key and, in the center of the Front view, click the grid eight times.
3. Press Enter to complete the first curve.

4. Type Y to get the Curve tool again and draw a second curve.
5. Position the cursor on the first curve, right-click, and select Control Vertex.
6. With the Pointer tool, select a CV (control vertex).
7. Press W to get the Move tool.
8. Hold down the C key. Notice that the center of the Move tool handles changes to a round shape.
9. Holding the C key down, middle-click-drag anywhere on the second curve. The selected CV should snap to the second curve (see Figure A.29).

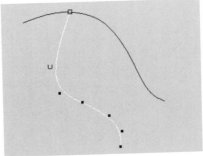

FIGURE A.29   A CV of the first curve snapped on the second curve.

Snapping points or curves can be a little tricky sometimes. Try it again if it did not work the first time. Don't be discouraged, it's just a matter of getting used to the tool.

The same process applies to snapping points.

SUMMARY

In this appendix, you learned the process of creating, lighting, previewing, and rendering a scene. This set of steps is so fundamental that you will use it for pretty much all work in Maya, and this level of understanding is assumed elsewhere in this book. Try to get comfortable with these tools and interface widgets before attempting the exercises elsewhere in the book. For a more detailed explanation about the Maya tools discussed in this appendix, consult the Maya documentation.

SAMPLE SYLLABI

In This Appendix

- Modeling Course for a 10-Week Quarter
- Integrated Modeling and Animation Course for a 10-Week Quarter
- Animation Course for a 10-Week Quarter
- Animation Course for a 16-Week Semester

Modeling Course for a 10-Week Quarter

WEEK	TOPIC	PRECLASS READING	ASSIGNMENT
Week 1	Maya boot camp	Appendix A	"Maya Boot Camp" tutorial: Design and model a cat using primitives
Week 2	Modeling a simple character	Chapter 3	Designing and modeling a flour sack
Week 3	Texturing, rigging, and test animating	Chapter 3 Chapter 4	Texturing the sack and posing it in three different poses
Week 4	NURBS modeling	Chapter 5	"Modeling a Fish" tutorial: Model a fish based on collected reference
Week 5	Character design	Chapter 1: "Character Design and Character Sketches"	Character sketches
Week 6	Modeling a head	Chapter 6: "Human Anatomy for Modelers," "Tools and Methods"	"Modeling the Head" tutorial: Create the head
Week 7	Modeling a torso	The rest of Chapter 6	Model the torso
Week 8	Texturing the model		Texture your model
Week 9	Rigging a humanoid	Chapter 7	Rig your model
Week 10	Facial expression	Chapter 9	Create facial expressions for your model

Integrated Modeling and Animation Course for a 10-Week Quarter

WEEK	TOPIC	PRECLASS READING	ASSIGNMENT
Week 1	Maya boot camp	Appendix A	"Maya Boot Camp" tutorial: Design and model a cat using primitives
Week 2	Preproduction	Chapter 1	Storyboard of light and heavy animation
Week 3	Principles of animation	Chapter 2	Animate light and heavy balls
Week 4	Modeling and texturing	Chapter 3	Model and texturing a sack
Week 5	Rigging, posing, and test animating	Chapter 4	Texture the sack, pose, and test animations
Week 6	NURBS modeling	Chapter 5	Model a fish
Week 7	Path animation	Chapter 5: "Motion Path Animation," "Hair Curves as Deformers"	Animate the fish
Week 8	Simple walk cycles	Chapter 8: "Muybridge's Observations of Motion," "The Process of Walking"	Tutorial 8.1: "A Normal Walk Cycle" Chapter 8 Challenge Assignment Part A
Week 9	Emotion in body language	Chapter 8: "Adding Emotion and Character to Your Walk Cycles"	Chapter 8 Challenge Assignment Part B
Week 10	Emotion in the face	Chapter 9	Chapter 9 Challenge Assigment

Animation Course for a 10-Week Quarter

WEEK	TOPIC	PRECLASS READING	ASSIGNMENT
Week 1	Preproduction	Chapter 1	Storyboard of light and heavy animation
Week 2	Principles of animation	Chapter 2	Animate light and heavy balls
Week 3	Path animation with secondary motion	Chapter 5: "Motion PathAnimation," "Hair Curves As Deformers"	Animate fish swimming
Week 4	Simple walk cycles	Chapter 8: "Muybridge's Observations of Motion," "The Process of Walking"	Animate Henry walking
Week 5	Emotion in body language 1	Chapter 8: "Adding Emotion and Character to Your Walk Cycles"	Create an emotional walk cycle
Week 6	Emotion in body language 2		Animate a sneak
Week 7	The jump	Chapter 8: "The Jump"	Chapter 8 Challenge Assignment 2
Week 8	Lifting weight	Chapter 8: "Lifting a Heavy Object"	Chapter 8 Challenge Assignment 3
Week 9	Pushing and pulling	Chapter 8: "Character Exerting Horizontal Force"	Chapter 8 Challenge Assignment 4
Week 10	Emotion in the face	Chapter 9	Chapter 9 Challenge Assignment

Animation Course for a 16-Week Semester

WEEK	TOPIC	PRECLASS READING	ASSIGNMENT
Week 1	Preproduction	Chapter 1	Storyboard of light and heavy animation
Week 2	Principles of animation	Chapter 2	Animate light and heavy balls
Week 3	Path animation with secondary motion	Chapter 5: "Motion Path Animation," "Hair Curves as Deformers"	Animate a fish swimming
Week 4	Simple walk cycles	Chapter 8: "Muybridge's Observations of Motion," "The Process of Walking"	Animate Henry walking
Week 5	Emotion in body language 1	Chapter 8: "Adding Emotion and Character to Your Walk Cycles"	Create an emotional walk cycle
Week 6	Emotion in body language in-class critique		Refine the emotional walk cycle
Week 7	Emotion in body language 2		Animate a sneak
Week 8	The jump	Chapter 8: "The Jump"	Chapter 8 Challenge Assignment 2
Week 9	Lifting weight	Chapter 8: "Lifting a Heavy Object"	Chapter 8 Challenge Assignment 3
Week 10	Pushing and pulling	Chapter 8: "Character Exerting Horizontal " Force"	Chapter 8 Challenge Assignment 4
Week 11	Working day—no lecture		Refine a selected assignment from prior three weeks
Week 12	Emotion in the face	Chapter 9	Animate Henry's face: first pass
Week 13	Emotion in the face in-class critique		Refine Henry's facial animation

Continued

Week 14	Final project preproduction	Chapter 1	Storyboard an animation conveying changing emotions
Week 15	Blocking and preliminary animation		Animate emotional changes: first-pass animation
Week 16	Final animation		Animate emotional changes: final animation

INDEX

License Agreement/Notice of Limited Warranty